WEAPONIZED RELIGION

From Latter Rain to Colonia Dignidad

JOHN ANDREW COLLINS

Dark Mystery Publications
ISBN: 978-1-7351609-4-8

"C. S. Lewis once said that almost all crimes of Christian history have come about when religion is confused with politics. Politics, which always runs by the rules of ungrace, allures us to trade away grace for power, a temptation the church has often been unable to resist."
— *Philip Yancey, Christians and Politics Uneasy Partners*

INTRODUCTION

The Latter Rain Movement of the late 1940s and 1950s created a new breed of Pentecostalism that dramatically impacted Christianity in the United States as well as many other countries around the world. Initially viewed as a movement by God, a number of well-respected men and women participated in the movement during its early years. Over time, however, many of those same men and women came to realize that there were wolves among the sheep. Political ideologies not aligned with sound biblical theology crept into the movement, causing the group to explode into several splinter groups. New sects were created, and while some of them reformed, others became very destructive and militant. Such is the case with Paul Schäfer Schneider, leader of the Colonia Dignidad compound in Chile.

In March 2005, Paul Schäfer was found hiding in the expensive gated community of Las Acasias, about 25 miles from Buenos Aires, Argentina. He had been on the run for nearly eight years and was extradited to Chile to face an array of charges from the rape and torture of children to his involvement with the 1976 disappearance of political activist Juan Maino. Two months later, after his Pentecostal community was raided by government officials, it was discovered that the men and women dressed in the style of Pentecostal-holiness fashion had been manufacturing, selling, and using weapons — including sarin gas — all from what appeared to be a humble religious community.

Schäfer was the leader of a splinter group of "The Message", the cult following of William Marrion Branham, aka William Marvin Branham,[1] from Jeffersonville, Indiana. In the early 1950s, German Baron Frary von Blomberg became one of

---

[1] Draft Card Serial 2342. 1940, Oct 16. Clark Co. No.1 Ind.

William Branham's campaign managers and organized a tour through Germany. Von Blomberg was a strong supporter of Branham's anti-communist revivals due to the horrific things that Russian soldiers did to his family.[2] Branham went to Germany, and Baron Von Blomberg helped William Branham establish a series of fifteen offices in Sweden, Finland, Germany, Africa, Norway, Belgium, France, and two in Canada.[3] Paul Schafer, the infamous leader of Colonia Dignidad, was assigned to be William Branham's security detail.[4] Schäfer was recruited into the "Message" cult and became programmed to believe Branham's End-of-Days prophecies, as well as his misogynistic and abusive doctrines.[5]

These were the same years that Rev. Jim Jones — who created a similar compound in South America — was rising to

---

[2] Branham, William. 1953, May 10. Testimony (53-0510). "A few days ago, I was setting with one of the managers, Baron von Blomberg, a baron of Germany in Saint Petersburg, Florida...?...And he's had a little German boy that he got out from behind the Russian lines, upon the—close to the American zone, where it connects with the Russian zone. He had two young sisters; the Russian soldiers run in was ravishing those girls on the floor. The father run in to take up for them. They shot the father. Taken the girls and the boys up in the camp, put them in a coal mine. Would make the girls push coal out in the daytime, strip off, dance before those soldiers at night, naked. One of them lost their mind, the other one, forgot what happened; she died. This little boy made an escape, one day. Though some way got hid over in some stuff, got near the border, slipped out from under a load of stuff, and got over into the American zone. It's been about eight or ten months ago since he come. He could speak pretty good English."

[3] Branham, William. 1953, May 6. Jesus Christ The Same Yesterday, Today, And Forever (53-0506). "So, we just had to get started, get a little office set up. Since then, now, we got around about fifteen of those offices across the world: Sweden, Finland, Germany, Africa, Norway, Belgium, France, two in Canada."

[4] Basso, Carlos. 2022. La Secta Perfecta. (Kindle Version, Spanish) p8. "Despite the fact that communication In those years was not as fast as today, Schäfer knew the Jeffersonville preacher very well and was elated by the prospect of his visit. So much so, that after much insistence, he and his followers were accepted as part of Branham's security detail."

[5] Basso, Carlos. 2022. La Secta Perfecta. (Kindle Version, Spanish) p8. "'In the year 1955, Paul Schäfer and some of his supporters participated in the Karlsruhe meetings of William Branham, evangelist and healer, and were very impressed by the large number of healings', adding that later, 'Schäfer had began practicing several of his doctrines.'"

become a leader in Branham's "Message" sect.[6] This is critically important for understanding Schäfer's authoritative control over his sect, as this was during the early years of Branham's "Manifested Sons of God" theology. Branham had recruited Jones into a militant version of Pentecostal extremism referred to as "Joel's Army",[7] a group of extremists on domestic terrorism watchlists such as the Southern Poverty Law Center.[8] Prior to 1963, this theology empowered numerous ministers with authoritarian control by manipulating congregants to believe that the deity was speaking directly to them as "The Spoken Word", or "The Voice of God" through the superhuman central figures. Both Jones and Schäfer used this to their advantage, and because of this, many of their congregants were either murdered or sacrificed their lives.

As the investigation into Schafer's cult compound continued, the level of domestic and international crimes discovered was mind boggling. The cult compound had harbored Nazi leaders fleeing to South America, and Colonia Dignidad became known as "the Colony" to fleeing Nazis.[9] The CIA and Nazi-hunter Simon Wiesenthal claimed to have evidence that Hitler's "Angel of Death", Josef Mengele, spent time in Colonia Dignidad.[10]

---

[6] Enemy in the Camp: The Inside Story Behind Jim Jones' 1957 Prophecy of Death. Accessed 2022, Nov 18 from https://jonestown.sdsu.edu/?page_id=117834. "Jones rose through the ranks of the 'Message' into a leadership role, officially ordained into the sect by Joseph Mattsson-Boze."

[7] Joel's Army: The Manifested Sons of God. Accessed 2022, Nov 18 from https://jonestown.sdsu.edu/?page_id=102213.

[8] Sanchez, Casey. 2008. TODD BENTLEY'S MILITANT JOEL'S ARMY GAINS FOLLOWERS IN FLORIDA. Accessed 2022, Dec 28 from https://www.splcenter.org/fighting-hate/intelligence-report/2008/todd-bentley%E2%80%99s-militant-joel%E2%80%99s-army-gains-followers-florida.

[9] Infield, Glenn B. 1981. Secrets of the SS. "an enclave known only as 'the Colony' to outsiders but officially named Colonia Dignidad (Noble Colony) by the Chilean government."

[10] Infield, Glenn B. 1981. Secrets of the SS. "Both the CIA and Simon Wiesenthal, the famed Nazi-hunter, state they have evidence that such fugitives as Dr. Josef Mengele, the Third Reich's 'Angel of Death', have spent time at Colonia Dignidad."

"Message" believers in Colonia Dignidad began torturing[11] and killing everyone from opponents of the current political regime to children who disobeyed Branham's cult rules.[12] They were also manufacturing and stockpiling weapons of war. During their searches of the compound, officials found surface-to-air missiles, rocket launchers, machine guns, submachine guns, hand and cluster grenades, rifles, anti-personnel mines, automatic pistols, and a large amount of ammunition.[13] Officials found traces of sarin gas[14] and learned that the "Message" believers were manufacturing chemical and biological weapons.[15] [16] Also found

---

[11] Laurier, Joanne. 2021, Nov 23. Colonia Dignidad: Nazi criminality exported to Chile. Accessed 2022, Jun 9 from https://www.wsws.org/en/articles/2021/11/24/colo-n24.html. "'Schäfer provided torture chambers for Pinochet's use in exchange for mining licenses and other perks,' explains the series. Colonia facilitated the infrastructure that supported the dictatorship's rampage in poor neighborhoods. For Pinochet's National Intelligence Directorate (DINA), Colonia Dignidad became one of the regular secret torture and execution centers for its kidnapped political opponents. In underground prisons, captives were tortured in numerous ways, including mutilation from savage dogs and electric shock. Samuel Fuenzalida of DINA comments in Colonia Dignidad that the Chilean fascists thought the Germans were more experienced with torture."

[12] Bensmann, Marcus. Fend, Ruth. Schlange, Bastian. 2019, Apr 5. Beatings, Torture, and singing.

[13] The Investigation on the Mysterious German Enclave in Southern Chile. 2005. Clarin. Accessed 2022, Jun 9 from https://www.clarin.com/ediciones-anteriores/arma-mato-kennedy-oculta-chilena-colonia-dignidad_0_ByLg95_yRKe.html. "The arsenal includes dozens of surface-to-air missiles, rocket launchers, machine guns, submachine guns, hand and cluster grenades, rifles, anti-personnel mines, automatic pistols and a large amount of ammunition. The finding was the product of an inspection order of the property of more than 16,000 hectares of Judge Jorge Zepeda, who investigates human rights violations in the German enclave during the dictatorship."

[14] Pisetta, Nicola. Colonia Dignidad: Pinochet's City-Lager in Chile. Accessed 2022, Jun 9 from https://www.vanillamagazine.it/colonia-dignidad-la-citta-lager-nel-cile-di-pinochet/. "Colonia Dignidad was therefore also one of the most ruthless places of detention for political prisoners in Chile: new bunkers, long underground tunnels and laboratories very similar to those of Auschwitz were born inside. According to the most recent documents, the well-known Nazi doctor Josef Mengele also found hospitality in the structure. Joseph Mengele Psychedelic drugs were tested on inmates and electroshock was common. In addition, the effect of sarin gas was also examined in the secret basement of the concentration camp. Those who died joined the long list of disappeared and ended up in mass graves."

[15] Wills, James. Dark secrets of Nazi paedo cult leader's commune where grisly torture methods were rife. Accessed 2022, Jun 9 from https://www.dailystar.co.uk/news/world-

were five hundred files on people who had been assassinated in Chile, from political leaders to entertainers. One file found had the name "John F. Kennedy" on it, and inside were two bullets of the same caliber of rifle used by Lee Harvey Oswald during the assassination of JFK.[17]

As historical analysts began to examine the many unusual details of the compound and began interviewing cult members, it became apparent that those participating had undergone under a deep level of mind control and were being manipulated through Schäfer's religious practices. Schäfer had used a weaponized version of religion, and it had the power to overthrow the Chilean government and to install the ruthless dictator Augusto Pinochet into power. Like Adolf Hitler controlled Nazi Germany — and with the help of many high-ranking Nazi officials — Schäfer was able to convince cult members to brutally torture political opponents.[18] At the same time, Schäfer was molesting Chilean boys, and the cult

---

news/dark-secrets-nazi-paedo-cult-25089683. "It has also been claimed the site, which had its own armoury, was used as centre to create biological weapons."

[16] Wills, James. Dark secrets of Nazi paedo cult leader's commune where grisly torture methods were rife. Accessed 2022, Jun 9 from https://www.dailystar.co.uk/news/world-news/dark-secrets-nazi-paedo-cult-25089683. "It has also been claimed the site, which had its own armoury, was used as centre to create biological weapons."

[17] The Investigation on the Mysterious German Enclave in Southern Chile. 2005. Clarin. Accessed 2022, Jun 9 from https://www.clarin.com/ediciones-anteriores/arma-mato-kennedy-oculta-chilena-colonia-dignidad_0_ByLg95_yRKe.html. "In the middle of a huge hidden arsenal, two bullets were found with a paper that had the name of the former president of the United States, assassinated in 1963, written on it. Now a possible connection between that assassination and the mysterious German enclave founded in Chile by the former Nazi Paul Schaefer."

[18] Pisetta, Nicola. Colonia Dignidad: Pinochet's City-Lager in Chile. Accessed 2022, Jun 9 from https://www.vanillamagazine.it/colonia-dignidad-la-citta-lager-nel-cile-di-pinochet/. "Colonia Dignidad was therefore also one of the most ruthless places of detention for political prisoners in Chile: new bunkers, long underground tunnels and laboratories very similar to those of Auschwitz were born inside. According to the most recent documents, the well-known Nazi doctor Josef Mengele also found hospitality in the structure. Joseph Mengele Psychedelic drugs were tested on inmates and electroshock was common. In addition, the effect of sarin gas was also examined in the secret basement of the concentration camp. Those who died joined the long list of disappeared and ended up in mass graves."

physician prescribed sedatives to assist in the sexual abuse when they resisted.[19]

> *Colonia Dignidad was therefore also one of the most ruthless places of detention for political prisoners in Chile: new bunkers, long underground tunnels, and laboratories very similar to those of Auschwitz were born inside. According to the most recent documents, the well-known Nazi doctor Josef Mengele also found hospitality in the structure. Psychedelic drugs were tested on inmates and electroshock was common. In addition, the effect of sarin gas was also examined in the secret basement of the concentration camp. Those who died joined the long list of disappeared and ended up in mass graves.[20]*

Yet what Schäfer was able to achieve in Chile was not unique or unusual. The Message cult and its doctrine had enabled leaders of other splinter groups around the world to do the same. Branham cult leader Robert Martin Gumbura, for example, established a Pentecostal/military compound in Zimbabwe that nearly overthrew the Zimbabwe government.[21] Like Schäfer, Gumbura was involved in sexual crimes, some of which were based

---

[19] Colonia Dignidad. Aus dem Innern einer deutschen Sekte. Documentary by Annette Baumeister und Wilfried Huismann. Part 2: Aus der Finsternis ans Licht. ARD, 23 March 2020.

[20] Pisetta, Nicola. Colonia Dignidad: Pinochet's City-Lager in Chile. Accessed 2022, Jun 9 from https://www.vanillamagazine.it/colonia-dignidad-la-citta-lager-nel-cile-di-pinochet/.

[21] 2015, Dec 4. Gumbura Plotted to Dethrone Govt: Witness. Accessed 2021, May 13 from https://www.herald.co.zw/gumbura-plotted-to-dethrone-govt-witness/. Jailed Independent End Time Message leader Robert Martin Gumbura communicated with alleged coup plotter and former army captain Albert Matapo from prison cells planning on how "they" would dethrone the Government, the court heard yesterday. State witness, Claudius Mutizwa, a convict, told the court during cross examination by Gumbura's lawyer that the Church leader communicated with Matapo through one prison officer, Chinake's mobile phone. He said Matapo's role was to gather manpower and to get guns from Morris Depot's armoury adding that the rioting at Chikurubhi was not about food, but a political scheme. On Tuesday the same witness said Gumbura communicated with former Vice President Dr Joice Mujuru from prison cells through letters, strategizing on how they were going to form their political party."

on William Branham's "Serpent's Seed" and polygamous[22] theology.

> *The End Time Message dictates various disturbing beliefs which include claims that women are inferior to men all because "the first female, Eve, in the book of Genesis, had intercourse with a live snake producing a half serpent, half human child, Esau". They also hold that their Church founder William Marrion Branham is the Last Prophet of the New Testament. This revelation comes shortly after End Time Message Pastor Robert Gumbura who had 13 wives was slapped with a half a century jail term for having raped several women last year. Gumbura was running his own sidekick but utilizing the same religious poison that demeans women and claims that women are responsible for the mankind's fall and so a man can marry as many women he wishes.[23]*

There are hundreds, possibly thousands, of groups that splintered from William Branham's Post WWII healing revivals. Those whose lineage branched directly from any of the original versions of William Branham's cult of personality seem to wander further into extremism than the more distant splinter groups, but

---

[22] Branham, William. 1965, Feb 21. Marriage And Divorce. "then when the double covenant was made by man and woman, through sex, another covenant altogether (not the original covenant, but another covenant), now what's introduced? Polygamy, in all. Then, after the beginning, polygamy was introduced both in man and in beasts; after the beginning, the fall. God now, secondarily, sets a new nature again, by sex. God created the first without sex. Do you believe that? [Congregation says, "Amen. "–Ed.] Now it's another covenant with nature, He sets it in another order, by sex. Second covenant: one male, many females; one buck deer, a whole harem of does. Is that right? One bull, a whole herd of cattle, cows; one rooster, a yardful of hens. Is that right? One David, after His Own heart, with five hundred wives; with a hundred children born to him, in one year, of different women, a man after God's Own heart. One Solomon, with a thousand wives. But notice now, it wasn't so at the beginning, but now it's "after" the beginning. The woman has done this, then she just becomes what she is now. See?"

[23] 2015, Jan 18. EXCLUSIVE: Gumbura Agents Infiltrate Stanbic Bank, Harare. Accessed 2021, May 13 from https://www.zimeye.net/2015/01/18/exclusive-gumbura-agents-invade-stanbic-bank-harare/

with the vastly different versions of doctrine used by different versions of William Branham's stage persona, the spider web of siblings and cousins to the group seem countless. Collectively, they are called the New Apostolic Reformation, nicknamed "The Christian Taliban".[24]

Looking the opposite direction in history, however, prior to William Branham's leadership in the Post WWII healing revival, the doctrinal genealogy looks much the same. There was nothing that William Branham introduced that was new; every version of doctrine that was introduced as "new" by Branham came from other sources that were influential among Branham's peers. Even the "Serpent's Seed" doctrine which would cause over three hundred ministers to denounce William Branham after an event hosted by Jim Jones in Chicago[25] — a doctrine many believe to have been Branham's own creation — was a re-branding of the Christian Identity Doctrine of one-time Angelus Temple minister Rev. Wesley A. Swift under the manipulation of cult leader Amy Semple McPherson. According to Swift, the serpent in the Garden of Eden mated with Eve to produce Cain, and from Cain came all races with black skin. Swift's theology was weaponized by white supremacists during the 1950s and 1960s in the battle against Civil Rights. Branches from the Christian Identity tree include the neo-

---

[24] Exposing the New Apostolic Reformation's roots: William Branham & his heretics. 2016, Feb 13. Accessed 2022, Dec 28 from https://churchwatchcentral.com/2016/02/13/exposing-the-new-apostolic-reformations-false-ecclesia-false-authority/."Chris Rosebrough has done a series of Fighting for the Faith programs analyzing the key features of the New Apostolic Reformation (NAR) cult (aka Christian Taliban)."

[25] Branham, William. 1961, October 15. Questions And Answers (61-1015M). "And I asked the other day in Chicago before three hundred ministers that stood over there to debate and to ask that...I...And the Lord told me, He give me a vision, and told me where we'd be and what to do. I stood before three hundred trinitarian ministers, and I said, 'Now, if I am so wrong in this doctrine, some of you man stand up here and show me where I'm wrong by the Scripture without textbook. If there is no such a thing as Serpent's Seed or something like that that I've been teaching, just come here and show me by the Scriptures.' Nobody moved (see?), because it can't be done. That's true. Not to be different, but just it's the Truth; it's the Word. And there's where...No one can debate that; that's the Word of God; nobody can do it. See?"

Nazi Aryan Nations and other hate groups.[26] Though Branham convinced his cult of personality that the doctrine was original and given to him by "divine revelation",[27] many of his mentors, peers, and contemporaries had the same "revelation". Once integrated into their theology, it became a weaponized form of religion targeting people with black skin.

Yet Wesley Swift did not create the notion that the Biblical mother of all living had a sexual affair with an animal; before the Christian Identity Doctrine took its form and became popularized (and weaponized) in the United States, British Israelism was used to target Jewish People. According to British Israelism, the offspring of Eve and the serpent were the Jews that we see today, and the people of Great Britain are *"genetically, racially, and linguistically the direct descendants"*[28] of the Ten Lost Tribes of Israel. This was the theology weaponized by Adolf Hitler during the Holocaust. In his book, Mein Kampf, Hitler stated:

> *The nationalization of our masses will succeed only when, aside from all the positive struggle for the soul of our people, their international poisoners are exterminated*[29] {...} *If at the*

[26] Christian Identity. 2017. Accessed 2022, Dec 28 from https://www.adl.org/resources/backgrounder/christian-identity. "By the 1960s, a new group of Christian Identity leaders had emerged. In the ensuing decades, they would spread Identity throughout the far right. Most prominent among them were California disciples of Wesley Swift: James K. Warner, William Potter Gale and Richard Butler. Warner (1939-), who moved to Louisiana and became active in the segregationist struggle against civil rights, was the head of the Christian Defense League and the New Christian Crusade Church. Gale (1917-1988) was an early leader in the Christian Defense League as well as its paramilitary arm, the California Rangers. In the 1970s he founded the Posse Comitatus (the group that helped spawn the sovereign citizen movement), while in the 1980s he created the Committee of the States and served as the "chief of staff" of its "unorganized militia." Most famous of all, Butler (1918-) moved Swift's Church of Jesus Christ Christian to northern Idaho in 1974, where he recast it as the neo-Nazi group Aryan Nations."

[27] Branham, William. 1964, Aug 16. Proving His Word. "I want you to check my revelation on Serpent's Seed."

[28] Cottrell-Boyce, Aidan. 2021. Israelism in Modern Britain.

[29] Hitler, Adolf. 1925. Mein Kampf, Volume One – A Reckoning, Chapter XII: The First Period of Development of the National Socialist German Workers' Party

beginning of the war and during the war twelve or fifteen thousand of these Hebrew corrupters of the nation had been subjected to poison gas, such as had to be endured in the field by hundreds of thousands of our very best German workers of all classes and professions, then the sacrifice of millions at the front would not have been in vain."[30]

Looking back through time at the horrific extinction of Jewish people at the hands of the Germans in Nazi concentration camps, and now understanding Adolf Hitler's deep burning hatred for Jewish people, one would assume that only a very small minority of people in the United States would have agreed with Adolf Hitler before, during, and after WWII. The sad truth is that, with the exception of murder and genocide, many Pentecostals and fundamentalists in the United States were in full agreement. So much so that Gerald Burton Winrod, the "Jawhawk Nazi"[31] and "Kansas Hitler",[32] built an entire religious organization on that very premise. Winrod was so popular among fundamentalists that F. F. Bosworth, William Branham's spiritual mentor in the Post WWII healing revival, invited Winrod to submit articles for his "Exploits of the Faith" magazine.[33] Paul Rader, the second president of the Christian and Missionary Alliance, held conferences with Winrod

---

[30] Hitler, Adolf. 1926. Mein Kampf, Volume Two - A Reckoning, Chapter XV: The Right of Emergency Defense, p. 984,

[31] Justification by Race: Wesley Swift's White Supremacy and Anti-Semitic Theological Views in His Christian Identity Sermons. Accessed 2022, May 5 from https://jhs.press.gonzaga.edu/articles/10.33972/jhs.183/. "Minister Wesley Albert Swift (1913-1970), one of the original and leading proponents of Christian Identity, a racial theology movement which emerged in the United States after World War II. I

[32] Foursquare Church. 1954, Apr 17. Fresno Bee. "William Branham: 'The Story of a 20th Century Prophet: A Sound Film in Color".

[33] Barnes, Roscoe III. 2018, Dec 31. Reading with F. F. Bosworth. Accessed 2022, Dec 28 from http://roscoereporting.blogspot.com/2018/12/. "Bosworth's magazine also featured the writings of his wife, Florence, and his brother, B.B. Bosworth. Other writers included Evangelist A.G. Jeffries, Harry Hodge, C.C. Fitch, Rev. William T. MacArthur, Rev. Herbert Dyke, Rev. P. Gavin Duffy, Bishop Charles H. Brent, James Moore Hickson, Carrie Judd Montgomery, Rev. J. P. Roberts, Mary Lowe Dickinson, Rev. W. J. Bennett, Ethel E. Tulloch, E. West, Charles H. Usher, John Harris, Fannie J. Rowe, J. Albert Libby and Dr. Gerald B. Winrod.'

— some of which opened at the Cadle Tabernacle,[34] Indiana Klan Headquarters. Rader was a member of Winrod's "Defenders of the Christian Faith" movement.[35] Gordon Lindsay, Branham's first campaign manager, was a member of the "Anglo-Saxon Christian World Movement", a British Israelism organization.[36]

During WWII, this movement was weaponized, politically, against Franklin D. Roosevelt. Religious leaders began openly declaring the Jewish race to be the cause of communism and that Jews were working with Russia to invade the religious and political systems of the United States. The weaponized doctrine quickly spread through fundamentalist Christianity leading to a severe impact on the morale of the United States military. Most of the people organizing the effort were from California, and in Los Angeles during December of 1941, a series of mock trials impeaching Roosevelt were held. Mixing politics, religion, and anti-Semitism through British Israelism, weaponized religion began to undermine government systems. This led to the Great Sedition Trial of 1944.[37]

Ironically, not only was weaponized religion used against the United States Government, but Richard Nixon also recognized the level of influence achieved by the groups involved and chose to use weaponized religion — by many of the same groups involved in or connected to defendants of the Sedition Trial of 1944 — to spread domestic fear of Communism in the United States by using members of the Full Gospel Businessmen's Fellowship International

---

[34] An Intellectual and Religious Treat! 1929, Feb 2. Indianapolis Times. (Paul Rader and Gerald B. Winrod Pictured).

[35] Chicago Gospel Tabernacle World Defenders' Convention. 1930, May 17. Chicago Tribune. "Gerald R. Winrod: 'The Church and its Parasites' {...} Paul Rader"

[36] Annual Conference of Anglo-Saxon Christian World Movement. 1940, Aug 17. The Vancouver.

[37] Sedition Trial of 1944. Accessed 2022, Dec 28 from https://digital-library.csun.edu/in-our-own-backyard/sedition-trial-of-1944. "On January 3, 1944, thirty opponents of American involvement in the war against Germany went to trial for charges of violating the Smit Act of 1940. The charges stemmed from their involvement in fascist movements and from cooperation with German forces. The defendants opposed war against Germany and espoused rabid anti-Semitism. A high percentage of the defendants came from California, including Noble, Jones, Schwinn and Diebel."

(FGBMFI). FGBMFI was founded by Demos Shakarian, the nephew of Kardashian Family patriarch Tatos Kardashian.[38] The Kardashians and Shakarians sponsored William Branham's revivals in 1947,[39] and William Branham is photographed attending the FGBMI convention[40] where then Vice President Nixon appealed to the weaponized religion to help fight the *greatest battle ever fought: the battle of the minds.*

> *Now in the National Security Council, we consider, of course, the military policy, the economical policy, the political policies that the United States can adopt to meet this threat. But all of us know that the great battle in which we are engaged today is one which is not only military, economic, and political in character and it is that, but that in the final analysis, it is a battle for the minds, and the hearts, and the souls of men.*[41]

The group's success is not only evident from the historic fears of Communism that spread throughout the United States

---

[38] Oppenheimer, Jerry. 2017. The Kardashians. "The sprawling Kardashian family had arrived in America from their village in Armenia in the early 1900s. It was in California where Tatos Kardashian met his future wife, Hamas Shakarian, the matriarch and the great-grandmother of the famous Kardashian siblings. Hamas's brother, Isaac Shakarian, had made a fortune in the dairy business in Downey, California. His son, Demos Shakarian, took over the business, but would earn his greatest fame as a Pentecostal evangelist who believed in miracles and healings,"

[39] The "Full Gospel" Origins of Peoples Temple. Accessed 2022, Dec 28 from https://jonestown.sdsu.edu/?page_id=92702. Tatos "Thomas" Kardashian, great grandfather of Kim Kardashian, sponsored Hagopian's tour through the United States, and the highly publicized activities of the "healer" caused a flurry of interest from coast to coast. They teamed up with avowed anti-Semite and Ku Klux Klansman Clem Davies to sponsor Avak, and when Arkelian's son was not cured, sponsored a Pentecostal evangelist from Jeffersonville, Indiana named William Branham.

[40] Branham, William. 1954, July 18. The Great Coming Revival and The Outpouring of The Holy Spirit (54-0718A). "Some time ago, a few weeks ago, having Breakfast or—in the room at Washington, DC, and a speaker, Mr. Nixon, the Vice President of the United States, was speaking at this time. And he was talking of how Communism was sweeping the land and the space we had to—to travel. For instance, the goal that the world faces like that...Communism has this much of it already."

[41] Vice-President Richard Nixon's Message to the Full Gospel Businessmen's Convention. 1954, Sept. Voice of Healing.

through religious propaganda, but also from the fact that Richard Nixon engaged the group once more when he became President. Specifically, Nixon engaged Branham's splinter group in Chile — Paul Schäfer's Colonia Dignidad compound. Declassified documents confirm that Presidents Nixon, Ford, and Carter were all in collaboration with the Pinochet Regime from 1973 to 1981.[42] After a meeting held between Chilean media tycoon Agustin Edwards, Pepsi Cola owner Donald Kendall, and the CIA, the United States Attorney General convinced Nixon to form a "Task Force" for staging a military coup in Chile.[43] The CIA worked directly with DINA (Pinochet's Intelligence Agency), which used Colonia Dignidad as *"a national intelligence training center run by Germans"*[44]. It was *"the central receiver of all of the information from the external apparatus of DINA"*.[45]

---

[42] Salviato, Serena. 2020. How did the American Administrations (Nixon, Ford, Carter) react to the human rights violations of Pinochet's dictatorship? An account of the United States' relation with Chile (1973-1981) through its declassified files. Accessed 2022, Dec 28 from https://unipd-centrodirittiumani.it/en/schede/How-did-the-American-Administrations-Nixon-Ford-Carter-react-to-the-human-rights-violations-of-Pinochets-dictatorship-An-account-of/443. "The United States' ties to Chile in the first and most repressive phase of the Augusto Pinochet's dictatorship, from 1973 to 1981, represent a complex and controversial history for the U.S. In this seven-year period major human rights violations were registered in Chile as the American administrations of Richard Nixon, Gerald Ford and Jimmy Carter entertained a relationship with General Pinochet."
[43] Basso, Carlos. 2022. La Secta Perfecta. (Kindle Version, Spanish) p65. "The conspiracies were activated between September 15 and 17, 1970, when the Chilean journalistic businessman Agustin Edwards traveled to Washington DC and, with the owner of Pepsi Cola, Donald Kendall, managed to meet with the director of the Central Intelligence Agency (CIA) and the United States Attorney General, who took Edwards' petition to Richard Nixon. Nixon agreed, remembering his old friendship with Kendall, and as a result, the CIA put together a 'Task Force', which ultimately designed an absurd plan for a coup, which began with the kidnapping of the commander-in-chief of the Army, Reno Schneider."
[44] Basso, Carlos. 2022. La Secta Perfecta. (Kindle Version, Spanish) p178. "According to his testimony, he was detained anyway, but 'later, I was released on the condition that I cooperate. They took me to Colonia Dignidad', a place about which he stated, 'there is a national intelligence training center run by Germans and nationalized Chileans."
[45] Basso, Carlos. 2022. La Secta Perfecta. (Kindle Version, Spanish) p178.

CHAPTER 1

THE WAR BEGINS

❖

"Zion City is overrun with new 'prophets' some of whom appear to be gaining followings. Five of these prophets have arisen within the last two weeks." - Chicago Press

The year was 1907. The World Series was only four years old, and twenty-year-old Ty Cobb, nicknamed "The Georgia Peach", was earning his record for stealing bases on the path leading to a competition between his Detroit Tigers and the Chicago Cubs at West Side Park. That year, Cobb stole second, third, and home bases. The baseball legend would repeat that performance five more times in his career.[46]

Oklahoma was not yet officially part of the United States. It wasn't until November 1907 that the Indian Territory and Oklahoma Territory were combined to form the 46th State in the Union. After the American Civil War, most tribes of native Americans having sided with the South, the Indian Territory had been under the control of the United States military. President Teddy Roosevelt welcomed Oklahoma into the United States on November 17, 1907.[47]

---

[46] Ty Cobb - Baseball Legend. 2003, Jul 22. H2G2. "Six times in his life, Cobb reached first base, stole second, stole third and then stole home. He did it for the first time in 1907. Very few people can do this."

[47] Oklahoma enters the Union. Accessed 2022, Dec 19 from history.com/this-day-in-history/Oklahoma-enters-the-union. "In 1907, Congress decided to admit Indian

The rest of the country was in an economic recession and stocks were struggling. In October, the New York Stock Exchange would drop fifty percent causing the Panic of 1907. Fearing the worst, people across the nation started liquidating assets causing a collapse of the United States banking system. When the Knickerbocker Trust Company fell, it sent shockwaves through regional banks leading to the 8th-largest market decline in U.S. history.[48]   J. P. Morgan, E. H. Harriman, James Stillman, Henry Clay Frick, and other Wall Street financiers saved the day when they created a $25,000,000 investment pool that they pumped into the plunging New York Stock Exchange. Their quick decision ultimately led to the establishment of the Federal Reserve System.

The United States economy was not the only major concern of 1907. Fears of pandemic were quickly spreading in the East. So much so that one George Sober began stalking Irish born Mary Mallon to prove that she was hosting and spreading the Salmonella Typhi bacteria, giving typhoid fever to everyone in that she came in contact with.[49] Sober discovered that she had served as the cook for eight families that contracted the deadly disease, though she, herself, was asymptomatic. It is believed that three thousand New Yorkers were infected because of her spreading the disease, giving her the nickname "Typhoid Mary".[50] Under sections 1169 and

Territory and Oklahoma Territory into the Union as a single state. Representatives of the two territories drafted a constitution, and on September 17, 1907, it was approved by voters of the two territories. On November 16, Oklahoma was welcomed into the United States by President Theodore Roosevelt."

[48] Panic of 1907: J.P. Morgan Saves the Day. Accessed 2022, Dec 19 from http://www.u-s-history.com/pages/h952.html

[49] Marine, Filio. Tsoucalas, Gregory. Karamanou, Marianna. Androidsos, George. 2013. Mary Mallon (1869-1938) and the history of typhoid fever. "From March 1907, Sober started stalking Mary Mallon in Manhattan and he revealed that she was transmitting disease and death by her activity. His attempts to obtain samples of Mary's feces, urine and blood, earned him nothing but being chased by her. Sober reconstituted the puzzle by discovering that previously the cook had served in 8 families. Seven of them had experienced cases of typhoid. Twenty-two people presented signs of infection, and some died. That year, about 3,000 New Yorkers had been infected by Salmonella typhi, and probably Mary was the main reason for the outbreak."

[50] Typhoid Mary' Dies of A Stroke At 68. Carrier of Disease, Blamed for 51 Cases and 3 Deaths, but Immune". 1938, Nov 12. "Mary Mallon, the first carrier of typhoid bacilli

1170 of the Greater New York Charter, Mallon was arrested as a public health threat.

Millions of people were migrating to the United States, bringing with them new culture, new ideas, and a wide variety of religious beliefs. In 1907, during the busiest day of the year, Ellis Island processed over one million new immigrants.[51] A large number of those coming to America were Jewish. Between 1881 and 1924, over two-and-one-half million Jews immigrated into cities across the country, mostly clustering together in districts close to downtown.[52] Though they left native lands due to persecution, the Jewish migrants were soon to be the target for white supremacy. In 1907, however, this was not yet the case.

During the same time period, one of the most significant events in United States Christianity was underway in Los Angeles and had been since April of the year before. A series of revival meetings led by Louisiana-born African American William Joseph Seymour on Azusa Street were making waves through the holiness communities across the nation.

Seymour, a student of Pentecostal founder Charles Fox Parham, had adopted Parham's beliefs that speaking in tongues was the evidence of receiving the baptism of the Holy Spirit, and many early Pentecostals began referring to his revivals as the most significant outpouring of the Holy Spirit. Seymour had separated with Parham in 1906 over theological differences, and as the leader of the revivals, gained far more attention than his mentor. Parham, however, had his sights set much higher — which was likely the reason for the separation.

identified in America and consequently known as Typhoid Mary, died yesterday in Riverside Hospital on North Brother Island."

[51] "Ellis Island closes". This Day in History. Accessed 2022, Dec 19 from https://www.history.com/this-day-in-history/ellis-island-closes. "During the busiest year of operation, 1907, over 1 million people were processed at Ellis Island."

[52] From Haven to Home: 350 Years of Jewish Life in America

A Century of Immigration, 1820-1924. Accessed 2022, Dec 29 from https://www.loc.gov/exhibits/haventohome/haven-century.html

From 1906 to 1907, Parham was entertaining the religious crowds in Zion, Illinois. The year 1907 marked the fall of the one of the biggest religious empires in early American history, one which Parham and many other opportunists tried to claim for their own. Faith healer John Alexander Dowie, founder of the Christian Catholic Church sect, was near death. His communal city of Zion[53] — fully owned, operated, managed, and occupied by his cult of personality, had become a new prospect for other "faith healers" seeking wealth and power. In just ten years, by 1902, Dowie had amassed $15,000,000[54] earning him the nickname, *"Richest Man in the West"* and the *"Merchant Prince of Faith Healers"*. Dowie himself claimed the nickname "Elijah III" after convincing his cult of personality that he, like John the Baptist in the Old Testament, was empowered with the Spirit of Elijah.[55] In today's money, he was worth over a half of a billion dollars.[56]

Though the ongoing revival at Azusa Street in Los Angeles would ultimately be the event that most historians believed to have exploded into modern Pentecostalism, the fuse had been lit years earlier when Dowie first migrated to the United States from Australia.[57] And as it transitioned from a series of revivals to a religious movement, many of those same opportunists seeking

---

[53] Faith Healer Dowie to Establish a New "City of Zion": Will Remove His Tabernacle and Homes to a Country Location. 1895, Oct 10. Chicago Chronicle. "John Alexander Dowie will soon solve the vexed question of whether he is a nuisance in the community or not, and no more will it be necessary for citizens to swore out warrants for his arrest. He has decided to remove the Zion Tabernacle from its present location near Jackson Park to the old Cool farm, near Blue Island, eighteen miles from the center of the city.

[54] A Record of $15,000,000 Profit in 10 Years Makes John Alexander Dowie, Alias Elijah III the Merchant Prince of Faith Healers. 1902, Nov 30. Brooklyn Daily Eagle.

[55] Dowie Denounces City: Throngs See Elijah III., but Leave Before Sermon. 1903, Oct 19. Asbury Park Press. "His word being law with the members of his restoration host, Elijah III. Could not comprehend that his command to an audience to be seated or that doors be locked to retain it should not be obeyed."

[56] $15,000,000 in 1900 is worth $531,626,785.71 today. Accessed 2022, Dec 19 from https://www.in2013dollars.com/us/inflation/1900?amount=15000000

[57] The Faith Healer. 1888 Aug 25. Oakland Tribune. "Rev. J. A. Dowie, the faith healer proposes to return in a month and establish a permanent Faith Cure Mission home in Oakland or San Francisco, after which he intends to labor in the southern part of the State.

control of Zion fanned the flames in ways that fit their own agenda. A large number of people joined Dowie's sect in hopes of rising into power, while others tried very hard to replicate it. Among those who initially tried to clone Dowie's work was Charles Parham. From 1898 through 1900, Parham toured the United States visiting various religious communities in hopes of creating one of his own,[58] and Zion City was among those that he visited.[59]

When Dowie's health began to fail in 1906, and a transition of power from Dowie to Wilbur Voliva was announced, many other "prophets" sensed weakness among the ranks and began flooding Zion in hopes of claiming stake in Dowie's financial empire. Newspapers noted that Zion City was *"overrun with new 'prophets'"*.[60] It was during this time that Parham seized the opportunity and entered the city proclaiming himself to be the next "Elijah".[61]

---

[58] The Holy Ghost & Us Society. Accessed 2021, Dec 22 from https://www.apostolicarchives.com/articles/article/8801925/173155.htm. "In the summer of 1900, Charles Fox Parham, founder of the Bethel Bible School in Topeka, Kansas, the birthplace of the modern Pentecostal Movement, journeyed throughout the United States visiting various Christian utopias and Bible centers in an effort to identify a community which replicated the Apostolic experience of the New Testament Church. One stop on this spiritual odyssey was Frank Sandford's commune in Durham, Maine called Holy Ghost and Us Society."

[59] In 1898 Parham visited John Alexander Dowie's healing homes in Chicago. He was so impressed that he returned and founded a healing faith home called Beth-el in Topeka, Kansas. The couple also began to publish a holiness journal called "Apostolic Faith".

[60] Many and Vexatious Are Prophets in Zion: Five Rise Up to Add to the General Confusion. 1906, Sep 27. Indianapolis News. "Zion City is overrun with new 'prophets' some of whom appear to be gaining followings. Five of these prophets have arisen within the last two weeks. Overseer Wilbur Glenn Voliva, hoping to check the defection, announced at a divine healing meeting yesterday that he would 'lead Zion or it would fall.'"

[61] Was something Startling About Cures He Effected. 1906, Nov 3. Topeka Daily Capital. "A short time ago Parham received another vision from his spiritual source, and announced himself to be Elijah III, as Dowie had declared himself to be Elijah II. Parham left Topeka and went to Zion City. There, taking advantage of the time when Dowie and Voliva were wrangling over the job of overseer of Dowie's millions, he entered the sacred city and proclaimed his vision and his title."

It was said that Parham *"turned Zion City upside down"* when he imparted the gift of tongues to thousands of people.[62] Parham held his revival on the western outskirts of the city, attracting a large crowd and announcing that it was only a matter of days before he won the entire population of Zion.[63] Among those who defected to Parham's sect was John G. Lake, who spread Pentecostalism throughout South Africa, and F. F. Bosworth[64] who helped establish the Assemblies of God and later mentored revivalists in the Post WWII healing revival. Parham would ultimately be ejected from Zion City[65] after having been arrested for sodomy with a young J. J. Jourdan in San Antonio, Texas.[66] According to the newspaper accounts, there was a "mass of evidence" against Parham, which included his own confession.[67]

---

[62] Parham Denies Charges Made by Voliva. 1908, December 7. Waukegan Daily Sun. "Turned Zion City Upside Down: two years ago Parham turned Zion City upside down, inducing thousands to a belief in the 'gift of tongues', in a non-resistance, in the doctrine that the 'Lord will provide,' and in a missionary spirit that has carried some of the Zion people to remote corners of the earth, John G. Lake being in South Africa, others in China, Japan, Korea, Australia, and various parts of this country."

[63] Many and Vexatious Are Prophets in Zion: Five Rise Up to Add to the General Confusion. 1906, Sep 27. Indianapolis News. "Charles Parham, the last addition to the ranks of the new evangelists, attracted a large crowd to an open-air meeting which he held in the afternoon on the western outskirts of the city. He announced after his return to Elijah hospice that it would be a matter of only a few days before he had won the entire population".

[64] Deep Diplomacy: Overseer Voliva Apes Dowie Methods in Zion. 1907, March 5. Waukegan Daily Sun. "It is apparent that Voliva has become alive to the growing separations and scattering of the forces of Zion. Meetings were held yesterday in the college building, directed by such leading men as Alex Granger, C. A. Rominger, F. A. Fieden and Horace Cook. F. F. Bosworth, formerly conductor of the Zion City Band, is one of the head Parhamite preachers.

[65] Ejected From Zion. 1906, Nov 5. Coffeyville Daily Journal. "Charles Fox Parham, founder of the Apostolic Faith, worker of miraculous cures and physical phenomena, well known in this city and throughout this section, has been excommunicated and ejected from Zion City."

[66] Justice Ben Fisk's Court. 1907, Jul 20. Daily Express. "Charles F. Parham and J. J. Jourdan, charge sodomy, waived examination; bond placed at $1000 each. Both remanded to jail."

[67] Nameless Crimes in Texas Cause Arrest of Parham Who Makes Confession. 1907, Jul 27. Waukegan Daily Son. "Despite the mass of evidence which has been produced against him and his own written confession, many of his flock refuse to believe in his guilt."

He was arrested while giving special "lessons" to children.[68] During the court proceedings that followed, affidavits, letters, and the testimony of an eyewitness were submitted as evidence against Parham, and it was learned that Parham had also been accused of sodomy in Waco, League City, and Orchard, Texas. A certified copy of Parham's explanation of the charges in Orchard was also used as evidence in the San Antonio case.[69] Though charges against him were eventually dropped, the court of public opinion had already found him to be guilty. Parham did not deny the charges; according to Parham, the act was unintentional.[70]

This explosive news caused even more disruption in Zion City. From the early 1890s until his failing health in 1906, Dowie had fully militarized his sect. Dowie converts *"breathed vengeance upon"* all who opposed his cult of personality,[71] and were willing to kill those who stood in the path to Dowie's success.[72] Death was

---

[68] Nameless Crimes in Texas Cause Arrest of Parham Who Makes Confession. 1907, Jul 27. Waukegan Daily Son. "Arrested Giving Lessons to 'Kids': When Constable Stevens went to arrest the accused man, he found him giving a Bible lesson in the Majestic Theater to the junior members of the congregation."

[69] Nameless Crimes in Texas Cause Arrest of Parham Who Makes Confession. 1907, Jul 27. Waukegan Daily Son. "Affidavits, letters, the testimony of an eyewitness and the written confession of Parham himself were produced as evidence in the case. Both Parham and his companion, Jourdan, were unable to secure bond and are confined to county jail."

[70] Nameless Crimes in Texas Cause Arrest of Parham Who Makes Confession. 1907, Jul 27. Waukegan Daily Son. "I am a helpless degenerate physically. I will swear, however, that I never committed this crime intentionally. What I might have done in my sleep, I can not say, but it was never intended on my part."

[71] Dowie on Parade: Proprietor of Zion Attacks His Enemies Before an Audience of 3,000 Persons: Endorses Harrison. 1899, Aug 14. Inter Ocean. "The services opened with a song — a strong militant hymn, which breathed vengeance upon the enemies of Dowie and the Lord. Here is one verse: 'On every hand the foe we find, drawn up in dread array, Let the tents of ease be left behind, and onward to the fray.'"

[72] Dowie on Parade: Proprietor of Zion Attacks His Enemies Before an Audience of 3,000 Persons: Endorses Harrison. 1899, Aug 14. Inter Ocean. "Now Mr. Stevens, I am going to make a statement, and you can go against me for damages if I am wrong. I brand this man Stevens as a liar, as a seducer of a widow, and as a scoundrel. He ought to be disbarred. Sit down, Stevens, I am through with you."
As Mr. Stevens sat down Mary Casey lost control of herself and shrieked:
"He ought to be tarred and feathered!"

a frequent occurrence in Zion, to the extent that everyone was familiar with the bodies being whisked away from the commune[73] — many of them transported secretly under the cover of night.[74] Converts were willing to kill for their new brand of Christianity, and they were trained to assist in sweeping murder under the rug. Parham, having spent over a year in Zion with his unique style of glossolalia and exorcisms, created an even more deadly mixture at his own command. Once Parham was expelled from Zion, that power went to one Harold Mitchell.

After Charles Fox Parham was exposed for the sinful acts allegedly committed against small boys, Mitchell seized his opportunity for power by declaring himself to be the one "chosen by God".[75] With the militant power of Dowie, the exorcism training of Parham,[76] and the flood of "faith healing" doctrines by the many prophets of Zion, Mitchell quickly became drunken with a very militant and deadly religious cocktail. The Parhamites in Zion, now under Mitchell's control, decided to forcibly "cure" one

---

"Yes, yes," came back the response from all over the building. "Tar and feather him; throw him from over the railing."

[73] Law to Reach Dowie. 1899, Aug 16. Inter Ocean. "In another case, Mrs. Canaris took her young son, who had dislocated his shoulder, to Dowie's resort for treatment. Dowie pulled off all the bandages and pretended to pray for the boy. Later the mother saw that he was suffering intense agony, and Dr. Gentry was called to reduce the fracture. The boy got well all right, but if he had continued under Dowie's treatment, he would have been carried out of that side door of Zion into the hearse which visits the place so often. This fight will be to a finish and will be on practical lines. Dowie's days are numbered."

[74] Faith Healers Jailed. 1899, Aug 18. Worthington Advance. "'It's claimed that corpses were taken away at night, when Dr. Dowie had his sanitarium at Sixty first street,' remarked the reporter. 'Do you know whether anything like that goes on here?' 'No, I don't. A dealer near me on Twelfth street, told me that they were carrying out corpses often at night, but I don't know.'"

[75] In Religion's Name. 1907, Sep 23. Coffeyville Daily Journal. "When Parham was arrested in San Antonio recently, some of his adherents deserted him. Mitchell denounced him and a little more than a month ago declared he himself had been 'chosen of God.'

[76] Five Held to Jury for Zion Horror. 1907, Sep 22. Chicago Tribune. "We, the jury, further find by investigating the death of Mrs. Greenhalgh that certain practices under the leadership of one Charles F. Parham and his followers which are both disgraceful and dangerous to society; and we believe that these practices should be thoroughly investigated by the proper authorities."

Letitia Greenhaulgh of rheumatism and paralysis by painfully *straightening* her bones to exorcize the "demons" out of her feeble body. Even through her cries of excruciating pain, the group continued snapping her bones. Post-mortem examination of the body showed that both knees, both elbows, and the left collarbone were broken, and other parts of her body were injured. The bones were broken longitudinally, giving such intense pain that doctors determined the bone-breaking shock was the cause of death.[77]

After a loud prayer by Mitchell, his wife took hold of one of the old woman's legs, gripped it tight, and by twisting, pulling, and pressing down upon the knee, forced it nearly straight. The screams of agony rang through the house, but the same cruel treatment was given the other limb, and as both showed signs of returning to their former positions, the son seated himself on the knees to hold them straight.

As he did so he heard a breaking sound made by the fractures of the bones. "What was that?" he demanded, shaking Mitchell by the arm. "It's only corruption coming out with the devils", was the answer. "Don't hurt her," pleaded the son, and Mitchell pushed him away, saying: "Those are not her cries. They are the cries of the demons," and he put his hand over her mouth, stifling her screams." As they ceased for a moment he took his hand away, and the dying woman muttered:

"I was in hell, but soon will be heaven." With that, thinking she meant she was being cured, Mitchell began with her

---

[77] Five Held to Jury for Zion Horror: Coroner's Body Finds Against Those Responsible for Mrs. Greenhaulgh's Death: Criticism for the Cult; Recommends State Health Authorities Take a Hand to Prevent Repetition. 1907, Sep 22. Chicago Tribune. "Dr. Taylor's statement to the jury was that there was no question as to the cause of Mrs. Greenhaulgh's death. 'The shock coming from those fractures alone,' he stated, 'would be enough to cause death to a much stronger person than she. Each and every one of them was a complicated fracture that would not have healed normally. The bones, through long invalidism, were like dry sticks, and they broke not only crosswise but longitudinally. They splintered and pieces of bone several sizes are found in each of them."

deformed arms. The screams broke out again, and as they did, he made a signal to his wife, who with Mrs. Smith began to dance around the room, waving their hands and striking at the air. They said afterward they were "driving out the room the bad devils as they left the body."

Each arm cracked as it was bent away from the body where rheumatism had kept it locked for years. The victim seemed almost unconscious, but a spasm of pain more severe than the rest passed through her frame and the broken arms and legs rose in the air, seeming to push at Mitchell. He covered her head with a pillow, and as the motions ceased, he removed it, and seizing her by the head gave her neck a severe wrench that dislocated the vertebrae. The body sank back motionless. They continued working at the senseless muscles until they saw no response was given.[78]

Harold Mitchell, his wife Anna, Greenhaulgh's son Walter and daughter Jennie, and one Louise Smith were arrested and sent to the Grand Jury for manslaughter. The Parhamite sect in Zion imploded, but certainly did not die. Parham himself escaped almost unscathed and is remembered by some as one of "God's Generals",[79] as are other leading figures among the Parhamites such as F. F. Bosworth, John G. Lake, and more. Some of the men involved truly believed they were endowed with power from God. Others recognized the power that this new religion gave to those that harnessed it, and the control over those who accepted their spiritual authority. That authority, as evil minds would soon learn, was more physical than spiritual.

---

[78] - Tortured in Rite of Fanatics. 1907, Sep 21. Chicago Tribune.
[79] Liardon, Roberts. God's Generals: Charles F. Parham and William J. Seymour (video)

CHAPTER 2

VICTIM OF THE FLAMING SWORD

❖

"From the time of the expulsion from Eden till the Exodus from the land of Egypt the way of the tree of life had been kept from Adam's posterity. No man had ever been able to pass the flaming sword." - Genesis 3:24

The United States changed very rapidly between the time of the Azusa Street Revival and the early 1920s. Only sixteen percent of American households had electricity in 1912, but by the early 1920s, over sixty percent of households had modernized.[80] Women had advantages which never existed before; electric washing machines, freezers, and vacuum cleaners turned daily chores into simple tasks. The 19th Amendment to the Constitution passed in 1920, secured freedom for white women to vote, though black women in the South would be limited in their freedom for decades due to the Jim Crow segregation laws.

The first commercial radio station went live in 1920. Pittsburgh's KDKA thrilled listeners with information about the Harding-Cox Presidential election on the evening of November 2,

---

[80] The Roaring Twenties. Accessed 2022, Dec 23 from https://www.history.com/topics/roaring-twenties/roaring-twenties-history.. "In 1912, an estimated 16 percent of American households had electricity; by the mid-1920s, more than 60 percent did."

1920.[81]   Two years later, Warren G. Harding became the first president to address the nation by radio, and by the end of the 1920s, more than twelve million households in the United States owned radios.[82]   This new form of communication was heavily utilized by evangelists, and Pentecostal evangelists were no exception to the rule. Aimee Semple McPherson erected her own radio station with a 250-foot tower on top of the Angelus Temple and her sermons were broadcast throughout Los Angeles and the surrounding area.[83]

In January of 1923, Indiana Pentecostal Bishop Garfield Thomas Haywood published his tract entitled *Victim of the Flaming Sword*. Haywood, a black leader in the Pentecostal Religion, made significant progress towards removing racial barriers in Indiana during a time when the state was filled with members of the white supremacy groups. In 1909, Haywood became pastor and founder[84] of the Christ Temple Apostolic Faith Assembly[85], the first Pentecostal church built in the Midwest.[86]   His conversion to the

---

[81] Growth of Commercial Radio. Britannica. The first commercial radio station was KDKA in Pittsburgh, which went on the air in the evening of Nov. 2, 1920, with a broadcast of the returns of the Harding-Cox presidential election."

[82] The Roaring Twenties. Accessed 2022, Dec 23 from https://www.history.com/topics/roaring-twenties/roaring-twenties-history. "The first commercial radio station in the United States, Pittsburgh's KDKA, hit the airwaves in 1920. Two years later Warren G. Harding became the first president to address the nation by radio—and three years later there were more than 500 stations in the nation. By the end of the 1920s, there were radios in more than 12 million households."

[83] Kay, William K. 2009. Pentecostalism and religious broadcasting. Accessed 2022, Dec 23 from https://www.researchgate.net/publication/248999139_Pentecostalism_and_religious_broadcasting. Direct preaching was part of the religious scene from 1924 when Aimee Semple McPherson, a Pentecostal evangelist, erected her own radio station and placed a 250-foot-high transmission towers on the top of Angelus Temple, "

[84] Compromise proposes honoring deceased with memorial signs. 1989, Apr 18. Indianapolis Star. "Bishop Thomas Haywood, founder of Christ Temple Apostolic Faith Assembly"

[85] Ray Boomhower. 1994". Haywood, Garfield Thomas" The Encyclopedia of Indianapolis. "In 1907, Haywood attended a gathering of PENTECOSTALS in Indianapolis and became part of that movement. Two years later, he founded the Christ temple Apostolic Faith Assembly."

[86] Christ Temple Apostolic Faith Assembly: The Mother Church of the Pentecostal Assemblies of the World. Accessed 2022, Feb 23 from https://christtempleac.org/.

Pentecostal faith just two years prior ignited a flame that would burn so brightly that Haywood would rise quickly through the ranks of Pentecostalism to become one of the recognized Pentecostal founders[87] and Presiding Bishop of the Pentecostal Assemblies of the World.[88] Because of Haywood's skin color and his unusual faith,[89] however, Christ Temple found itself under heavy persecution and was forced to relocate several times.

Haywood's home state of Indiana in the 1920s was a hotspot for Ku Klux Klan activity and white supremacy. To be an "upstanding citizen" in Indiana, a person either joined the Klan, supported the Klan, or aligned with the ideologies that the Klan supported. The Klan was strongly opposed to Catholicism, the Jewish faith, and integration of races, even in religious settings. Haywood would have been respected by his religious peers as a leader of blacks, but the moment a white person attended one of his services, he would have been seen as a threat to society for *"influencing a white person"*. As he became even more influential as a leader of the now worldwide Pentecostal movement, white supremacists would have recognized his advancement as a huge threat to their preferred way of life. Not only was Haywood a leader in a black community for a black church, but he was also a "leader among leaders" of multiple races in a movement now advertising no racial boundaries. This was seen as a threat by white supremacy groups.

Haywood's *Victim of the Flaming Sword* tract focused upon the third chapter of the Book of Genesis from the Old Testament

---

[87] Pentecostals Prove Staying Power. 1982, Jul 25. Indianapolis Star. "Indianapolis also was the home of one of the major founders of the Pentecostal Assemblies of the World, the late Bishop Garfield Thomas Haywood. He became pastor in February 1909, of Christ Temple, which was the target of considerable persecution and several relocations."

[88] Ray Boomhower. "Haywood, who published numerous articles and tracts on behalf of his faith, rose to become Presiding Bishop of the Pentecostal Assemblies of the World."

[89] Points of Interest. 1985, Jun 16. Indianapolis Star. "Bishop Garfield Thomas Haywood, for whom a portion of Fall Creek Parkway is named, was one of the major founders of Pentecostal Assemblies of the World at a time when the denomination was the target of ridicule and persecution. Early Pentecostals were unpopular with other religious groups because they believed in speaking in tongues, disapproved of many 'worldly things' and did not believe in the Trinity teaching."

which described mankind being driven out of the Garden of Eden.[90] For a black man living in a world of white supremacy, the passage held greater meaning for Haywood and his black converts than their white counterparts. Especially for those with black skin in the State of Indiana at the time, the United States was certainly no *"Eden"*. It was a world filled with daily racial conflict and reminders that people with white skin did not view people with black skin as their equals. "White" bathrooms could not be entered by blacks, specific sections of restaurants and other venues were designated to be "for coloreds", and people with white skin had special privileges that were not available to those with black skin. Haywood made no significant attempt to change society or overturn the racial injustice in Indiana. His only hope was that someday the conflict might end. Hayward did not, however, feel that any ending would happen during his lifetime. Instead, he looked toward his new faith and the new freedom it promised after transitioning from this life to the next. Haywood found peace in believing that Jesus Christ fought a heavenly battle that purchased his right for freedom in paradise.

> *In the heat of the struggle He cried, "I thirst," and as darkness settled upon Him the lamentable cry, "My God, my God, why hast thou forsaken me," brought the terrible conflict to an end. And when He cried with a loud voice, "It is finished," He gave up the ghost and entered into paradise. Thus, he braved the flaming sword and gained for us a right to the tree of life in the midst of the paradise of God. (Revelation 2:7, 22:14). Whether we live or die, that life is for us, and He shall raise us up in the last day. (John 6:54; Revelation 2:10.)[91]*

---

[90] Genesis 3:23-24. "Therefore, the Lord God sent him forth from the garden of Eden, to till the ground from whence he was taken. So, he drove out the man; and he placed at the east of the garden of Eden Cherubims, and a flaming sword which turned every way, to keep the way of the tree of life."

[91] Haywood, Garfield Thomas. 1923. The Victim of the Flaming Sword.

This is not to say that Haywood was not influential, or that he was weak or was a pacifist. Persecuted or not, Garfield Thomas Haywood made a huge impact on the Pentecostal movement during its early years, and a profound impact on Pentecostal history. Only a few years after Pentecostalism began to spread throughout the United States, the movement began to split over divisions in doctrines over baptism.[92] Some Pentecostals decided to denounce the traditional Trinitarian baptism to further separate themselves from other Christian denominations of faith. For Pentecostals in Indiana especially, this would have been a popular opinion; Klan propaganda against the Catholic Church influenced religious leaders of the era against anything that even resembled Catholicism, and the doctrine of the Trinity was believed by some Indiana religious leaders to have Catholic origins.[93] Born and raised in Greencastle and Indianapolis, Indiana, Haywood likely would have shared that opinion without associating it to white supremacy. The Klan was so deeply intertwined with Christianity and nationality that it was often difficult to distinguish between the white supremacy and religion.[94]

---

[92] Church History. Accessed 2022, Feb 24 from https://christtempleac.org/church/history. "In 1913, the Pentecostal Movement across the country split because of the revelation of the deity of Jesus Christ. Revealed by the Holy Ghost through the Scriptures, baptism in the Name of Jesus Christ rather than the Trinitarian formula of the Father, the Son and the Holy Ghost separated assemblies."

[93] Branham, William. 1954, May 15. Questions and Answers. "First thing, this will straighten out you on your "trinity," Father, Son, Holy Spirit. Now, in the first place, not one place in the Bible was trinity ever mentioned. You find it and show it to me. There's no such a thing. It's Catholic error, and you Protestants bow to it."

[94] Stephens, Randall J. The Klan, White Supremacy, and the Past and Present. Accessed 2022, Mar 26 from https://voices.uchicago.edu/religionculture/2017/06/26/the-klan-white-christianity-and-the-past-and-present-a-response-to-kelly-j-baker-by-randall-j-stephens. "Kelly Baker rightly reminds us that the second Klan drew deep from the well of white Protestantism and nationalism. The organization's fierce religious bigotry and xenophobia appealed to millions of Americans in the 1920s. The era marked by social experimentation, prohibition, a new morality, nativism, and drastic social change witnessed the rise of America's most notorious homegrown brand of fascism. Klansmen and women, Baker notes, celebrated hearth and home, white America and patriotic nationalism, or "one hundred percent Americanism," as they put it. "The maintenance of white supremacy," says Baker, "becomes particularly obvious in the artifacts that white

Haywood was eventually convinced, and while disagreeing with their position on race, he stood beside certain leaders in the Klan that denounced the doctrine of the Trinity as being a *"Catholic error"*. He was one of the early adherents of the "Jesus Name" doctrine, the belief that converts to Christianity should be baptized in the name of "Jesus" instead of the "Father, Son, and Holy Spirit" as the Catholics (and most of their Protestant counterparts) did. Haywood became a founding member of what would later be named "Oneness Pentecostalism", bringing the issue of baptism front-and-center in Pentecostal circles. His Christ Temple Apostolic Faith Church in Indianapolis became one of the prominent centers for revivals of the Apostolic faith, resulting in the establishment of Oneness Pentecostal evangelists, converts, pastors, and churches throughout the State of Indiana and eventually the entire Midwest United States and beyond.[95] Over time, Indianapolis became a major international center for adherents of Oneness Pentecostalism, and because of Haywood's doctrinal position, many people around the globe abandoned the doctrine of the Trinity.[96]

In the spring of 1916, Glenn Cook from the Azusa Street Mission in Los Angeles migrated to Indianapolis and became an active leader[97] in Christ Temple. In the Pentecostal faith, people

---

supremacists, like the Klan, create and use." The American flag, the hood and robe, and the burning cross were their symbols of choice."

[95] The Bio of Garfield Thomas Haywood. Accessed 2022, Feb 23 from https://www.apostolicarchives.com/articles/article/8801925/173303.htm. "Undoubtedly, nearly every Apostolic knows the name of Bishop Garfield Thomas Haywood. Bishop Haywood's early alignment with the Oneness camp during the difficult years when the "New Issue" was dividing the Pentecostal Movement along doctrinal lines, is a well-known chapter in our unique history. He was a revered Bible teacher, apologist, and hymn writer. The church that Bishop Haywood founded and pastored until his death in April 1931, Christ Temple Apostolic Faith Church in Indianapolis, Indiana, was a center of Apostolic revival and was seminal in the establishment of other Oneness Pentecostal churches and ministries throughout Indiana and the entire Midwest."

[96] Church History. Accessed 2022, Feb 24 from https://christtempleac.org/church/history. "Because of his bold stance, Indianapolis quickly became the major international center for the "oneness" doctrine."

[97] Christ Temple Apostolic Faith Assembly: The Mother Church of the Pentecostal Assemblies of the World. Accessed 2022, Feb 23 from https://christtempleac.org. "The

who attended the Azusa Street Revival — especially those from the Azusa Street Mission — were viewed as "founding fathers" whose opinions were favored. The 1906 Revival at Azusa Street was believed by many in the Pentecostal movement to be the origin of the faith, though they ultimately traced their origins to the "Day of Pentecost" in the New Testament. Pentecostals believed that God "poured out His Spirit" among those who attended the revival, and as a result, their opinion was a result of that "Spirit" no matter what that opinion might be.

As an elder involved with the Azusa Street Revival, Cook's doctrinal positions would have been favored, and Cook had converted to the Oneness theology. Whether convinced by Cook's "Azusa Street authority" or from the Klan's influence on Indiana theology or both, Haywood was converted. On March 6, 1916, Haywood and 465 members of his church were re-baptized in the name of Jesus, abandoning their Trinitarian beliefs.[98] Their conversion had a significant impact on the Pentecostal movement. Not long after, Haywood's publication The Voice in the Wilderness became the official organ of the Pentecostal Assemblies of the World (PAW), and the PAW as a whole followed Haywood into the Oneness faith,[99] separating from the broader Assemblies of God sect of Pentecostalism.[100]

---

mission's overseer, Brother Glenn A. Cook, was one of the persons involved in the revival that began at an Azusa Street Mission in Los Angeles, California in 1906, a meeting which ushered in the Pentecostal movement throughout the country."

[98] The Bio of Garfield Thomas Haywood. Accessed 2022, Feb 23 from https://www.apostolicarchives.com/articles/article/8801925/173303.htm. "In early spring 1916, Bro. Glenn Cook, an elder from the Azusa Street Mission who had accepted the revelation of the mighty God in Christ and baptism in the Name of Jesus arrived in Indiana and was received by Bishop Haywood and his congregation at 11th and Senate. On 6 March 1916, Bishop Haywood and 465 members of his church were baptized in Jesus' Name in Eagle Creek, marking the first Apostolic baptisms east of the Mississippi River (Dugas 17). J. Roswell Flower, the General Secretary of the Assemblies of God and a prolific opponent of the Oneness movement, sent a telegram to Haywood warning him of Bro. Cook's "error." The message arrived too late, and Bishop Haywood, fully convinced of the veracity of Cook's message, became one of the most avid and effective proponents and propagators of Oneness theology."

[99] The Bio of Garfield Thomas Haywood. Accessed 2022, Feb 23 from https://www.apostolicarchives.com/articles/article/8801925/173303.htm. "In 1910,

Having earned the respect of many of his peers in the Pentecostal faith, and combined with his leadership role in the PAW, Haywood was able to move proverbial mountains that stood in the way of the paradise described in *Victim of the Flaming Sword*. In the Jim Crow era of segregation, and especially during the Ku Klux Klan's Indiana heyday, Haywood's integrated church services stood out as a beacon of hope[101] for black communities under such brutal oppression. It was also a very risky path of evangelism; as Haywood popularized integrated revival services, he was perceived as a threat by his white supremacist peers – both in religious circles during the day and their terrorist operations at night.

During the early 1900s after his conversion, Haywood conducted tent revivals throughout Indiana. As a result of his efforts, Pentecostalism quickly spread throughout Indiana and churches were planted in the wake of his meetings.[102] To some extent, Haywood improved the racial issue within White Supremacy in Indiana; white attendees once convinced that mixing faith with black Christians was "unholy" or "unclean" were now trained to believe in (at least religious) racial equality. As a result, in the State of Indiana, the Klan's fight against Catholicism appeared to take much higher priority than racial discrimination.

Haywood's church began publishing The Voice in the Wilderness. After 1916, this became one of the most influential Oneness circulars, and was the official organ of the Pentecostal Assemblies of the World (PAW), which followed Bishop Haywood into the Oneness movement."

[100] Hymns / Music: Garfield Thomas Haywood. Blue Letter Bible. Accessed 2022, Feb 23 from https://www.blueletterbible.org/hymns/bios/bio_h_a_haywood_gt.cfm. "He eventually became associated with an unorthodox group that denied the Trinity and left the Assemblies of God into the Pentecostal Assemblies of the World."

[101] French, Talmadge L. 2014. Early Interracial Oneness Pentecostalism: G.T. Haywood and the Pentecostal Assemblies of the World (1901-1931). "Haywood was undoubtedly a most remarkable man whose achievements in attaining racial integration in an era of Jim Crow segregation laws that were de jury in the South and de facto in the North, were nothing short of amazing."

[102] ex: Taylor, Dave. 2017, Nov 12. Terre Haute church honors the past, looks to future. Princeton Daily Clarion. "The church as its roots in a tent revival conducted by Bishop G.T. Haywood in 1917."

Regardless, Haywood's church was an early adopter of a much larger effort to promote equality. As much as forty percent of his congregation was white.[103] In 1912, 40 white Protestant congregations joined to form the Church Federation of Indianapolis[104] to promote unity, but that unity seldom crossed racial barriers.[105] In church services and revivals held by Haywood, however, both blacks and whites joined together.[106] From the mixture of skin colors to the mixture of worship styles, Haywood created a new breed of Pentecostalism that paved the way for future generations[107] while planting seeds that would quickly grow into local Pentecostal assemblies. Many of those assemblies also chose to break down racial barriers, largely due to the efforts of Haywood.[108]

By 1923, the year that *Victim of the Flaming Sword* was published, the congregation had outgrown their first building and relocated. Haywood, an architect, designed and engineered the construction of a larger church. Haywood was a firm believer in evangelism, and supplemented his ministry by printing and publishing tracts, booklets, outlines, and charts from his own print

---

[103] Cebula, Judith. 2002, Mar 17. It's not about color for this congregation in Indianapolis. "It was a lovely atmosphere, a time when 60 percent of the congregation was black and 40 percent was white."

[104] Religion. 1999, Nov 21. Indianapolis Star. "As early as 1912, Protestant churches joined forces for civic change. That year, members and clergy from 40 white Protestant congregations formed the Church Federation of Indianapolis to promote Protestant unity, according to Edwin Becker's 1987 history of the organization."

[105] Religion. 1999, Nov 21. Indianapolis Star. "Still, for most of the 20th century in Indianapolis, races prayed apart."

[106] Religion. 1999, Nov 21. Indianapolis Star. "Blacks and whites came to hear Haywood preach pure Pentecostalism."

[107] Religion. 1999, Nov 21. Indianapolis Star. "'Bishop Haywood was a tremendous trailblazer and someone who was 50 years ahead of his time', Tyson says. 'Anywhere you see contemporary worship services, modern music in churches or efforts to bring together black and white Christians, you are seeing the Bishop's legacy.'"

[108] Cebula, Judith. 2002, Mar 17. It's not about color for this congregation in Indianapolis. "The same conviction inspired the now-deceased Golder. In 1953 he founded Grace Apostolic, dreaming of a color-blind congregation. The vision grew from his childhood at Christ Temple Apostolic. In that Indianapolis church, Golder watched Bishop Garfield Haywood baptize blacks and whites in a creek. That was in the 1920s and 1930s."

shop.[109]   His printed materials became so popular throughout Indiana, nationally, and abroad, that Christ Temple and the name Garfield Thomas Haywood became recognized in Pentecostal assemblies around the globe. Before long, Christ Temple had a *"Foreign Missions Department"* and began sending missionaries to all parts of the world.[110]   As a result, Christ Temple earned the nickname "The Mother Church".[111]

Still, Indiana had quickly become a battleground for white supremacy. It soon gained national attention as the Klan began to seize political control of the state. The battle had many fronts, and though Haywood made significant progress in moving the racial boundaries towards the proverbial Eden, he was but one of many that opposed the "Invisible Army" of the Ku Klux Klan. The Klan had silently gained control of Indianapolis government, and had its sights set much higher. The Klan had successfully positioned political leaders in Indiana for a Presidential run.

---

[109]   Church   History.   Accessed   2022,   Feb   24   from https://christtempleac.org/church/history. "Having outgrown their tabernacle in numbers at Eleventh Street and Senate Avenue, in December 1923 a new location was found at Fall Creek and Paris Avenue, which was then a city dump. Bishop Haywood designed and engineered the construction of the new church. Bishop Haywood taught the importance of evangelizing the world and through his profession as a printer; his literature became in demand throughout the United States and internationally. He used his own print shop to publish tracts, booklets, outlines, and charts as additional means of spreading the Gospel. Through its continued growth, Christ Temple became and remained the only genuinely interracial church in the city."
[110]   Church   History.   Accessed   2022,   Feb   24   from https://christtempleac.org/church/history.   "Christ   Temple's   Foreign   Missions Department sent out and supported missionaries to foreign countries, continents and islands. Missionary blessings have gone out to Russia, Israel, Nigeria, Liberia, the Philippines, and other areas because of the foundational teachings of Bishop Haywood."
[111]   Church   History.   Accessed   2022,   Feb   24   from https://christtempleac.org/church/history. ". Nicknamed "The Mother Church," Christ Temple continued to be involved in the Home Missions Field of spreading the Gospel by supporting new assemblies throughout the city, state and country."

CHAPTER 3

THE INDIANA KU KLUX KLAN

❖

"Mulatto women were depicted as emotionally troubled seducers and
mulatto men as power-hungry criminals"
- The Tragic Mulatto Myth

While G. T. Haywood built his culturally diverse religious empire in Indianapolis, other religious leaders joined together to build quite the opposite. From 1910 to 1930, the black population of Indiana doubled,[112] creating what many Hoosiers viewed as a threat to Indiana culture. This was true to the extent that even Haywood's interracial revivals could not stop the rising growth in white supremacy. Especially after the 1915 D. W. Griffith film "Birth of a Nation" popularized the notion that the sexual union of a person having white skin and a person having black skin would create the perfect villain. The film was but one of many fictional stories of the era projecting the "tragic mulatto myth" on American society; interracial women were frequently portrayed as "female seducers" while interracial men were portrayed as power hungry criminals.[113] This myth seemed to take hold in several areas on the

---

[112] Segregation in Indiana during the Klan Era of the 1920s. Accessed 2022, Mar 27 from https://www.jstor.org/stable/1889600. "In the years from 1910 to 1930 the colored population of Indiana doubled."

[113] The Tragic Mulatto Myth. Accessed 2022, Mar 27 from https://www.ferris.edu/HTMLS/news/jimcrow/mulatto/homepage.htm. "Mulatto women were depicted as emotionally troubled seducers and mulatto men as power hungry

United States, and with the quickly rising number of recruits in the Indiana Klan, it was no doubt a hot topic of the 1920s in Indiana.

The quickly growing black population in Indiana was not the only concern for Hoosiers in 1920, however. On a religious front, white supremacists faced another "enemy" besides Haywood and his integrated revivals: Catholicism. American Catholics were the most frequent target of the Klan's hatred.[114] Klan literature frequently painted the Catholic Church as authoritarian, corrupt, and intent on taking control of the United States.[115] Fears of Armageddon quickly spread in the years leading up to and following the First World War, and with that fear came a sudden surge in church attendance. Though the Catholic population in Indiana may have seen no significant growth when compared to the quickly spreading popularity of Pentecostalism, church attendance certainly benefitted from the religious propaganda of the coming End of Days. For Klansmen, the doomsday scenario included a Roman Catholic invasion of the United States, and pamphlets were circulated proclaiming that *"Rome has no right to force upon Christian America her pagan ideals and propositions."*[116] This, the Klan claimed, would happen through assimilation of students in the public school systems.[117] Klansmen in Indianapolis especially feared that the Catholic members of the public school

---

criminals. Nowhere are these depictions more evident than in D. W. Griffith's film The Birth of a Nation (1915)."

[114] Moore, Leonard J. 1997. Citizen Klansman: The Ku Klux Klan in Indiana, 1921-1928. "American Catholics were the most frequent targets of the Klan's ethnocentric propaganda."

[115] Moore, Leonard J. 1997. Citizen Klansman: The Ku Klux Klan in Indiana, 1921-1928. "Klan literature focused most often on the traditional charge that the Catholic Church was authoritarian, corrupt, and intent on taking over the United States. 'Rome has no right', one Klan pamphlet proclaimed, 'to try and force upon Christian America her pagan ideals and propositions."

[116] Moore, Leonard J. 1997. Citizen Klansman: The Ku Klux Klan in Indiana, 1921-1928.

[117] Moore, Leonard J. 1997. Citizen Klansman: The Ku Klux Klan in Indiana, 1921-1928. "One pamphlet warned that 'in many of the largest cities in this country the parochial schools outnumber our on American public schools', thus allowing countless immigrant children to avoid the 'surest process of assimilation. Klan literature also accused Catholics of exerting undue influence on public education."

board were secretly working to undermine the improvement of the schools.[118]

This "assimilation" of white students was, according to the Klan, to come into fruition through a mixture of races in the younger generations. Through interracial marriage the United States would, according to Klan propaganda, fall victim to an "inferior race".[119] The Indiana Klan successfully convinced the public that America was under attack by the Catholics, and the conspiracy theory surrounding that threat was even more powerful than the literature. Hoosiers joined the quickly growing movement to "defend the nation".

Protestant leaders in Indiana, even those who did not openly support the Indiana Klan, joined in the fight against Catholicism — which though partly unintentional, empowered the Klan. The Indiana Baptist convention of 1920, for example, claimed that Catholic children *"received over eight times religious instructions than Protestants"*.[120] Protestant ministers united to find ways to increase Sunday school attendance, and the Klan was more than willing to use their political pull to support that idea. Klan legislators proposed a bill to allow early release from public schools for the purpose of religious instruction.[121] Very few white Protestants actually believed the propaganda, and most did not fear Catholicism invading the Indiana public school system. They

---

[118] Moore, Leonard J. 1997. Citizen Klansman: The Ku Klux Klan in Indiana, 1921-1928. "The Fiery Cross, for example, frequently claimed that, at the direction of the church, Catholic members of the Indianapolis school board were working to undermine improvements in the city's schools."

[119] Moore, Leonard J. 1997. Citizen Klansman: The Ku Klux Klan in Indiana, 1921-1928. "The United States was 'established by White Men ... for White Men' and was never intended to 'fall into the hands of an inferior race.' Mixing of the races was 'biologically disastrous.'"

[120] Moore, Leonard J. 1997. Citizen Klansman: The Ku Klux Klan in Indiana, 1921-1928. "A report presented in the Indiana Baptist Convention of 1920 concluded that Catholic youths received over eight times more religious instruction than Protestants and that churches must work to increase Sunday school attendance."

[121] Moore, Leonard J. 1997. Citizen Klansman: The Ku Klux Klan in Indiana, 1921-1928. "In 1925, the Baptist Observer supported a bill proposed by Klan legislators that would allow early release from public schools for the purpose of religious instruction."

did, however, fear the doomsday rhetoric, and eagerly supported the Klan if only for their militant protection.[122] This created the perfect opportunity for the religious side of the Indiana Klan; by capitalizing on religious fears of doomsday, the religious communities became easy targets for recruitment. Klan leaders realized that religion could be weaponized.

The Klan began appealing to the religious communities through its vigilante enforcement of prohibition. Prohibition was, by far, the most effective social and religious issue for the Klan's agenda. The Klan not only endorsed the liquor laws, but it also enforced them.[123] Klan propaganda declared alcohol to be *"one of the greatest evils that threatened our homes"*.[124] The Indiana Klan declared war on the alcohol industry and those who consumed it. Klansmen were instructed to enforce the liquor laws *"without fear or favor"*.[125] Spokesmen for the Klan blamed Chicago, immigrants, and organized crime on a large percentage of the illegal consumption and transfer of alcohol in Indiana.[126] For Indiana religious leaders of the era who were strongly in favor of the liquor laws, this would have made the Klan seem like religious heroes ordained by God for the cleansing of the nation. It also placed the Klan in favor with the Anti-Saloon League and its disciples. The Indiana Anti-Saloon League endorsed several Klan candidates in

---

[122] Moore, Leonard J. 1997. Citizen Klansman: The Ku Klux Klan in Indiana, 1921-1928. "Few white Protestants actually believed that 'white civilization' was on the brink of collapse or that the pope was about to destroy Indianapolis's public schools. At the same time, doomsday predictions and conspiratorial accusations, however incredible, captured the attention of white Protestants and heightened their identification with the cause defending ethnic values and traditions."

[123] Moore, Leonard J. 1997. Citizen Klansman: The Ku Klux Klan in Indiana, 1921-1928. By far, the most important of these was Prohibition enforcement. Klan recruiters, backed by editorial support from the Fiery Cross, endorsed the liquor laws, condemned those who violated them, and called upon Klansmen to do what they could do to support enforcement."

[124] Moore, Leonard J. 1997. Citizen Klansman: The Ku Klux Klan in Indiana, 1921-1928.

[125] Moore, Leonard J. 1997. Citizen Klansman: The Ku Klux Klan in Indiana, 1921-1928.

[126] Moore, Leonard J. 1997. Citizen Klansman: The Ku Klux Klan in Indiana, 1921-1928. "Spokesmen for the Klan blamed immigrants and organized crime for much of the liquor problem. The Fiery Cross pointed to Chicago as the source of a large percentage of Indiana's illegal alcohol."

Indianapolis and worked closely with the Klan to strengthen Indiana's liquor laws.[127]

In May of 1924, the Indiana Klan held a public display of strength and political power through a parade and picnic in downtown Notre Dame — the most densely populated Catholic region in the state. Notre Dame students lashed out at the Klan's display of force when fifty students forcibly unmasked Klansmen and staged their own parade of captured robes.[128] Five hundred university students joined in the fight, catching the Klan members off guard as they arrived by bus and by car only to be disrobed. Newspaper reporters captured photographs of the embarrassing scenes as students leaped onto moving vehicles to steal the Klan's regalia as battle trophies.[129] Klansmen temporarily retreated to the headquarters on the corner of Wayne and Michigan streets in South Bend, but quickly regrouped for a strong force of power that would make the history books. In 1925, the Indiana Klan took full control of the Indianapolis government through Klan-appointed Governor Ed Jackson, and Notre Dame was subjected to Klan governance.

As Indiana Secretary of State, and against the will of Indiana Governor Warren McCray, Ed Jackson approved a certificate of business for the Indiana Ku Klux Klan.[130] McCray was

---

[127] Moore, Leonard J. 1997. Citizen Klansman: The Ku Klux Klan in Indiana, 1921-1928. "The Indiana Anti-Saloon League and its president, Edward Schumaker, endorsed numerous Klan candidates in the state election of 1924 and worked closely with the Klan-dominated legislature to strengthen state liquor laws in 1925."

[128] Students Rout Klansmen. 1924, May 18. Chicago Herald and Examiner. "Masked and garbed in full Klan regalia, guards directed visitors at a Klan festival in South Bend until fifty university youths descended upon them. The students ripped off the robes of the guards and then paraded the streets with the captured costumes."

[129] A Clash Over Catholicism. 2018. University of Notre Dame. Accessed 2022, Mar 27 from https://www.nd.edu/stories/a-clash-over-catholicism/. "About 500 University of Notre Dame students showed their objections by storming downtown and ripping the hoods and robes off surprised Klan members. As the Klan arrived in trains, buses and cars, the students roughed members up in alleys and stole their regalia for battle trophies. They chased the rest to the Klan headquarters downtown at the corner of Wayne and Michigan streets."

[130] Retro Indy: KKK in Indiana and their leader D.C. Stephenson. Accessed 2022, Mar 27 from https://www.indystar.com/story/news/history/retroindy/2014/02/20/d-c-

---

not necessarily against the white supremacy agenda; he viewed the reconstruction-era Ku Klux Klan favorably. The 1915 Ku Klux Klan, however, was much different. Instead of targeting blacks, the "new Klan" cast a wider net of hatred towards Catholics, Jews, labor unions, and any foreign-born citizen.[131] In the years leading up to his term as governor, Jackson used his authority as the Secretary of State to appoint Klan members into various non-elected but highly influential positions within Indiana state government.[132] The strategy was very effective, and before long, the Klan had positioned itself as an invisible government that was making decisions using elected officials as proxies. The "invisible empire' gained the upper hand when Jackson, an active member of the Klan and strong supporter of Klan policy, entered office as governor.[133]

stephenson/5641029/. "In 1921, Indiana Gov. Warren McCray, in a bold move, voiced his opposition to the Ku Klux Klan because of their "lawless deeds of the old Klan of the reconstruction period." The tension came after Secretary of State Ed Jackson granted the Klan a certificate of business in Indiana. McCray recalled the original Klan that organized after the Civil War and targeted newly enfranchised blacks. But this "new" Ku Klux Klan, which was founded in 1915 and entered Indiana via Evansville in 1921, cast a wider net of hate that included Catholics, Jews, labor unions and the foreign-born.:"

[131] Retro Indy: KKK in Indiana and their leader D.C. Stephenson. Accessed 2022, Mar 27 from https://www.indystar.com/story/news/history/retroindy/2014/02/20/d-c-stephenson/5641029/. "In 1921, Indiana Gov. Warren McCray, in a bold move, voiced his opposition to the Ku Klux Klan because of their "lawless deeds of the old Klan of the reconstruction period." The tension came after Secretary of State Ed Jackson granted the Klan a certificate of business in Indiana. McCray recalled the original Klan that organized after the Civil War and targeted newly enfranchised blacks. But this "new" Ku Klux Klan, which was founded in 1915 and entered Indiana via Evansville in 1921, cast a wider net of hate that included Catholics, Jews, labor unions and the foreign-born."

[132] Holzwarth, Larry. 2017, Oct 3. Accessed 2022, Mar 26 from https://historycollection.com/10-well-known-us-figures-affiliated-with-the-ku-klux-klan/5/. "While still Secretary of State Jackson attempted to bribe the governor to appoint Klan members to various non-elected but influential positions in the state government."

[133] Holzwarth, Larry. 2017, Oct 3. Accessed 2022, Mar 26 from https://historycollection.com/10-well-known-us-figures-affiliated-with-the-ku-klux-klan/5/. "Former attorney and judge Edward L. Jackson was the Governor of the State of Indiana for a single term, 1925 – 1929. He had previously served as Secretary of State. Throughout his political career, he was an active member of the KKK and was supportive of Klan goals and policies in the performance of his political offices."

Along with their political power, the Indiana Klan was a financial powerhouse. Recruits were asked to pay $10 to join ($165.92 in today's money)[134], and the organization gained as many as 200,000 new members per year in the 1920s.[135] They collected over thirty-three million dollars (in today's money) in initiation fees alone[136] — not to mention membership dues, donations, fundraising, or other areas in which the Klan funded operations. The Klan was truly a force to be reckoned with in Indiana. They had gained both religious and political control of the state, which gave them funding to support their initiatives, and a sizable army of recruits to do battle. In 1923, the "general" of this army, so to speak, was David Curtis Stephenson, the Klan's "Grand Dragon" for the State of Indiana. During the 1920s, D. C. Stephenson was the most powerful man in Indiana.[137]

On the Fourth of July 1923, during one of the largest Klan events in history, Imperial Wizard Hiram Evans officially declared D. C. Stephenson to be the Grand Dragon of the Indiana Klan. Over 100,000 Klan members and their families joined the celebration in Kokomo, Indiana. It was as much of a public display for the Klan as it was for Stephenson; Indiana was viewed as the "heartland" of the domestic terrorist group.[138] Stephenson was also granted

---

[134] $10 in 1924 is worth $165.92 today. Accessed 2022, Mar 26 from https://www.in2013dollars.com/us/inflation/1924?amount=10.

[135] Retro Indy: KKK in Indiana and their leader D.C. Stephenson. Accessed 2022, Mar 27 from https://www.indystar.com/story/news/history/retroindy/2014/02/20/ d-c-stephenson/5641029/. In 1928, according to official figures filed in Marion County court by Klan attorneys, 200,000 Indiana men became members of the Knights of the Ku Klux Klan, paying a "klectokon" ($10 fee)."

[136] $2,000,000 in 1924 is worth $33,183,157.89 today. Accessed 2022, Mar 26 from https://www.in2013dollars.com/us/inflation/1924?amount=2000000.

[137] Retro Indy: KKK in Indiana and their leader D.C. Stephenson. Accessed 2022, Mar 27 from https://www.indystar.com/story/news/history/retroindy/2014/02/20/ d-c-stephenson/5641029/. "In 1925, David Curtis Stephenson was the most powerful man in Indiana. He owned politicians, up to and including the governor. He could send hundreds of hooded Klansmen marching through the streets."

[138] Moore, Leonard J. 1997. Citizen Klansman: The Ku Klux Klan in Indiana, 1921-1928. "On the Fourth of July 1923, at a massive Klan rally in Kokomo, one that symbolized both the growing national importance of the Klan and Indiana's place at the center of the movement, D. C. Stephenson received his compensation. In front of more than 100,000

control of seven northern states, including their membership fees.[139]

Stephenson was, by all appearances, the devil incarnate when compared to G. T. Haywood and his army of peaceful converts. Before moving from Houston to Indiana, Stephenson had already married and abandoned two wives.[140] He abused his power to rape multiple women. Any who opposed his authority were brutally beaten or would simply "disappear".[141] While the Klan pushed the non-alcoholic vision of the Church, Stephenson himself was a drunkard.[142]

For blacks in Indiana during Stephenson's reign, G. T. Haywood's *Victim of the Flaming Sword* would have had a profound effect on their lives. Symbolically, the events in Indiana were a near match to the biblical fall from grace and banishment from the Garden of Eden. Stephenson would have represented the serpent, the devil, and every evil described in the Holy Book. There is no doubt that Klansmen were aware of this symbology and the Haywood/Stephenson opposition, simply based on the historical timeline. In 1924, William Joseph Simmons, the founder of the 1915 Ku Klux Klan, started a second white supremacy group named the "Knights of the Flaming Sword".[143] The symbolic

---

Klansmen and their families from throughout the Midwest, Evans officially declared Stephenson to be the grand dragon of the Indiana Klan."

[139] Moore, Leonard J. 1997. Citizen Klansman: The Ku Klux Klan in Indiana, 1921-1928. "At the same time, he privately agreed to make Stephenson the head of recruitment in seven other northern states east of the Mississippi. The second part of the reward – more specifically, the share of membership fees that was to accompany it."

[140] Leonard J. Moore, Citizen Klansmen: The Ku Klux Klan in Indiana, 1921-1928, Chapel Hill: University of North Carolina Press, 1997, p. 14

[141] Retro Indy: KKK in Indiana and their leader D.C. Stephenson. Accessed 2022, Mar 27 from https://www.indystar.com/story/news/history/retroindy/2014/02/20/ d-c-stephenson/5641029/. "He could have a man beaten up or make him disappear. He raped women and got away with it."

[142] Retro Indy: KKK in Indiana and their leader D.C. Stephenson. 2014, Feb 20. Indy Star. Accessed 2022, Dec 29 from https://www.indystar.com/story/news/history/retroindy/2014/02/20/ d-c-stephenson/5641029/. "Stephenson had been drinking heavily -- as he often did."

[143] Date Set for "Flaming Sword" Knights' Debut. 1924, Feb 14. The Times. Col. Joseph Simmons, founder of the Ku Klux Klan, who relinquished his offices in that body following

meaning for the Klan was just as powerful for white supremacy as it was for those seeking freedom from oppression; some white supremacists in Indiana believed that that Adam's son Cain had sexual relations with an ape to produce the "colored race".[144] People with black skin were viewed as one of the "negative consequences" of mankind's fall from grace and banishment from the Garden of Eden.

Despite his immoral actions, however, many religious leaders in Indiana, did not view Stephenson as an immoral person or a threat to religion at all. In fact, as leader of the Klan, Stephenson was seen as a hero by Protestants in Indiana. During Stephenson's reign in Indiana, Protestant ministers were granted free membership in Indiana, and many of them accepted the offer to show their allegiance.[145] By engaging the religious leaders in Indiana, Stephenson was able to maintain his public image of a public defender of "Protestant womanhood" — though his private life would later be exposed to show the exact opposite. Stephenson boasted of his strong support of prohibition, which was a popular hot topic for ministers in Indiana at the time. During all of this, Stephenson was an alcoholic and hosted drunken orgies in his mansion in Indianapolis.[146] He was nearly arrested once for offering hundreds of dollars to staff members for sex.[147]

---

the sale of royalties he held, will organize 'The Knights of the Flaming Sword' in Atlanta, February 26, the date set for their first Georgia gathering".

[144] Branham, William. 1953, July 29. Questions And Answers on Genesis. (53-0729). And so, now, that's how I come...Her boy, George, the boy was a medium, Ed, also. They were in the store, and I heard a discussion back there, where the first...where Cain got his wife. Well, the one that had the floor seemed to be the best of the argument, he said, "I tell you where Cain got his wife," said, "Cain went over and married a great big female ape." And said, "Out of that ape come forth the colored race." Said, "You notice the colored person's head is kind of peaked like that, like–like the ape is, in the head."

[145] Hamlett, Ryan. 2013, Sep 24. The Graham Stephenson House. Accessed 2022, Mar 27 from https://historicindianapolis.com/the-graham-stephenson-house/. "Stephenson relocated to Indianapolis in 1922, where he helped to grow the scope of the Indiana Klan, offering Protestant ministers free membership and helping to create the Klan newspaper The Fiery Cross."

[146] Hamlett, Ryan. 2013, Sep 24. The Graham Stephenson House. Accessed 2022, Mar 27 from https://historicindianapolis.com/the-graham-stephenson-house/. "Though Stephenson was an outspoken Prohibitionist and defender of "Protestant womanhood"

Just as Haywood held revivals throughout Indiana recruiting Pentecostals, Stephenson held rallies throughout Indiana recruiting for the Klan. Stephenson and his henchmen hit the road in the summer of 1922 promoting the "White Knights", distributing Klan propaganda in churches,[148] men's clubs, and other venues. Through the work of Stephenson, the "secret society" became far less secret. Stephenson advertised Klan activities in an Indianapolis newspaper named "The Fiery Cross", and Klan activities were heralded as fun, family-friendly events. Very quickly, the once infamous domestic terrorist group – the same group that had recently been exposed in the New York Times as a violent threat to the United States – transitioned into a smiling, friendly face to Hoosiers. Thanks to Stephenson, the Indiana Klan was synonymous with "community", "family", and "morality" in Indiana.[149] Under Stephenson's leadership, even the local Klan chapters came out of the shadows and published advertisements in local newspapers. The Klan held local parades, picnics, and holiday celebrations to reinvent themselves as family-oriented protectors of the Indiana communities. Most white supporters would have seen the white robes as a blanket of security and protection while Catholics, blacks, and Jews in the surrounding communities would have seen them as a growing threat to their survival and very existence.

---

behind closed doors he was an alcoholic and sexual predator, reportedly hosting booze-filled orgies in his new mansion."

[147] Hamlett, Ryan. 2013, Sep 24. The Graham Stephenson House. Accessed 2022, Mar 27 from https://historicindianapolis.com/the-graham-stephenson-house/. "At the Deschler Hotel, a whiskey fueled Stephenson had offered the staff manicurist a hundred dollars to have sex with him. When she refused, he said "You will, or I'll kill you." The manicurist escaped his room. Stephenson escaped prosecution."

[148] Moore, Leonard J. 1997. Citizen Klansman: The Ku Klux Klan in Indiana, 1921-1928. "That summer, Stephenson and his men crisscrossed the state, doing everything they could to stimulate public interest in their organization. They spoke and distributed Klan literature at church meetings and men's clubs."

[149] Moore, Leonard J. 1997. Citizen Klansman: The Ku Klux Klan in Indiana, 1921-1928. "While the new Klan chapters were ostensibly secret, Stephenson and his fellow recruiters were actually eager to draw as much attention as possible to their membership campaign. The Fiery Cross heralded the growth of klaverns at every opportunity, and individual chapters took out ads in local newspapers to promote upcoming Klan parades, picnics, and holiday celebrations."

Stephenson made this threat even more visible by publishing recruitment numbers. Blacks watched in horror as the new recruits for the Klan numbered as many as 9621 per week.[150]

The social, religious, and political landscape of the 1920s created the perfect storm. After D. C. Stephenson fell from grace when he was arrested for the murder of Madge Oberholtzer in 1925, a noticeable void was created in the Indiana Klan that appealed to several opportunists. The Klan was dealt a strong blow when Stephenson was convicted, and Haywood's "Jesus Only" converts seemed to gain the upper hand. As the Klan's political control of Indianapolis government was brought to national attention, and the terrorist organization was once again viewed as a threat instead of protectors of "safe" communities, Haywood's new religion became much more of a threat to white supremacy than the Klan had anticipated. It was a threat that could only be stopped from within, and infiltrating the Pentecostal movement apparently became a priority among white supremacy leaders. Once on the inside, however, leaders in white supremacy suddenly realized the power given them by weaponizing the religious views of the people for political gain.

---

[150] Moore, Leonard J. 1997. Citizen Klansman: The Ku Klux Klan in Indiana, 1921-1928. "New Klansmen for Selected Weeks."

CHAPTER 4

INDIANA KLAN HEADQUARTERS

❖

"If you can't beat 'em, jine 'em"
- Indiana Senator James Eli Watson

From the time that the soldiers came home from the first World War in 1919 until the stock market crash in 1929, Indianapolis, Indiana was experiencing what historians consider to be its golden age.[151] Indianapolis luxury auto giants Marmon, Stutz and Duesenberg were pushing the limits on what automakers of the era thought possible, winning the hearts of auto enthusiasts by running cars in the Indianapolis 500 and earning the pocketbooks of every wealthy businessman that could afford the expensive cars. Duesenberg won the Indy 500 in 1924, 1925, and 1927, and the Duesenberg Model J introduced in 1929 had 265 horses under the hood. It was priced between $14,000 and $20,000.[152]

In 1923, the Eli Lily Company in Indianapolis found a way to increase production of insulin, and insulin production and distribution became a medical miracle. What began as a simple

---

[151] Wall, J.K. Accessed 2022, Dec 29 from Indy's Golden Age in 1920s shows way forward. "From 1919, when the soldiers returned home from World War I, until the stock market crash in 1929, Indianapolis enjoyed the fruits of what historians call the city's Golden Age—a 40-year period starting in about 1880 that saw Indianapolis flourish economically and culturally."

[152] Buttermore, Gregg. 1994, Nov 22. Duesenberg. pp. 513-514.

discovery in a university quickly turned into a treatment for diabetics around the globe.[153]

The Indianapolis jazz community produced several big names and influenced songwriters and musicians throughout the nation. During the segregated years of Indianapolis, the African American community congregated on Indiana Avenue, which became known as the "Indianapolis Harlem". The city was so filled with music that it continued to produce jazz legends for years to come. Music giants such as J.J. Johnson, Freddie Hubbard, David Baker, Slide Hampton, and Wes Montgomery all rose to fame because of Indianapolis's deeply rooted music culture.[154]

In the 1920s, however, Indianapolis had a much more sinister culture growing in the background, an underground movement that would fill history books with new villains for years to come. Indiana had the largest concentration of members of the Ku Klux Klan in the 1920s, and through the efforts of key figures, the Klan had full control of Indianapolis government. This fact combined with the unusual mixture of religious influence from all directions to fully blur the fine line between Church and State in Indiana. To many "Hoosiers", the Klan was *part of* their religion.

In 1915, the same year that the Ku Klux Klan was reorganized in Atlanta under the leadership of William Joseph Simmons, the Pentecostal Assemblies of the World was reorganized in Indianapolis.[155] During this time, the Oneness or "Jesus Only"

[153] Wall, J.K. Accessed 2022, Dec 29 from Indy's Golden Age in 1920s shows way forward. "It was in Indianapolis in 1923 that Eli Lilly and Co. figured out how to scale up production of insulin, turning a university discovery into a treatment available to diabetics around the globe. In so doing, Lilly pioneered the R&D-based model that undergirds the modern pharmaceutical industry.

[154] Johnson, David Brent. 2012. The Once-Thriving Jazz Scene Of ... Indianapolis? "In the segregated years of the 20th century, many American cities with significant black populations had what was known as a "main stem": a primary boulevard of business and cultural activity for the African-American community. In Los Angeles, it was Central Avenue; in Detroit, it was Hastings Street; in Harlem, it was 125th Street; and in Indianapolis – the city that bequeathed us jazz greats such as J.J. Johnson, Freddie Hubbard, David Baker, Slide Hampton and Wes Montgomery – it was Indiana Avenue."

[155] The A.B.S.A. Council. Accessed 2022, Mar 29 from http://www.absacouncil.org/home.html. "The Apostolic Bible Students Association

version of Pentecostalism with its interracial message of unity began to spread throughout Indiana. Under Haywood's leadership, Pentecostalism became known as a driving force for an interracial commitment to *"all-flesh, all-people, counter-cultural Pentecost."*[156] That same year in Indiana, another figure began making waves throughout the Indiana religious community: E. "Emmett" Howard Cadle. Cadle would be forever remembered in Indiana history as a rags-to-riches, crime-to-Christianity evangelist, but the name Cadle would become even more famous for all the wrong reasons. It was at E. Howard Cadle's church, the Cadle Tabernacle in Indianapolis, where the Ku Klux Klan would take control of the Indianapolis government and it would eventually become the headquarters for the Klan. At the Cadle Tabernacle. Indiana's Rev. William Branham would also help launch the career of Indiana's infamous Rev. Jim Jones and Peoples Temple.

E. Howard Cadle was born in Fredericksburg, Indiana, about thirty miles northwest of Louisville near the Kentucky border.[157] The Cadle family moved to Utica, Indiana,[158] where William Branham was raised producing liquor in the Clark County underworld.[159] William's father, Charles Branham, drove[160] for

---

(A.B.S.A.) of Indiana is the 4th Episcopal District of the Pentecostal Assemblies of the World, Inc. (P.A.W.), the oldest Oneness Pentecostal organization in existence, founded in 1906, and re-organized as a Oneness Pentecostal organization in 1915. The PAW was originally headquartered at Azusa Street in Los Angeles, California, moved to Oregon, and eventually moved to Indianapolis, Indiana where it was legally incorporated and remains today."

[156] French, Talmadge L. Anderson, Allen H. 2014. Early Interracial Oneness Pentecostalism: G. T. Haywood and the Pentecostal Assemblies of the World (1901–1931). "The study of the first thirty years of Oneness Pentecostalism (1901-31) is especially relevant due to its unparalleled interracial commitment to an all-flesh, all-people, counter-cultural Pentecost."

[157] Melton, Gordon (1999). Religious Leaders of America. Gale Group. p. 98.

[158] Tabernacle Built Here by Indianapolis Man. 1920, May 28. Courier Journal. "His mother, Mrs. Thomas Cadle, lives near Utica, Ind."

[159] Branham, William. 1953, Nov 8. Life Story. (53-1108A). "When I was about seven years old, I was packing water one day. you've heard that part of the story. Sorry to say, packing it to a moonshine still for my daddy, two little half-a-gallon molasses buckets."

[160] Branham, William. 1964, Apr 27. A Trial. (65-0427). "He come out there to break some hackney ponies, for a—a rich man named O. H. Wathen, lives on the Utica Pike. He's a

Otto H. Wathen of the R. E. Wathen Distilleries.[161] Those same distilleries supplied Grand Dad whiskey[162] to the Chicago mob, with which Cadle was later intimately familiar. In the years leading up to his Indianapolis fame, Cadle gained notoriety as a gambler[163] and saloonkeeper.[164] His ties to the Chicago underworld earned him the title "slot machine king" and Cadle was well known in Chicago's Levee district.[165] It was the same notorious, mob-controlled district where Al Capone built his criminal empire. There, in Chicago's underground, Cadle was known as a *"wonderworker with the dice — a marvel with the cards — fingers trained to manipulate to 'trim the sucker'"*[166].

Once the Indiana Klan had successfully put soon-to-be Governor Ed Jackson in position in Indianapolis government as Secretary of State, Cadle received a substantial loan of $25,000[167]

---

great owner of the Colonels, and also the R. E. Wathen Distillery, and all them in Louisville, and O. H. and R. E. And daddy was breaking saddle horses for him. And then he got hurt, and he went to being a private chauffeur for him."

[161] Branham, William. 1964, Apr 27. A Trial. (64-0427). Three years later, we come to Indiana, and papa got a job. He was a rider, breaking horses for the ranchers and farmers, and so forth. He come out there to break some hackney ponies, for a–a rich man named O. H. Wathen, lives on the Utica Pike. He's a great owner of the Colonels, and also the R. E. Wathen Distillery, and all them in Louisville, and O. H. and R. E.

[162] Federal Agents Face Arrest in Rum Ring. 1920, Oct 23. Newport Mercury. "Chicago ... Sadler is said to have told the jury something of his dealings with the Wathen Distillery at Louisville, whence were shipped the supplies of Old Grand Dad whisky, seizure of which brought about his confession. Badler said his deal was made with Otto H. Wathen, secretary of the Wathen Company of which Otto's brother, R. E. Wathen is president."

[163] Tabernacle Built Here by Indianapolis Man. 1920, May 28. Courier Journal. "in his early life was a drinker, a notorious gambler, who sowed wild oats in many fields."

[164] Cadle Tabernacle. 1920, Jun 5. Courier Journal. "E. Howard Cadle, the converted gambler and saloon-keeper."

[165] Cadle Tabernacle. 1922, Aug 17. News And Observer. "He had been known in the sporting fraternity as the 'slot machine king', a hound after the easy money of the sucker. Cadle was reputed on the 'levee'."

[166] Cadle Tabernacle. 1922, Aug 17. News And Observer. "Cadle was reputed on the 'levee', the rendezvous of the sporting people, as wonder-worker with the dice – a marvel with the cards – fingers trained to manipulate to 'trim the sucker' in the vernacular of the underworld."

[167] This Mother's Prayers Won. 1921, Oct 29. The Dearborn Independent. "He went to James P. Goodrich, former governor of Indiana under whose administration in the state house he was a wielder of the mop and told him of his business affairs. He asked for $25000, and Mr. Goodrich, impressed with the story, wrote a check for that amount."

(a half of a million dollars in today's money)[168] from former Indiana governor James P. Goodrich, the acting governor when Jackson was appointed as Secretary. With the money received, Cadle started sixteen shoe repair stores in Illinois, Indiana, and Ohio,[169] and eventually put down $375,000[170] (almost ten million dollars in today's money)[171] for the Cadle Tabernacle in Indianapolis. Cadle put up $305,000 in cash,[172] which some noticed to be an unusually high amount for a man earning his wealth from a shoe repair business.[173] According to the story given by Cadle, he had been given only a few months to live after contracting Bright's disease (the same disease that claimed his life in 1942), had lost all of his money, and was living in poverty.[174] Clearly there was a disconnect between Cadle's story and reality. After attending a revival meeting by Gypsy Smith, Cadle claimed that he abandoned his life of alcohol and crime for the work of the Lord. As a result, Cadle became wealthy almost overnight. Interestingly, Gypsy Smith had invaded the Levee District in Chicago a few years earlier, bringing with him thousands of both pious and curious individuals to his revival — after which many of

---

[168] $25,000 in 1918 is worth $469,728.48 today. Accessed 2022, Mar 28 from https://www.in2013dollars.com/us/inflation/1918?amount=25000.

[169] This Mother's Prayers Won. 1921, Oct 29. The Dearborn Independent. "Today, Cadle's firm has a string of sixteen shoe repair stores in nine cities in Illinois, Indiana, and Ohio."

[170] This Mother's Prayers Won. 1921, Oct 29. The Dearborn Independent. "It cost approximately $375,000."

[171] $375,000 in 1876 is worth $9,943,317.76 today. Accessed 2022, Mar 27 from https://www.in2013dollars.com/us/inflation/1921?amount=375000.

[172] Misc. news. 1922, Aug 17. News And Observer. "I was more interested in the man Cadle who put $305,000 in cash in the building."

[173] Letter to the Editor. 1922, Aug 17. News And Observer. "It is a big business – that of making as good as new a shoe which, otherwise would be worthless. The business has been profitable – highly profitable – otherwise, Cadle could not have done the things he has, such as building the Cadle Tabernacle."

[174] This Mother's Prayers Won. 1921, Oct 29. The Dearborn Independent. "Only five years ago Cadle, his wife, and children were living in poverty in Orleans, Indiana."

the latter stayed in the Levees to partake in the sin Cadle had abandoned.[175]

E. Howard Cadle began holding revivals throughout Indiana telling his "Life Story" account from rags to riches,[176] and these revivals created some serious competition for Haywood's meetings. Cadle's evangelism promoted the United Brethren Church, which maintained racial segregation until the late 1960s.[177] His meetings were so popular that he left his gambling nicknames behind to become known as the "Tabernacle Man" and announced plans to build "tabernacles" throughout Southern Indiana and Kentucky.[178]

> *I made money in gambling in wine rooms, where the elite spent their money in slot machines. I tell this in all humility, and only to show what a great savior Christ is. Once a year, I always went back to the old home and mother always treated me the same, though she must have suffered with a knowledge of my waywardness. Finally, my luck changed. The slot*

[175] Jacob, Mark. 2007, Nov 25. 10 things you might not know about famous evangelists. "British preacher Gipsy Smith's visit to Chicago in 1909 was a textbook example of the danger of spotlighting sin. Smith invaded Chicago's vortex of vice, the Levee District on the Near South Side, to conduct a prayer rally. The event attracted thousands of the pious and the curious, and many of the latter stayed around after prayers to conduct their own fact-finding tours."

[176] Ex: Story of Life Will Be Told. 1920, Jan 4. Indianapolis Star.

[177] Astle, Cynthia. 2020, Aug 5. Amid its own racist history, United Methodist Church unites against racism. Accessed 2022, Mar 27 from https://baptistnews.com/article/amid-its-own-racist-history-united-methodist-church-unites-against-racism. "In 1968, today's United Methodist Church was formed through the merger of the Methodist Church and the Evangelical United Brethren Church, spiritual descendants of German-speaking colonial-era Methodists. In a reversal of fortune, the historically abolitionist EUB's price of merger was the dismantling of the racially segregated Central Jurisdiction. This action was met with jubilation among Black Methodists and with dismay and outright anger among remnants of the former southern branch. A few dozen congregations exercised their option to leave the new denomination because of it, joining the more theologically conservative Wesleyan Church or even the Southern Methodist Church, which advocated racial separation as part of its doctrine."

[178] Tabernacle Built Here by Indianapolis Man. 1920, May 28. Courier Journal. "He is planning a chain of tabernacles throughout Southern Indiana and parts of Kentucky."

machines were legislated out of business. I lost at the table;
my saloon melted away and when our second child came, a
sweet baby girl, I was so far out that I was in the company of
the degraded. Instead of at home with my wife, and we were
lacking in the comforts of life. I started life anew, working for
$14 a week. In the six years that have passed, I have had
many temptations and battles, but, by God's help, I have
won.[179]

The crowds that attended Cadle's "tabernacle meetings" gladly looked beyond the math calculating how many shoes would have to have been repaired to earn the large sums of money required for the expensive buildings and other operations that Cadle was involved with. They were more interested in his back story, and Cadle told it often. Black Pentecostal leader G. T. Haywood would likely have never given Cadle a second thought, though at the time, Cadle was erecting a house of enemies to Haywood's cause. Cadle was just one of many revivalists attracting crowds with fascinating conversion stories all over the country. Even though large sums of money flowed through Cadle's hands, other revivalists operated with similar finances in their ministries, and the "life story" that Cadle used in his revivals was not that much different from those told by the others.[180]

When Secretary of State, Ed Jackson, was elected President of the Cadle Tabernacle Evangelistic Association in 1921,[181] Cadle's operation still would not have been seen as a threat to the interracial revivals, at least for their religious services. The Cadle Tabernacle meetings were *"undenominational in character"*,[182] which could have been interpreted as breaking away from the segregated background and permitting open fellowship with the

---

[179] Starts New Life, Is Now Wealthy. 1921, Jan 24. Muncie Morning Star.

180 Ex: Revivalist Peter Cartright was a gambler-turned-preacher. Cartright helped start America's Second Great Awakening 1790-1840

[181] Jackson Tabernacle Head. 1921, Nov 10. The Indianapolis Star. "Ed Jackson Secretary of State was elected president of the Cadle Tabernacle Evangelistic Association."

[182] Jackson Tabernacle Head. 1921, Nov 10. The Indianapolis Star.

racially-united Pentecostals of Indiana. This sentiment would have quickly faded, however, when rumors began to spread that men in white robes were seen joining the evangelistic meetings[183] at the Cadle Tabernacle. Mayor Samuel L. Shank, who tried unsuccessfully to halt the Klan's invasion of Indianapolis government,[184] issued an order to the chief of police instructing them to stop citizens from wearing of masks in public places. It was an order that would never be enforced in Indianapolis — especially at the Cadle Tabernacle where high-ranking Klan members conducted business. When the Indiana Klan began producing films to indoctrinate the public with Klan ideology, the Indiana-produced film[185] *The Traitor Within* played for an extended time at the Cadle Tabernacle in 1924.[186] Soon after, it became public knowledge that Cadle's Tabernacle was a *"Klan Center"*. The film, which angered Catholics in Indianapolis for its anti-Catholic themes, resulted in a published statement in the Indiana Catholic and Record newspaper exposing the Klan operations at the Cadle

---

[183] Misc. News. 1923, May 12. The Indianapolis News. "Mayor Shank, recently, on the day after a group of masked men, supposedly members of the Ku Klux Klan, had visited a revival meeting at the Cadle Tabernacle, issued an order to the chief of police forbidding the wearing of masks in public places."

[184] Samuel Lewis (Lew) Shank. Accessed 2022, Mar 28 from https://indyencyclopedia.org/samuel-lewis-lew-shank. "In an effort to break the Klan statewide, Shank entered the Republican gubernatorial primary against the Klan's candidate, Ed Jackson. In the May 6, 1924, primary election, Jackson easily gained the nomination over Shank and other anti-Klan Republicans, defeating the Indianapolis mayor in Marion County by a total of 38,668 to 20,306 votes".

[185] Rice, Tom. 2008. The True Story of the Ku Klux Klan: Defining the Klan through Film. "While the Klan in Ohio was completing the production of The Toll of Justice, Cavalier Moving Picture Company, a Klan enterprise in Indiana, was attempting to produce its own picture, The Traitor Within."

[186] Rice, Tom. 2016. White Robes, Silver Screens: Movies and the Making of the Ku Klux Klan. "The Klan presented these films within a myriad of non-theatrical venues – The Traitor Within played at baseball parks, country clubs, and even the Knights of Pythias lodges – and, in particular, in churches and religious venues. The Traitor Within played at the Scoville Tabernacle in Muncie, The First Christian Church in Hammond, and the Universalist Church in Logansport. In March 1924, it enjoyed an extended run at the Cadle Tabernacle, an established Klan center in Indianapolis."

Tabernacle. *"The Traitors Within — the Cadle Tabernacle, being a Klan headquarters, is the natural home of traitors."*[187]

No announcement was necessary for the public to see what was happening at the Cadle Tabernacle. Klan meetings were held almost weekly in the building Cadle built with his "shoe repairs", and the meetings were no secret. The Imperial Wizard, Hiram W. Evans, appeared openly in public for the first time at a meeting in Indianapolis at the Cadle Tabernacle.[188] Evans fully supported the Indiana Klan's agenda to educate (indoctrinate) children, and his first public speech was on the subject of *"The Public School Problem in America"*.[189] The Klan was openly praised at Cadle Tabernacle, and though the group spread discrimination of people with black skin, Indiana ministers falsely claimed that the Klan had made huge strides towards the *"uplift of negroes"*.[190] After Ed Jackson became governor, he himself spoke at the Klan meetings that were held in the Cadle Tabernacle.[191]

Eventually, as the Klan gained control of the educational, religious, and business operations of the Cadle Tabernacle, E. Howard Cadle lost control of his church. James P. Goodrich and Ed Jackson, members of the "Tabernacle Association committee" were noticeably absent when certain members of the church met to

---

[187] Rice, Tom. 2016. White Robes, Silver Screens: Movies and the Making of the Ku Klux Klan.

[188] To Speak at Cadle Tabernacle. 1924, Feb 12. The Indianapolis News. "It has been announced that Hiram W. Evans, Imperial Wizard of the Knights of the Ku Klux Klan, will appear for the first time at an open meeting in Indianapolis Wednesday evening at Cadle Tabernacle."

[189] To Speak at Cadle Tabernacle. 1924, Feb 12. The Indianapolis News.

[190] For Immigrants Vote. 1924, Mar 29. The Indianapolis News. "'The immigrant is no better than your son or my son', the Rev. Mr. Andrews said. 'And should be made to wait as long as you to vote.' He praised the Ku Klux Klan for what he said it had done for the uplift of the negroes."

[191] Stephenson Criticized. Klan Official Says He Cannot Represent Organization. 1924, May 9. The Indianapolis News. "Grover A. Smith, titan of the seventh province kleagle, Ku Klux Klan of Marion County {...} called the audience in order at the Cadle Tabernacle last Friday night when Ed Jackson spoke."

protest.[192] In June of 1923, Cadle sold the Tabernacle to be used for the purposes of *"civic, municipal, religious, and educational meetings"*.[193]

The transition of the Tabernacle ownership was but one small part of a much larger plan. In the weeks leading up to the trial of Indiana Klan's Grand Dragon, D. C. Stephenson for the murder of Madge Oberholtzer, Stephenson began sharing Klan secrets for leverage. Some of that information included secrets about the Klan's plot to shift political power to specific government officials, transitioning control away from Stephens to Klan Imperial Wizard Hiram Evans. Apparently, former Indiana Governor James P. Goodrich — who had given Cadle the initial investment for his "shoe repair" business — was being primed for control of the Indiana Klan.[194] The transfer of Klan leadership to Goodrich was allegedly for the purpose of placing Goodrich in the United States Senate, overthrowing Indiana Senator James Eli Watson. Watson, whose original slogan, *"If you can't beat 'em, jine 'em"*[195], was growing increasingly popular among the white supremacists, and Stephenson sought out to overthrow his seat in the Senate. Stephenson issued a public statement asking *"every Protestant minister in the State of Indiana to be present"*[196] at the Cadle Tabernacle Klan meeting to discuss the issue. Stephenson, angry at being stripped from power by Evans, began organizing Indiana

---

[192] Choir Upholds Cadle in Split. 1921, Nov 23. The Indianapolis Star. "James P. Goodrich and Secretary of State Ed Jackson, members of the Tabernacle Association committee, were out of the city."

[193] Tabernacle Sold by Howard Cadle. 1923, Jun 20. The Indianapolis News.

[194] Plot Against Watson Seen by the Old Man. 1 924, May 10. The Indianapolis News. "That Walter Bossert, Imperial representative of the Knights of the Ku Klux Klan in twenty-one states, is attempting to deliver the Klan influence in Indiana to James P. Goodrich, former Governor and Republican leader, in that order, that Goodrich may defeat United States Senator James E. Watson in 1926."

[195] Billington, James H. 2010. Respectfully Quoted: A Dictionary of Quotations. "If you can't lick 'em, jine 'em. Attributed to Senator James E. Watson."

[196] Plot Against Watson Seen by the Old Man. 1924, May 10. The Indianapolis News.

Klansmen to separate from the Atlanta Klan organization[197]. At a meeting at the Cadle Tabernacle in May of 1924, Stephenson declared for a reorganization of the Klan and was able to gain a large number of supporters who lifted him back into power as the Grand Dragon of the "Indiana Realm" of the Klan.[198] Stephenson's return to power was short-lived, however, and Walter Bossert was re-elected Grand Dragon during a meeting at Cadle Tabernacle in September.[199]

Just days later, it was announced that E. Howard Cadle was unable to meet debts in his "American Shoe Rebuilders" company,[200] and he was sued by creditor Edward H. Mayo. A similar suit was filed the following week against the Cadle Tabernacle by E. Howard Cadle for $50,000.[201] In the course of the suit, it was announced that the organization holding the new title for the Cadle Tabernacle was the "Indiana Holiness Association"[202] — a more direct competitor to G. T. Haywood's quickly growing Pentecostal Holiness sect.

---

[197] 1924, May 16. The Fairmount News. Klan the Issue in Indiana Now. "D. C. Stephenson Starts Movement Within Klan Ranks to Break Away from Southern Domination Thereby Intensifying the Already Complex Political Situation."

[198] 1924, May 16. The Fairmount News. Klan the Issue in Indiana Now. "At a meeting held in the Cadle Tabernacle in Indianapolis last Monday, Indiana Klansmen joining with Stephenson declared for a reorganization on which Klan membership should have a voice, and in which the officers should be elected instead of 'appointed' by some one who stood in the position of 'sole owner' of the organization. At this meeting, Stephenson was elected grand dragon of the Indiana realm."

[199] Indiana Klan Re-Elects Bossert Grand Dragon. 1924, Sep 18. The Hancock Democrat.

[200] Cadle Company Receiver. 1924, Oct 1. The Indianapolis News. "The company was unable to meet debts in the ordinary course of business. Cadle was out of the city."

[201] Ask for Receiver for Big Cadle Tabernacle. 1924, Oct 11. The Alexandria Times Tribune.

[202] Ask for Receiver for Big Cadle Tabernacle. 1924, Oct 11. The Alexandria Times Tribune. "Editor's note: The D. L. Speicher above referred to, is connected with the Indiana Holiness Association, who controls Beulah Park, in this city."

CHAPTER 5

THE HOLINESS ASSOCIATION

❖

"With the purchase yesterday at Indianapolis of the Cadle Tabernacle from Howard Cadle, Daniel L. Speicher, president of the Indiana Holiness Association at Beulah Park, and Walter Hansing, secretary of the Holiness Association, came into possession of one of the largest religious structures in the United States" - Muncie Evening Press

The sudden growth, influence, and power of the Indiana Klan accomplished by mixing politics and religion in Indianapolis became the prototype for similar strategies for years to come. Though the white supremacists knew that they would never again be able to plant a majority of proxies in government positions, most of their target audience had been influenced through the propaganda campaigns pushed through Indiana churches. Leaders in the Klan realized that by weaponizing fundamentalist Christianity, whether they themselves lived by the Christian standards or not, they gained almost unlimited control of their followers.

E. Howard Cadle could no longer be used as the vehicle that carried the movement, however. Not only were people losing interest in his bars-to-riches story, Cadle had some fierce competition. Paul Rader and members of the Christian Missionary Alliance, for example, were entertaining crowds of thousands, with as many as 12,000 converts in a single meeting.[203]   Cadle's audiences continued to dwindle. The Tabernacle began hosting well-known white supremacists and Nazi conspirators such as Gerald Burton Winrod, who was nicknamed *"The Jayhawk Nazi"*[204] and "The Kansas Hitler"[205]. Together with Paul Rader, Winrod held conferences at Cadle[206] discussing Christian Fundamentalism — the Indiana Klan's primary religious platform. As time continued, Winrod rose to be a key player in the spreading of white supremacy through various religious ministries. In the 1920s, however, leaders of the movement appeared to have shifted their strategic focus from that of E. Howard Cadle's planting of "tabernacles" to the old time "Camp Meetings".

The Holiness Movement in the United States with its exciting camp meetings won wide popularity in some parts of the country in the early 1920s. Though the movement's origins were heavily influenced by the Methodist Church, the Holiness Movement consisted of several participating denominations. Traditional Methodists did not agree on the doctrinal positions of those advocating for what was required to achieve "holiness", and as a result, Methodism splintered into several denominations.[207]

---

[203] Ex: F. F. Bosworth. Christ the Healer. Accessed 2022, Aug 8 from https://healingandrevival.com/BioBosworth.htm. "In 1924, approximately 12,000 people responded to the salvation message, in one meeting alone in Ottawa, Canada."

[204] The Winrod Legacy of Hate. Anti-Defamation League. Accessed 2022, Dec 26 from https://www.adl.org/sites/default/files/documents/assets/pdf/combating-hate/The-Winrod-Legacy-of-Hate.pdf. "Gordon Winrod, now in his late 60s, who has declared that "Not Jew-wise, the American citizenry always gets Jewed," is the current patriarch of the Winrod clan. His father was the late Rev. Gerald B. Winrod of Wichita, Kansas, a propagandist so notorious for his pro-Nazism and anti-Semitism in the 1930s and 1940s. that he earned himself the sobriquet of the "Jayhawk Nazi," ("Jayhawk" is a nickname for a Kansas native.)"

[205] Protection Sought by 'Kansas Hitler'. 1940, May 29. San Bernardino County Sun. "Mrs. Gerald Winrod today appealed for police protection for her husband, the Rev. Gerald Winrod, who was called the 'Kansas Hitler' when he was candidate for the U. S. senate in 1938. She said he feared violence but did not explain what source."

[206] An Intellectual and Religious Treat! 1929, Feb 2. Indianapolis Times. (Paul Rader and Gerald B. Winrod Pictured).

[207] Bricked, Sophia. 2021, Jul 21. What Is the Holiness Movement and Is it Biblical? "Many traditional Methodists did not agree with the teachings and emphasis of the

Following the pattern of the "camp meeting revivalists" during the Second Great Awakening of the late 1700s and early 1800s, many of these denominations joined together in unity to form inter-denominational "Holiness Associations." These associations often held large annual camp meetings and sometimes smaller meetings throughout the year. Families from each geographical region would travel to the chosen campgrounds, taking extended breaks from their jobs and household duties for nonstop preaching, singing, praying, and other forms of worship. The meetings resulted in a very emotional experience or even a trance,[208] while it produced hundreds, sometimes thousands, of religious conversions. It was the perfect vehicle for pushing Klan agenda, especially since G. T. Haywood had created roadblocks in the Pentecostal revivals.

Whether because of the Klan agenda or not, the Indiana Holiness Association of the early 1900s was far more restrictive and controlling with the rules and regulations governing "holiness" than their counterparts in other states. In 1905, the Indiana association made national news when it threatened to break away from the general conference of the Holiness Association over doctrines of church discipline.[209] Indiana had banned *all secret*

---

movement, which to them was focused too much on emotions. Because of this growing tension, those in the Holiness Movement broke away from the Methodist church and developed their own denominations.
Denominations of the Holiness Church. Multiple denominations were formed within the Holiness Movement and Church once they broke away from Methodism. One of the largest denominations within the Holiness Church is the Church of the Nazarene."

[208] J. William Frost, "Part V: Christianity and Culture in America, Christianity: A Social and Cultural History, 2nd Edition, (Upper Saddle River: Prentice Hall, 1998), 430. "Several ministers, sometimes from different denominations, provided virtually nonstop preaching and hymn singing during the day, in the evening, and late into the night. Attenders anticipated and had emotional conversion experiences, with crying, trances, and exaltation."

[209] Members Divided: Two Factions in Holiness Church Association: Church Discipline Causes Dissension Between the Indiana and Eastern Members. 1905, Oct 5.

societies, life insurance companies, the use of tobacco and liquor, and in fact, everything that does not properly belong to church life.[210]

For the black community in Indiana, the *"everything that does not properly belong to church life"* clause was problematic. While the Methodist faith in America was initially aligned with John Wesley's stance against the injustice of slavery and discrimination, it took the opposite position in 1844 after bishop James Osgood Andrew refused to give up his slaves, causing a deep division in the Methodist denomination.[211] The result was a very racially segregated central and southern Methodist community that was predominately white.[212] Blacks who remained Methodist were assigned to all-black churches, creating friction at inter-denominational and cross-district functions such as the Holiness Associations and the camp meetings. The split among Methodists over segregation was not reconciled until 1939, at which time the "resolution" was to remain segregated, and the Methodist church continued to be segregated until the United Methodist Church was formed in 1968.[213] Racial separation was deeply rooted in the Holiness theology of the era.[214] Though the group banned "secret

---

[210] Members Divided: Two Factions in Holiness Church Association: Church Discipline Causes Dissension Between the Indiana and Eastern Members. 1905, Oct 5.

[211] Astle, Cynthia. 2020, Aug 5. Amid its own racist history, United Methodist Church Unites Against Racism. "In 1844, the white Methodist Church split into southern and northern branches because a bishop, James Osgood Andrew, refused to give up his slaves. This split wasn't resolved until 1939 when three predominantly white Methodist branches reunited into a single Methodist church."

[212] Astle, Cynthia. 2020, Aug 5. Amid its own racist history, United Methodist Church Unites Against Racism. "In 1844, the white Methodist Church split into southern and northern branches because a bishop, James Osgood Andrew, refused to give up his slaves. This split wasn't resolved until 1939 when three predominantly white Methodist branches reunited into a single Methodist church."

[213] Astle, Cynthia. 2020, Aug 5. Amid its own racist history, United Methodist Church Unites Against Racism. "In 1968, today's United Methodist Church was formed through the merger of the Methodist Church and the Evangelical United Brethren Church, spiritual descendants of German-speaking colonial-era Methodists. In a reversal of fortune, the historically abolitionist EUB's price of merger was the dismantling of the racially segregated Central Jurisdiction."

[214] Astle, Cynthia. 2020, Aug 5. Amid its own racist history, United Methodist Church Unites Against Racism. "This action was met with jubilation among Black Methodists and

societies" which would have included the Klan, it would have been impossible to prevent Klan members from infiltrating the camp meetings. Their work with the Holiness association is evident by the fact that the Indiana Holiness Association was strongly linked to the Cadle Tabernacle Klan headquarters.

In the very same section that announced Speicher's purchase and involvement with the Cadle Tabernacle, newspapers announced that the Indiana Klan would be holding their next meeting in Alexandria, the heart of Indiana's Holiness movement and Beulah Park campgrounds where thousands of people met each year for religious activities.[215] At the same time, a sudden and unexpected explosion of new participants in the organization took place. In 1923, the Indiana Holiness Association announced that the big event at Beulah Park was expected to be *"one of the largest attendances in years"*.[216]

It is critical to understand the religious backgrounds of the demographic of people in Indiana who participated in the camp meetings. It was not so much that it was a *Holiness Association Camp Meeting vs. Haywood's Pentecostal Revivals* event. Even Pentecostals participated in the camp meetings, giving the Klan opportunity to influence those attending and undermine the work Haywood was doing towards racial equality.

---

with dismay and outright anger among remnants of the former southern branch. A few dozen congregations exercised their option to leave the new denomination because of it, joining the more theologically conservative Wesleyan Church or even the Southern Methodist Church, which advocated racial separation as part of its doctrine."

[215] Klan to Parade. 1923, Jun 22. Muncie Evening Press. Advertising material appeared in the city announcing a Ku Klux Klan meeting to be held in Alexandria next Tuesday night. The bills telling of the meeting states that a naturalization ceremony will be on the program together with a big parade of white robed figures. The place of the naturalization ceremony has not been announced as of yet, but it is understood that it will be in a nearby field."

[216] Alexandria Plan for Meeting. 1923, Jun 21. Muncie Evening Press. "Preparations are being made at Beulah Park for the annual meeting of the Indiana Holiness Association for ten days during the latter part of August. The main auditorium in the park is to be cleaned from one end to the other. The program for the annual meeting will be mailed to all members of the Holiness Association in a short time. Officials of the Association look for one of the largest attendances in years."

During the years leading up to the Indiana Holiness Association's purchase of the Cadle Tabernacle, the Holiness Camp Meetings were extremely popular. From 1890 to 1920 the Holiness Association experienced increased attendance as the movement spread and local holiness organizations also began to grow and spread.[217]   This was at least in part due to the controversial "Doctor" John Alexander Dowie from Zion City, Illinois, whose Christian Catholic Church cult of personality had a strong foothold in the state of Indiana.

Dowie was a religious conman who created quite a stir in newspapers from San Francisco to New York as he convinced large numbers of people to leave their churches, abandon any form of medical attention — including medication, no matter how badly it was needed — and join his new breed of militant religion. Dowie's Indiana control stretched as far as Evansville along Indiana's southern border.

The Christian Catholic Church, in no way connected to the Roman Catholic Church, infiltrated many Christian denominations by doctrinally positioning itself against "apostate" religion. Ironically, the word "Catholic" in the cult's name meant "universal", which was the opposite of the group's doctrine. Dowie publicly attacked all denominations, especially the Methodist Church, because they had allowed congregants to use medication. The alternative, according to "Doctor" Dowie, was to bring converts to his "healing homes" in Chicago and later Zion City for his own brand of "healing" for not such a small fee.

In many ways, John Alexander Dowie's empire was a prototype for the events taking place in Indianapolis in the 1920s. Fundamentalist Christian leaders, using a platform of apocalyptic fear, were able to sway political outcomes by placing (or buying)

---

[217] Danielson, Robert A. Tenting by the Cross: The History and Development of the Methodist and Holiness Camp Meeting. "This period from about 1890 to 1920 was a period of great growth and expansion for the holiness camp meeting. With the organizational effort of what became the Christian Holiness Association and the rise of local holiness organizations, regular meetings were established to promote the teaching of holiness."

people into positions of power. Dowie used a divide-and-conquer strategy of singling out and attacking a specific person or Christian denomination, and then labeling any person who did not join his attack as "enemies". For Dowie and his Christian Catholic Church cult, the Methodists were initially the enemy. When other groups did not rise against the Methodists, all Christians became viewed as enemies of his "Gospel of Divine Healing". Similarly, the Indiana Klan initially focused on anti-Catholicism propaganda, rallying churches against the spread of Roman Catholic Churches. That same strategy was used for other agendas, such as the Klan's support of prohibition, which became deeply embedded in Indiana fundamentalist religion. Christians in Indiana were either for prohibition or they were reprobates worthy of Klan retribution.

Though Dowie was openly attacked by religious leaders of his time, after his death it was apparent that his ministry wielded a strong influence — especially within the fundamentalist Christian community in Indiana. The Beulah Park Indiana Holiness campground often hosted "Divine Healing" revivals. On special occasions one of the leading figures in Dowie's cult,[218] Rev. F. F. Bosworth, held "Divine Healing" revivals at the Beulah Park Tabernacle.[219] Fred F. Bosworth and his brother, Bart B. Bosworth, both out of Dowie's Zion commune in Illinois, were also intimately familiar with the Cadle Tabernacle. During the Klan's reign using the Cadle Tabernacle as headquarters, the Bosworth Brothers held revivals up to forty days long at Cadle.[220] Prior to the revivals, F. F.

---

[218]   Christ   the   Healer.   Accessed   2022,   Apr   3   from https://www.healingandrevival.com/BioBosworth.htm. "F. F. became the band leader for the Zion City band."

[219] Drove Here from Florida in Hope of Divine Healing. 1929, Jun 7. Alexandria Times-Tribune. "The Bosworth evangelistic meetings at the Beulah Park tabernacle Thursday night were attended by another fair-sized audience, a large number of whom came from out of town. In the audience were a man and his son, who stated that they had come by auto all the way from Florida in order that the elder man, who is suffering from cancer, might be prayed for in the meetings."

[220] Bosworth Close Local Campaign: Life Story of Evangelist Told at Final Service in Cadle Tabernacle. 1924, Dec 30. Indianapolis Star. "The forty-day Bosworth evangelistic campaign closed last night in the Cadle Tabernacle with an attendance estimated at

Bosworth had already been endorsed[221] and financially supported by[222] the Klan.

As one of the founding members of the all-white Assemblies[223] of God,[224] F. F. Bosworth's doctrinal positions would have been closely aligned with those of other Klan-backed ministers hosted in the Cadle Tabernacle. It would not be until 1962 that the Assemblies would begin ordaining black ministers, and even then the church still permitted the doctrinal support of segregation[225] until a 1965 resolution discouraging *discriminatory practices wherever they exist*.[226] Some historians believe the segregation within Pentecostal Movement to have come directly from the movement's founder, Charles Fox Parham, when he discovered *southern darky camp meetings*[227] at the Azusa Street Revival, and claim that Parham was a *Ku Klux Klan sympathizer*.[228] Historians sympathetic to Parham disagree, but

---

10,000. All available seats in the tabernacle were taken and many were standing in the aisles and along the walls."

[221] Living In Bible Times: FF Bosworth and Pentecostal Per suit of the Supernatural, by Christopher J. Richmann, C. Douglas Weaver, 2015, Baylor University. "Meetings in Detroit, where Bosworth preached over the radio probably for the first time; endorsed by local Ku Klux Klan".

[222] Living In Bible Times: FF Bosworth and Pentecostal Per suit of the Supernatural, by Christopher J. Richmann, C. Douglas Weaver, 2015, Baylor University. "When their letter reached Bosworth, he was surprised to find $25 in cash and a note of well-wishes. The Klan apparently appreciated the Christian values promulgated in Bosworth's revivalism."

[223] Sack, Kevin. 2000, June 4. Shared Prayers, Mixed Blessings. New York Times. "The Assemblies of God is still virtually all white."

[224] Christ the Healer. Accessed 2022, Apr 3 from https://www.healingandrevival.com/BioBosworth.htm. "In 1910 Bosworth began pastoring the First Assembly of God Church in Dallas, Texas."

[225] Sack, Kevin. 2000, Jun 4. The Pentecostal Church in America. "With a very few exceptions, the denomination did not ordain black ministers until 1962. And in 1964, when pressed to take a stand on integration, the group's executive presbytery adopted a statement leaving such positions up to individual churches."

[226] Sack, Kevin. 2000, Jun 4. The Pentecostal Church in America.

[227] Sack, Kevin. 2000, Jun 4. The Pentecostal Church in America. New York Times.

[228] Sack, Kevin. 2000, Jun 4. New York Times. The Pentecostal Church in America. "When Mr. Parham came to visit his former student's revival in October 1906, he was dismayed to find scenes of ecstatic praying and frenzied dancing. A Ku Klux Klan sympathizer, he was particularly displeased by the mixing of the races at services that he derided as 'Southern darky camp meetings.'"

shortly after the Azusa Street Revival, Pentecostals split along racial lines to transition the Church of God in Christ to the "black group" while establishing the predominately white Assemblies of God.[229]

John Alexander Dowie's fierce religious competition and sudden demise was a double boost of popularity for the Holiness Association. During the heat of the battle raging with the Christian Catholic Church, many Methodists rallied their support for the Methodist Church – including those who would have otherwise been indifferent. After the very public exposure of Dowie's deceptive practices, including many deaths that the Christian Catholic Church had kept secret, and especially after Dowie's premature death rendered his End-of-Days prophecy a complete failure, Dowie's cult of personality imploded. In the aftermath, his groups of indoctrinated cult members became fertile fields for harvesting fundamentalist-minded converts. The inter-denominational Holiness groups experienced a surge in members, but ultimately it was the Pentecostal Movement that reaped the greater harvest. The interracial revivals in Indiana — that were quickly spreading through the nation from Indianapolis — had become unstoppable.

G. T. Haywood and his interracial Pentecostal revivals were in the perfect position to dominate Indiana fundamentalist religious groups and had become a real threat to the Klan-supportive religious leaders. As the popularity of the Pentecostal movement overtook that of the Indiana Holiness Association, and Haywood continued breaking down racial barriers, leaders in the Klan knew that a different strategy must be used. Indiana Senator James Eli Watson said, "If you can't beat 'em, jine em", and leaders of white supremacy groups did just that. High ranking leaders of

---

[229] Sack, Kevin. 2000, Jun 4. New York Times. The Pentecostal Church in America. "not long after the revival ended the Pentecostals split along racial lines into two major denominations, one black, the Church of God in Christ, and one white, the Assemblies of God, with which the Tabernacle in Atlanta affiliated in the 1940's. The Pentecostal faith spread like fire, most rapidly in the deeply segregated South, but white Southerners were far from ready to embrace the multiracial ethic of Azusa Street."

the 1915 Ku Klux Klan joined into the Pentecostal Movement in Southern Indiana and began attacking the Pentecostal movement from the inside to ensure that their racist agenda continued to move forward.

CHAPTER 6

THE KNIGHTS OF THE FLAMING SWORD

❖

*"I now, by virtue of my authority as royal ambassador, states at
large, Knights of the Flaming Sword, ask all Sir Knights to lay down
your arms and cease to prosecute your efforts in developing the
principles of an organization sole propagated for financial gains."*
- Rev. Roy E. Davis

In September of 1921, New York World published a series
of articles that brought national attention to the Ku Klux Klan and
exposed the organization as a domestic terrorist group that
threatened national security. At least eighteen other newspapers
across the nation picked up the story and helped spread the news
about very disturbing activities that went on under the cover of a
white hood.[230] The series brought an estimated two million readers
nationwide[231] and caused an immediate investigation into the Ku
Klux Klan. Interestingly, it initially caused a surge in Klan
membership.[232]

---

[230] Blow, Charles M. (2021-09-05). "Opinion | From 'Ku Kluxism' to Trumpism". The New York Times. ISSN 0362-4331. Retrieved 2021-09-06.
[231] "The New Ku Klux Klan." Baltimore Sun 07 Sep 1921: 6. Print.
[232] Blow, Charles M. (2021-09-05). "Opinion | From 'Ku Kluxism' to Trumpism". The New York Times. ISSN 0362-4331. Retrieved 2021-09-06.

The articles covered everything, such as its structure as a pyramid scheme collecting $10 a head for membership, $4 of which went to the Klan salesmen, called Kleagles. By 1921 the Klan had raised over five million dollars.[233] The Klan used the word "Americanism" as a word with overloaded meaning to include the entire Klan agenda and used the slogan "One Hundred Percent Americanism" to recruit members of the United States Military via the Army and Navy Club in New York City using a semi-secret mailbox.[234] The Klan was exposed as a pseudo-Christian extremist group with unusual religious practice. Klan recruits were literally baptized, for instance, into a *transparent, life-giving, powerful, God-given fluid, more precious and far more significant than all the sacred oils of the ancients"* — which was actually nothing more than water.[235] Many Klansmen in northern states were not fully aware that the organization was targeting Jews and blacks until the New York World articles,[236] as the Klan's primary target in most states was Catholicism. When it was learned that high-ranking government officials were under Simmons' control,[237] however, the nation could no longer turn a blind eye to the Invisible Empire. They were, by all standards, a domestic terrorist organization that threatened National Security.

Georgia Congressman William D. Upshaw, leader of the prohibitionist movement in the South, defended the Ku Klux Klan in the Congressional Inquiry[238] that followed. (Upshaw would later

---

[233] Ku Klux Klan Wars on Catholics, Jews; Reap Rich Returns. 1921, Sep 6. New York World.

[234] Ku Klux Klan Plot Alleged to Reach Army and Navy" – "Officers Club in New York Used for Mail Headquarters for Membership Solicitors – Men in Service Invited to Join Secret Order. 1921, Sep 8. New York World.

[235] Christian Baptism Ceremony Parodied in Klux Klan Ritual. 1921, Sep 12. New York World.

[236] Ku Klux Made Jews and Negroes Target for Racial Hatreds" – "Not all of 'Colonel' Simmons' Warfare was Directed Against Americans Who are Catholics for He Sought 'White Supremacy. 1921, Sep 16. New York World.

[237] High Officials Hold Ku Klux Membership. 1921, Sep 21. The Evening Sun (Baltimore)

[238] KLAN IS ASSAILED IN HOUSE FEARING; Imperial Wizard Simmons Only Smiles When Witnesses Call Ku Klux Un-American. CONGRESS INQUIRY UNLIKELY Investigation by

become a Latter Rain supporter claiming to be healed in William Branham's revivals.) Upshaw defended the Imperial Wizard, William Joseph Simmons, as *"one of the knightliest, most patriotic men [he had] ever known."*[239] In the aftermath, Simmons and several others were ousted by the Ku Klux Klan, and the Klan itself fell into disarray. Among those ousted from the Klan was the Official Spokesperson and Simmons' second-in-command,[240] Roy E. Davis. Davis, the man who ordained, mentored, and toured with William Branham, was also the man who sent Upshaw to Branham's healing revival in what ultimately ended in an advertisement for Branham's campaigns.

This did not stop Simmons, Davis, and Upshaw, however. While the Indiana Klan was strategically planting proxies into Indianapolis Government in Indiana, Simmons, Davis, and Upshaw went to work. Upshaw, who already had a widely popular ministry as a Christian evangelist,[241] had become famous by publishing an "undenominational" publication called the "Golden Age." He used that fame to hit the road pushing prohibition. Upshaw would eventually run for President of the United States for the Prohibition party, but at the time, he said that he would settle for a Vice President nomination.[242] The end game, as it turned out, was another white supremacy attempt to seize control of Washington

---

Department of Justice and Postal Officials Are Said to Be Sufficient. 1921, Oct 12. New York Times.

[239] Congressman Backs Klan. 1921, Oct 8. Courier Journal.

[240] Knights Flaming Sword Asked to Lay Down Arms. 1925, Jan 19. Chattanooga Daily Times.

. "Immediately thereafter I became quite active in conferring this second degree, which resulted in banishment papers being made out against me for entering into a conspiracy to disrupt or overthrow the Klan. I immediately replied to the charges filed against me, took this reply along with my banishment papers to 1840 Peachtree Road, Atlanta, laid them before the colonel and the then chief of staff, Dr. Fred B. Johnson, of San Antonio, Tex., and was assured that I was right in standing by the colonel."

[241] Georgia Congressman A Law Maker by Day and Revivalist at Night. 1919, Jun 11. Running The Charlotte Observer.

[242] Who's Who in the Days News. 1921, June 21. "That he would be willing to run as vice president on the Democratic Ticket if nominated."

through the 1924 election.[243]   While Upshaw hit the campaign trails, Simmons and Davis began organizing a new white supremacy group.

Just months after Haywood referenced Genesis 3:23-24 in his *Victim of the Flaming Sword* tract describing being symbolically driven from the Garden of Eden, Col. William Joseph Simmons and Rev. Roy E. Davis formed a new, more militant sect of white supremacy elites under the title, "Knights of the Flaming Sword." The new terrorist group officially gathered for the first time on February 14,1924, in Atlanta,[244] and by the name chosen, declared themselves to be an army to force blacks, Catholics, and Jews out of the proverbial "Eden" with modern weapons that symbolized "flaming swords".

Simmons's and Davis's new militant group prided themselves on being extremists, even when compared to the Atlanta-based Ku Klux Klan. As the Knights of the Flaming Sword began to gain a foothold in the South, violence broke out between the Knights of the Flaming Sword and the Ku Klux Klan. Klansmen were openly shot during their "peaceful" displays of power in local parades,[245] and they implemented a strategy within American white supremacy *"calculated to disturb the peace and tranquility".*[246]

Roy E. Davis was greatly angered by his banishment from the 1915 Ku Klux Klan, and became very vocal against the new leadership that had replaced Simmons and himself. Joined by Dr. Fred B. Johnson of San Antonio, Texas, Simmons and Davis sent

---

[243] United States Presidential Election of 1924. Britannica. Accessed 2022, Dec 30 from https://www.britannica.com/event/United-States-presidential-election-of-1924.

[244] Date Set for "Flaming Sword" Knights' Debut. 1924, Feb 14. The Times. Col. Joseph Simmons, founder of the Ku Klux Klan, who relinquished his offices in that body following the sale of royalties he held, will organize 'The Knights of the Flaming Sword' in Atlanta, February 26, the date set for their first Georgia gathering".

[245] Knights of Ku Klux Klan and the Knights of Flaming Sword Clash. 1924, Nov 1. The Eagle. "Four Been Shot: The warfare between the Ku Klux Klan and the Knights of the Flaming Circle resisting plans for a Klan parade through the city streets, blazed into a series of street disorders today in which four men were shot and three were injured by mob violence."

[246] Knights Flaming Sword Asked to Lay Down Arms. 1925, Jan 19. Chattanooga Daily Times. "a movement calculated to disturb the peace and tranquility."

eight thousand copies of a letter (written by Davis) describing their discontent with the Klan's leadership and direction.[247] Simmons appointed Davis as one of the twelve leaders of the group, and asked Davis to prepare an address specifically designed to anger members of the Ku Klux Klan throughout the United States.[248] After the public address, Davis was invited by various leaders of the Ku Klux Klan to speak at regional Klan meetings, further dividing the Klan and recruiting members to the Knights of the Flaming Sword.[249] From there, Davis went on tour to the West and the North as an official spokesman for Col. William Joseph Simmons.[250] All the while, Davis did so under the guise of religion — Davis was also an evangelist, soon to be banished by the Southern Baptist Convention for immorality.[251]

---

[247] Knights Flaming Sword Asked to Lay Down Arms. 1925, Jan 19. Chattanooga Daily Times. "I immediately replied to the charges filed against me, took this reply along with my banishment papers to 1840 Peachtree Road, Atlanta, laid them before the colonel and the then chief of staff, Dr. Fred B. Johnson, of San Antonio, Tex., and was assured that I was right in standing by the colonel. Eight thousand copies of my reply to the wizard concerning my banishment was printed at the suggestion of the royal castle and was sent broadcast through the United States."

[248] Knights Flaming Sword Asked to Lay Down Arms. 1925, Jan 19. Chattanooga Daily Times. "Immediately after the publication of my reply I was notified to meet Col. Simmons in Jacksonville, Fla., and was also instructed to prepare an address to be delivered before this convention of Klansman assembled from over nation, which address did disturb or was calculated to disturb the peace and tranquility of the minds of the Klansmen over the country."

[249] Knights Flaming Sword Asked to Lay Down Arms. 1925, Jan 19. Chattanooga Daily Times. "The next night I was billed to deliver an address in the principal theater of that city, being the first public address ever delivered in the world setting forth what at that time were believed to be the aims, principles, and purposes of the Knights of the Flaming Sword. After the meeting, I was invited to attend a Klan meeting in that city, and I did attend this Klan meeting, Judge Preston B. Reynolds, of Dallas, Tex., accompanying me, and organizing the first court of the Knights of the Flaming Sword in all the world."

[250] Knights Flaming Sword Asked to Lay Down Arms. 1925, Jan 19. Chattanooga Daily Times. "Soon after this meeting, I was sent to the west and the north on a speaking tour in the interest of the colonel and his organization. Great results accompanied my efforts, particularly in the north."

[251] 1927, February 18. The Nugget. "August 12, 1926: Important Notice, The State Board of Missions through its Ex. Com. regrets to say that in its best judgment Mr. Roy E. Davis, now operating in and around Jacksonville and posing as a Baptist preacher, is not worthy of the confidence of the brotherhood, nor the public at large. A thorough investigation has been made and from the many personal letters and affidavits in hand

In a move similar to the Indiana Klan's attempt at taking Washington through Governor Ed Jackson's presidential run, the Knights of the Flaming Sword attempted to place either a Klansman or a proxy in the White House. While Davis proclaimed his support of *"one of the presidential nominees"*,[252] the Klan made waves throughout the United States in what would later become known as the Teapot Dome scandal. Republican Calvin Coolidge nearly lost re-election when it was learned that Navy oil fields were being secretly leased to private business owners.[253] With Coolidge seemingly out of the picture, the Democratic Party was a sure win. One runner up, New York Governor Al Smith was a Catholic and bitterly opposed by Democrats in the South and West.[254] Strongly opposing prohibition and toeing the Northern Democrat party line by supporting Catholics and Jewish immigrants, Governor Smith quickly became the Klan's public enemy number one. The Democratic Party split along lines for and against white supremacy, with defenders of the Ku Klux Klan creating the strongest opposition.[255] Northeastern Democrats wanted the party to

---

from trustworthy brethren it is evident that Mr. Davis is an excluded member of a Baptist church, and he has a long and black record behind him. W. L. C. Mahan, Pres. C. M. Brittain, Acting Sec'y"

[252] Knights Flaming Sword Asked to Lay Down Arms. 1925, Jan 19. Chattanooga Daily Times.

[253] The Democratic Convention of 1924. Accessed 2022, Apr 3 from https://www.digitalhistory.uh.edu/disp_textbook.cfm?smtID=2&psid=3393. "In 1924, Democratic prospects in the upcoming presidential election seemed promising. The administration of Republican Calvin Coolidge was rocked by a scandal, the Teapot Dome, which involved secret leasing of the Navy's oil fields to private businesses."

[254] The Democratic Convention of 1924. "The two leading candidates symbolized a deep cultural divide. Al Smith, New York's governor, was a Catholic and an opponent of prohibition and was bitterly opposed by Democrats in the South and West."

[255] The Democratic Convention of 1924. "On one side were defenders of the Ku Klux Klan, prohibition, and fundamentalism. On the other side were northeastern Catholics and Jewish immigrants and their children. A series of issues that bitterly divided the country during the early 1920s were on display at the 1924 Democratic Convention held at Madison Square Garden in New York City from June 24 to July 9, 1924."

denounce the Ku Klux Klan, and former Secretary William Gibbs McAdoo refused to do so.[256]

This resulted in a violently heated scene at the Democratic Convention of 1924. Twenty thousand Klan supporters gathered in New Jersey to protest Northern Democrats by throwing baseballs at an effigy of Al Smith after the Democratic Convention deadlocked. When a cross was burned at the event, newspapers began calling the Democratic Convention a "Klanbake".[257] The fierce battle between Klan and Anti-Klan factions within the Democratic Party continued until both Al Smith and William Gibs McAdoo withdrew from the contention — leaving the Democratic convention in complete disarray. As a result of the "Klanbake", only half of the eligible Democratic voters participated, and incumbent President Calvin Coolidge won by seven million votes.[258]

The battle between northern and southern Democrats continued after the election, however, and Col. William Joseph Simmons and the Knights of the Flaming Sword were suddenly in

---

[256] The Democratic Convention of 1924. "The two leading candidates symbolized a deep cultural divide. Al Smith, New York's governor, was a Catholic and an opponent of prohibition and was bitterly opposed by Democrats in the South and West. Former Treasury Secretary William Gibbs McAdoo, a Protestant, defended prohibition and refused to repudiate the Ku Klux Klan, making himself unacceptable to Catholics and Jews in the Northeast."

[257] The Democratic Convention of 1924. "Newspapers called the convention a "Klanbake," as pro-Klan and anti-Klan delegates wrangled bitterly over the party platform. The convention opened on a Monday and by Thursday night, after 61 ballots, the convention was deadlocked. The next day, July 4, some 20,000 Klan supporters wearing white hoods and robes held a picnic in New Jersey. One speaker denounced the "clownvention in Jew York." They threw baseballs at an effigy of Al Smith. A cross-burning culminated the event."

[258] The Democratic Convention of 1924. "Al Smith and William Gibbs McAdoo withdrew from contention after the 99th ballot. On the 103rd ballot, the weary convention nominated John W. Davis of West Virginia, formerly a US Representative from West Virginia, Solicitor General for the United States, and US Ambassador to Britain under President Woodrow Wilson. The nomination proved worthless. Liberals deserted the Democrats and voted for Robert La Follette, a third-party candidate. Apathy and disgust kept many home, and just half of those eligible went to the polls. The Democrat candidate, John Davis, received 8 million votes. The Republican candidate, incumbent president Calvin Coolidge, received 15 million votes."

the crosshairs of the angry Democrats in New York. They began collecting criminal evidence against Simmons for what was sure to be an indictment by a New York Grand Jury.[259] Roy E. Davis began holding a series of conferences to defend Simmons, which apparently succeeded in eliminating Simmons' risk of prosecution.[260] After doing so, Davis canceled his tours in the West to play a leading role in the Knights of the Flaming Sword. Davis travelled to Chattanooga and established the state headquarters,[261] where he promoted Simmons as *"one of America's greatest Christian statesmen, and the Moses of the present order of things".*[262] Within a short period of time, four thousand Klansmen renounced the Ku Klux Klan in Chattanooga[263] creating a pattern that quickly spread. By October 1924, the Knights of the Flaming Sword had recruited 642,000 members[264] and a rally of fifty thousand strong was

---

[259] Knights Flaming Sword Asked to Lay Down Arms. 1925, Jan 19. Chattanooga Daily Times. "While in Atlanta, incidentally, I learned the same gentleman had just been in conference with certain New York officials of the law and that he was going to be forced to appear before the New York grand jury and submit certain evidence alleged to be in his possession which would result in the indictment of my friend."

[260] Knights Flaming Sword Asked to Lay Down Arms. 1925, Jan 19. Chattanooga Daily Times. "I set in motion a series of conferences with the gentleman referred to above and with the royal castle, which finally resulted in a cessation of this gentleman's hostilities to the colonel and his movement.

[261] Knights Flaming Sword Asked to Lay Down Arms. 1925, Jan 19. Chattanooga Daily Times. "I canceled all my engagements in the west, accepted my portfolio and came to Chattanooga, and established the state headquarters for Knights of the Flaming Sword."

[262] Knights Flaming Sword Asked to Lay Down Arms. 1925, Jan 19. Chattanooga Daily Times.

[263] Klan is Renounced By 4,000 at Chattanooga. 1924, Oct 6. The Tennessean. "The meeting was attended by Dr. Fred B. Johnson, of San Antonio, Texas, chief of staff of Colonel Simmons and Dr. R. E. Davis, former ambassador at Washington for the Klan."

[264] Klan is Renounced By 4,000 at Chattanooga. 1924, Oct 6. The Tennessean. "The meeting was attended by Dr. Fred B. Johnson, of San Antonio, Texas, chief of staff of Colonel Simmons and Dr. R. E. Davis, former ambassador at Washington for the Klan."

expected that year.[265] Roy E. Davis himself enlisted most of those recruited into the organization.[266]

Less than thirty days later, the Knights of the Flaming Sword imploded. Newspaper reporters began investigating the organization and learned that Simmons had personally increased his wealth by $150,000 from the Klan and was doing the same for the Knights of the Flaming Sword.[267] Worse, Simmons had allegedly set up a bank account under the name of a family member and had been depositing funds allegedly collected by the Knights of the Flaming Sword into that account.[268] The deposits exceeded the organization's debt, making the Knights look like a den of thieves. All of these problems were dramatically compounded by the fact that the group's accounting was in disarray after "supreme recorder" Capt. M. A. Moore was killed in an automobile accident. Simmons was badly injured in the crash and unable to defend himself.[269]

Davis, who had been promoting the group as a charitable organization, was caught red-handed in one of the largest pyramid

---

[265] Simmons Says Old Klan is Dead. 1924, Oct 10. Chattanooga News. "It was learned from Col. Simmons that in the latter part of October there would take place on one of the historic mountains of Georgia near Chattanooga one of the most gigantic meetings ever held in the south. Fifty thousand people, it is expected, will rally to the call of the flaming sword."

[266] Knights Flaming Sword Asked to Lay Down Arms. 1925, Jan 19. Chattanooga Daily Times. "Dr. Davis said that he, personally, had enlisted most of the recruits of the organization."

[267] Knights Flaming Sword Asked to Lay Down Arms. 1925, Jan 19. Chattanooga Daily Times. "Less than thirty days after this conversation, and, utterly unknown to me, the newspapers were alleging that Col. Simmons had actually sold out the second degree for $150,000!"

[268] Flaming Sword Turns Against Col. Simmons: Receiver Is Appointed for Offshoot of Klan; Founder is "Whole Cheese". 1925, May 29. Muncie Post Democrat. "They further allege that by 'information and belief' Col. Simmons had a bank account in the name of some other member of his family, and that deposits exceed the debts."

[269] Flaming Sword Turns Against Col. Simmons: Receiver Is Appointed for Offshoot of Klan; Founder is "Whole Cheese". 1925, May 29. Muncie Post Democrat. "Col. Simmons is said to be still confined to his sick bed by reason of injuries received last January in an automobile crash near Gainesville, Ga., when Capt. M. A. Moore, supreme recorder of the new order was killed. They were enroute to Col. Simmons' country home in northern Georgia at the time."

schemes of the era and forced to either defend Simmons against the angry mob or separate himself. Davis chose the latter and issued a public statement declaring his innocence and discontent.[270]

> *I now, by virtue of my authority as royal ambassador, states at large, Knights of the Flaming Sword, ask all Sir Knights to lay down your arms and cease to prosecute your efforts in developing the principles of an organization sole propagated for financial gains. Dr. Fred B. Johnson, chief of staff to Col. Simmons, has resigned; Judge T. O. Tuttle, head of the propagation department of this order, has resigned, and Judge Preston P. Reynolds, national evangel, has resigned, and many others, for reasons I can explain by all Sir Knights conferring with me.*
>
> *(Signed) - DR. ROY E. DAVIS, Royal Ambassador, States at Large, Knights of the Flaming Sword, Incorporated.*[271]

This did not stop Roy E. Davis from continuing his mission, however. As the former ambassador in Washington for the Ku Klux Klan,[272] and escaping free from guilt as the former ambassador for the Knights of the Flaming Sword, Davis had many connections in several states. The Knights of the Flaming Sword would no longer be a threat to G. T. Haywood and his converts who were the "victims of the Flaming Sword". By leveraging the divisions within

---

[270] Knights Flaming Sword Asked to Lay Down Arms. 1925, Jan 19. Chattanooga Daily Times. "This organization was supposed, as announced by Col. William Joseph Simmons, as an eleemosynary institution. Not one dime to date of the $150,000 appropriated by the Klan to Col. Simmons, and the money he has derived from the Knights of the Flaming Sword has been given to justify this doctrine. It was said to be a fraternal organization. Fraternalism is an unknown quality of this organization, in that practically every worker on the field for the colonel has had to resign his position with the order because he could not get what money was due him."

[271] Knights Flaming Sword Asked to Lay Down Arms. 1925, Jan 19. Chattanooga Daily Times.

[272] Klan is Renounced By 4,000 at Chattanooga. 1924, Oct 6. The Tennessean. "Dr. R. E. Davis, former ambassador at Washington for the Klan."

Pentecostalism over race relations, however, Davis found the perfect replacement: an opportunity to attack Pentecostalism from within. Though he had been a Baptist minister and evangelist for as long as his history had been recorded, Davis began establishing himself as a Pentecostal minister instead, and occupied the pulpit of a Pentecostal Church in Dahlonega, Georgia, every night for an entire month.[273]

Davis's time as a Pentecostal minister from Georgia was limited to just two months. When it was made public that Davis was a Baptist minister posing as a Pentecostal evangelist,[274] and that he had an extensive criminal and immoral history, Davis was run out of Dahlonega. Newspapers began publishing quotes from the Wise County Messenger in Texas, informing the public that Davis was an imposter who had been arrested for living a dual life in Texas and in Georgia — with multiple wives and multiple churches.[275]

After a laundry list of crimes against God and man were aired to the public, Davis fled Dahlonega to setup camp in Chattanooga. Davis planted the "Pentecostal Baptist Church",[276] and by 1928, had outgrew the building. With success using the Pentecostal name under his belt (and with his supporters in the white supremacy underworld) Davis then transitioned the

---

[273] Bad Record for a Preacher. 1927, Feb 18. The Nugget. "Near two months ago a stranger arrived in Dahlonega who said his name was Rev. Roy E. Davis D. D. evangelist, author, lecturer, etc., and the doors of the Pentecost church, which its members call the House of God, were thrown open to him and he went to preaching, occupying the pulpit every night except one for a month before taking a rest."

[274] Bad Record for a Preacher. 1927, Feb 18. The Nugget. "He is charged with deserting a wife and 3 children in Texas, and in some of the Georgia towns and cities, with having a red headed woman with him. Was turned out of one Baptist church for using language unbecoming a minister."

[275] Rev. Roy E. Davis, Again. 1927, February 25. The Nugget. "As the above imposter has been here about four weeks pretending to be a good man ... We will now give you a clipping from the Wise County Messenger, published at Decatur, Texas, concerning his trial there as follows: 'Rev. Roy E. Davis, Singer and Masher, Goes to Prison, drew a jury, verdict of swindling and was given two years sentence by the District Court. ... Davis deserted his wife and three children, who now reside in East Texas; and married a young Lady in Georgia."

[276] Pentecostal Baptists to Build a Church. 1928, August 6. Chattanooga Daily Times.

"Pentecostal Baptists" into a new denomination of faith and started planting multiple churches across the nation. In Nashville, Davis was the pastor of the "First Pentecostal Baptist Church of Nashville, Tennessee".[277] He also had a church in Louisville, Kentucky.[278] The Pentecostal Baptist Church that would define Davis's legacy, however, would be planted in Jeffersonville, Indiana, just minutes from Cadle's hometown of Utica.

---

[277] An Explanation. 1928, Sep 2. The Tennessean. "I am the pastor of the First Pentecostal Baptist Church of Nashville, Tenn."
[278] A Preacher on Prohibition. 1930, Feb 5. The Courier Journal. "I am pastor of a church in this city."

CHAPTER 7

THE PENTECOSTAL BAPTIST CHURCH

❖

"The man here who is carrying a Bible, hymn book, and a little bottle of healing oil, and has been traveling through Texas, Florida and parts of Georgia is using the pulpit as a shield acts contrary to both the laws of God and man, for years" - The Nugget

On "Black Monday"; October 28, 1929, the Stock Market crashed; bringing an end to the "Roaring Twenties".[279] The Dow Jones Industrial Average dropped nearly thirteen percent in a single day. The next day, "Black Tuesday", the markets tanked, losing nearly twelve percent. By November, the Dow had lost nearly half of its value, sending chaos through financial systems.

In Louisville, Kentucky, however, Black Monday was a day of celebration. The George Rogers Clark Memorial Bridge, built by the American Bridge Company of Pittsburgh, began construction in 1926 and cost approximately $4.7 million to complete. It was the first bridge construction of its kind; rather than being built out from the shore, the bridge was constructed from the center towards land. It was also the safest construction of its kind. Unlike the Big Four Bridge next to it, wherein *"sixteen men drown like rats"*[280] in 1890, not a single person drowned during its

---

[279] Stock Market Crash of 1929. Accessed 2022, Dec 31 from https://www.federalreservehistory.org/essays/stock-market-crash-of-1929.
[280] Sixteen Men Drown Like Rats. 1890, Jan 10. Evening Gazette.

construction. The entire city celebrated, and the Louisville Courier Journal Newspaper dedicated almost an entire newspaper to bridge-related articles.[281] Interestingly, decades later, William Branham claimed in the Latter Rain revivals to have prophesied that sixteen fell from the newer bridge, not the bridge built before his birth. This "prophecy" would be used to claim the "office of prophet" in the Latter Rain sect.

Louisville was the perfect place for a criminal on the run. Any undesirable person could easily slip across the river to Jeffersonville, Indiana, and blend in with the crowds of ne'er-do-wells in the casinos and speakeasies that were soon to be desolated by the Great Flood of the Ohio river in 1937. Jeffersonville was home to liquor tycoon Otto H. Wathen, president of the R. E. Wathen Distilleries and owner of the Louisville Colonels baseball team. During the height of prohibition during Branham's early childhood years, William Branham and his father Charles produced illicit liquor for Wathen.[282] On the record books, the R. E. Wathen distilleries operated under the guise of producing alcohol under a medicinal license. The R. E. Wathen distillery was caught supplying the Chicago mob with liquor multiple times during the reign of Al Capone in Chicago.[283] The Branham family lived on Wathen Farm,[284] on the Utica Pike, where E. Howard Cadle had lived before transitioning to the Chicago underground. According to the

---

[281] Courier Journal, Oct 28, 1929.

[282] Branham, William. 1959, April 19. My Life Story (59-0419A). "Later we moved to Indiana and Father went to work for a man, Mr. Wathen, a rich man. He owns the Wathen Distilleries. And he owned a great shares; he's a multimillionaire, and the Louisville Colonels, and—and baseball, and so forth. And then we lived near there. And Dad being a poor man, yet he could not do without his drinking, so he—he went to making whiskey in a—in a still. 61 And then it worked a hardship on me because I was the oldest of the children. I had to come and pack water to this still, to keep those coils cool while they were making the whiskey. Then he got to selling it, and then he got two or three of those stills. Now, that's the part I don't like to tell, but it's the truth."

[283] City Linked to Chicago Rum Deal Third Time. 1920, Dec 4. "Mr. Simon recently uncovered the transaction, which resulted in the indictment of Otto H. Wathen and William F. Knebelkamp, of R. E. Wathen & Company, Louisville distillers.

[284] Branham, William. 1961, Nov 5. The Testimony of a True Witness. "Mr. Wathen up there on the Utica Pike, and we knowed nothing about church. They were Catholic."

locals in Jeffersonville, Wathen Farm was a massive underground in and of itself, having a casino, horse track, and other illicit attractions. None of it was advertised — for obvious reasons.

In 1929, the Greyhound racing track opened in nearby Clarksville, Indiana, under the name "Jeffersonville Dog Mart". The locals referred to it as the "Falls City Kennel Club". Monday night was known as "Monkey Night", a mini-Kentucky Derby event featuring monkeys dressed like jockeys that rode on the backs of the greyhounds.[285]

When Roy E. Davis moved his Pentecostal Baptist Church of God headquarters to Jeffersonville, Indiana, the move was not without controversy. Not only was he the former ambassador for two nationally recognized white supremacy groups — in both of which he ranked second in command to the infamous Col. William Joseph Simmons — Davis's shady past had been made public several times and in several states. Most recently, before starting the Jeffersonville sect, during a highly publicized criminal trial in Louisville; Davis nearly earned prison time for violating the Mann Act by bringing his future wife Allie Lee Garrison across the Tennessee state lines for the purposes of sex.[286] Garrison was only seventeen at the time, and crossing state lines with an underaged girl for the purposes of sex was a federal offense.

---

[285] Boyle, John. RISE & FALL NOW AND THEN: Goons, gambling, Greyhounds in Little Las Vegas. 2019, Sep 15. Accessed 2022, Dec 31 from https://www.newsandtribune.com/news/now-and-then-goons-gambling-greyhounds-in-little-las-vegas/article_7ec5fc96-d7ce-11e9-a036-63975d1c7c00.html. "A Greyhound racing track by the name of the Jeffersonville Dog Mart – also referred to as the Falls Cities Kennel Club – opened up just off of what is now Eastern Boulevard in 1929. The track was quite popular, with a capacity of roughly 3,000 people who would come out for events like Monkey Night. What is Monkey Night, you ask? Think of it as a mini-Kentucky Derby, where monkeys dressed like jockeys even tinier than the human version would zoom around the track atop saddled dogs."

[286] Pastor Held in Mann Act Case: Man Nabbed at Revival Accused of Bringing Girl from Tennessee. 1930, Oct 12. Courier Journal. "Charged with violation of the Mann Act, the Rev. Roy E. Davis, 40 years old, 1525 River Road."

Davis had deserted a wife and three children in Texas while married to[287] and living with another woman in Georgia.[288] Using various aliases[289] to conceal his tracks as he worked through churches in multiple states, he was accused of everything from "divine healing" schemes[290] to stealing church funds.[291] He had spent some time in a Texas prison for defrauding a bank in Boonesville, Texas[292]

In Waco, Texas, under the alias "Lon", Roy Davis was charged with two counts of burglary, as well as for breaking into the United States Marshall's office and stealing a pistol. There was no question as to whether or not Davis was a criminal, even when he was acquitted in Louisville; his long history of criminal activity spoke for itself. Worse, his record was laundered and left to dry before the public during the trial. The real question was whether Davis even believed the Pentecostal religion he was selling.

In his church in Louisville, which he called the "Holy Bible Mission", Davis set up a racketeering scheme in which he claimed that couples married by the Justice of the Peace were "not acceptable" in the sight of God and must be reunited by him — for

---

[287] Bad Record for a Preacher. 1927, Feb 18. The Nugget. "He is charged with deserting a wife and 3 children in Texas, and in some of the Georgia towns and cities, with having a red headed woman with him."

[288] Bad Record for a Preacher. 1927, Feb 18. The Nugget. "When Davis first came to Lavonia, Ga, from Texas, he went by the name of T. R. Crawford. And at Acworth as Lon Davis. And at other places tacked Dr. onto Roy E. Davis."

[289] Bad Record for a Preacher. 1927, Feb 18. The Nugget. "The man here who is carrying a bible, hymn book, and a little bottle of healing oil, and has been traveling through Texas, Florida and parts of Georgia using the pulpit as a shield in acts contrary to both the laws of God and man, for years."

[290] Bad Record for a Preacher. 1927, Feb 18. The Nugget. "Carried a pistol, jumped board bills, and a lot of other things charged. Among them collecting $10 from one man and $25 from another over in Pickens County, Ga., to buy an organ for a church and left with the money."

[291] Rev. Davis, Singer and Masher, Goes to Prison. 1917, Jun 29. Wise County Messenger.

[292] Two Burglary Complaints are Filed in Case of Lon Davis. 1922, Sep 15. The Waco News Tribune. "Two complaints charging Lon Davis with burglary were filed in Justice J. J. Padgett's court Thursday. This is the same man who is said to have entered the office of the deputy United States Marshall located in the federal building and purloined a six-shooter, for which offense he is now in default of bond in the sum of $750."

a fee of $5.00.[293] Davis was arrested for "religious racketeering" in 1930. It was the first charges of such a crime and was reported in newspapers of multiple states. At that time, Davis told officials that he had been ordained in the Baptist church.[294] The official name of his church, however, was the "Pentecostal Baptist Church",[295] and Davis advertised it as a Pentecostal Assembly.[296]

Together with Jeffersonville Mayor Rader's son and evangelist Ralph Rader, Davis held a series of revival meetings claiming to expose spiritualism.[297] Davis claimed that he was a "converted spiritualist" and excited the crowds by performing several tricks that he claimed that spiritualists used. It would have been a hot topic to his Indiana audience considering the popularity of nearby Camp Chesterfield, home of the Indiana Association of Spiritualists. Camp Chesterfield just happened to be just over ten miles from the Beulah Park Holiness Association that was connected to the Cadle Tabernacle owners.

---

[293] Arrest Pastor as Racketeer: Sought Fee for Remarriage, Flock Charges. 1930, Mar 20. Indianapolis Times. "The defendant, the 'Rev' Roy E. Davis, 40, has been conducting missions in Texas and Georgia for more than ten years. Detectives who investigated the case charged that Davis advised members of his congregation who had been married by justices of the peace, that the ceremony was 'not acceptable' in the sight of God, and that they should be reunited by him – for a fee of $5."

[294] Arrest Pastor as Racketeer: Sought Fee for Remarriage, Flock Charges. 1930, Mar 20. Indianapolis Times. "Davis said he was a minister of the Baptist church, but admitted, police said, that he has no license. He claimed to have been ordained at Arabia, Tex., June 15, 1911."

[295] Davis Gives Low-Down on 'Spirit' Tricks. 1930, Oct 16. Jeffersonville Evening News. "Last night the rev. Roy E. Davis, pastor of the Baptist Pentecostal Church of Louisville."

[296] Wm. Branham's First Pastor - Roy E. Davis. 1950, Oct. The Voice of Healing. "I am the minister who received Brother Branham into the first Pentecostal assembly he ever frequented. I baptized him and was his pastor for some two years. I also preached his ordination sermon, and signed his ordination certificate, and heard him preach his first sermon."

[297] Davis Gives Low-Down on 'Spirit' Tricks. 1930, Oct 16. Jeffersonville Evening News. "Evangelist Ralph Rader announces that on Sunday night, the revival meetings now being conducted in the Army will come to an end. ... Last night the Rev. Roy E. Davis, pastor of the Baptist Pentecostal Church of Louisville, who said he is a converted medium, mystified the crowd by doing a number of alleged tricks of the Spiritualists, explaining how they were done."

In 1931, Roy E. Davis set up camp in Jeffersonville, Indiana as a Pentecostal minister. Along with his brothers Dan S. Davis and W. L. Davis, Roy began advertising a Pentecostal Revival in Jeffersonville under the auspices of the "Pentecostal Baptist Church", a Pentecostal sect that he claimed to have founded a few years prior with satellite churches in the South.[298] Together, they set up a printing company and began publishing "The Banner of Truth" promoting the new Pentecostal sect, and issued "write-ups" of his services to the Jeffersonville Evening News insisting that the local paper print his version of the events that took place in his church.[299]

Curious minds asked the Evening News to investigate Davis and his new Pentecostal sect. Upon investigation, it was learned that Davis had intended to move to Jeffersonville since December of 1930. On December 16, 1930, Davis purchased the First Church of the Nazarene on the east side of Watt Street between Maple and Chestnut. The deed was made out to *"Roy E. Davis, Henry Steedley, Clarence E. Meyers, and William Adler as Trustees of the Pentecostal Baptist Church of God of Jeffersonville."*[300] Meanwhile, as Jeffersonville citizens held Davis and his Pentecostal sect in skepticism under a watchful eye, the angered members of his former Louisville church — just minutes across the Ohio River in Kentucky — continued pressing authorities to charge Davis for an

---

[298] 3 Davis Brothers Plan a Pentecostal Revival. 1930, April 17. The Rev. Roy E. Davis said that he founded the Pentecostal Baptist Church a few years ago and that he has organized congregations in the South."

[299] Church Publicity Policy Explained. 1931, Apr 18. Evening News. "A publication with the name 'The Banner of Truth' at its head published by Roy E. Davis, of the First Pentecostal Baptist Church, claims to owe its existence to the refusal of the Evening News to take a 'write-up' of the services and Sunday School of his church. ... but he does not state that when he began preaching here a short time ago he brought his own write-up to us every morning following his meeting the previous night and written as though it was the product of our own force and that he continued this daily until we stopped it, wondering why he should expect us to give him daily publicity contrary to the policy of this paper."

[300] Pentecostal Church. 1931, Aug 14. Jeffersonville Evening News. "Upon request, we have made an examination of the records in the Recorder's office to ascertain the title to the Church building on the east side of Watt Street between Maple and Chestnut."

array of civil and criminal issues. Only a few months after the Davis brothers' Pentecostal Revival in Jeffersonville, Indiana, Governor Harry G. Leslie ordered the extradition of Roy E. Davis to Louisville to face trial for defrauding former congregant Lelia Cain.[301] Davis was defended by Jeffersonville State Senator Russell P. Keyhole who had previously been nominated by the Ku Klux Klan.[302]

This development made Jeffersonville citizens even more curious, including the local news media. Before long, congregants of Davis's Pentecostal Baptist Church of God sect and its history were investigated by investigative reporters. As Davis was sent to Louisville for trial, Jeffersonville newspapers began to publish details about the formation of the church. Apparently, Roy E. Davis served temporarily as a choir leader of Ralph Rader's church and began creating divisions there. When the church eventually split, Davis took a number of congregants with him to organize a church community and filled the pews of the church that he had previously purchased for this strategy.[303] Davis had used the funds provided by Lelia Cain to purchase the Jeffersonville church.[304] He

---

[301] Extradition of Davis Ordered. 1931, Sept 25. "Gov. Harry G. Leslie ordered the return of Roy Davis of Jeffersonville, an evangelist, to Louisville, Ky., for trial on a charge of defrauding Miss Lelia Cain there. State Senator Russell P. Keyhole of Jeffersonville defended Davis at the extradition hearing."

[302] Coots is Victor Without Ku Klux: Jeffersonville Primary Returns Show Coroner Is Only Such Nominee. 1924, May 8. Courier Journal. "From an M. Coots, for County Coroner, was the only candidate nominated who was not indorsed [sig] by the Ku Klux Klan … [names of those nominated listed] Russell P. Kehoe."

[303] Governor Holds Cleric Must Face Money Charge. 1931, Sep 25. Evening News. "Mr. Davis's first introduction to church people on this side of the river was as choir leader of the church services conducted by Rev. Ralph Rader. This was soon terminated, but in the meantime a friendship arose between him and a number of those who attended the services, and Davis organized a church community of those who would go with him. After conducting services at other places, he finally located his religious activities at the church on Watt Street between Chestnut and Maple."

[304] Governor Holds Cleric Must Face Money Charge. 1931, Sep 25. Evening News. "Several months ago, the News & Journal had occasion to investigate the title to the property and it was found that Mr. Davis and two members of his congregation had received a deed of conveyance for it as trustees of the Pentecostal Baptist Church and as we understand this is the property sought to be mortgaged to secure a loan of $450.00 made by Lelia Cain."

immediately returned the money to Mrs. Cain and his charges were dismissed in court.[305]

For a brief period of time, Davis advertised "Pentecostal Bible Searching" meetings in the homes of congregants,[306] and advertised them in the religious section of the newspaper under "PENTECOSTAL".[307] His Sunday services were advertised as "FIRST PENTECOSTAL BAPTIST".[308] Even with his shady past publicly exposed; while still living with an underaged girl that he was grooming to be his future wife, Allie Lee Garrison, and ongoing scandals almost weekly; the Pentecostal Baptist Church of God sect continued to attract new members and grow. By July of 1932, the church had its own baseball team.[309]

Music was a big part of Roy E. Davis's services. Even from the early years of his ministry, Davis was known as a *"Singer and Masher"*. When his brothers Dan and W. L. organized the Pentecostal revival in Jeffersonville, they advertised singing and the playing of several instruments.[310] Rev. Roy E. Davis and his daughter were nationally recognized singers and radio performers in a stage act known as "Jack and Granny". Combined with the church's eleven-piece orchestra, Roy's daughter as "Granny"

---

[305] Charge Dismissed. 1931, Dec 29. Courier Journal. "A charge of obtaining money under false pretenses was dismissed Monday against the Rev. Roy E. Davis, 41 years old, Jeffersonville, pastor of the Baptist Tabernacle of God. ... When it developed that Davis paid the money back three days after she swore to the warrant, acting county judge Reuben Ruthenburg dismissed the case."

[306] Searching. 1931, Dec. 16. Jeffersonville Evening News. "Pentecostal Bible Searching will meet at the home of Mr. Davis 1016 Locust Street."

[307] PENTECOSTAL. 1932, Jan 13. Jeffersonville Evening News. "Pentecostal Bible Searching will meet at the home of Mr. Spaulding."

[308] FIRST PENTECOSTAL BAPTIST. DR. ROY E. DAVIS, PASTOR. 1932, May 28. Jeffersonville Evening News.

[309] Jeff Team Wins 1st Tilt in Indiana Loop. 1932, Jul 6. Courier Journal. "The baseball team of the First Pentecostal Baptist Church of Jeffersonville won its first game in the Southern Indiana Church league by defeating the Henryville nine 8 to 3."

[310] 3 Davis Brothers Plan a Pentecostal Revival. 1931, Apr 17. Evening news. "The Rev. Dan Davis, who sings and plays several musical instruments, will assist his brother in a revival which is to open Sunday at the Jeffersonville church."

performed musical numbers in the church services and the music, according to the church advertisements, *attracted multitudes.*[311]

Davis was one of the original members of the Stamps Gospel Quartet, which had gained him recognition in gospel radio.[312] As "Jack", Roy Davis worked with religious celebrities — at least to the fundamentalist and white supremacy crowd. Davis was connected to Dr. John Roach Straton, pastor of the Calvary Baptist Church in New York. Straton and Davis worked with Dr. Caleb A. Riley, pastor of the Central Baptist Church in Atlanta,[313] former supreme religious chaplain of the Ku Klux Klan. Davis was a national director of the fundamentalists of the world[314], as was Gerald Burton Winrod, who toured with Paul Rader, president of the Christian and Missionary Alliance[315] and close relative of Jeffersonville's Ralph Rader. Winrod was a writer for Pentecostal giant F. F. Bosworth,[316] and Bosworth toured with Branham during

---

[311] FIRST PENTECOSTAL BAPTIST. 1932, May 28. Jeffersonville Evening News. "Special musical attraction along with the eleven-piece orchestra. Sister Lest will sing many of her popular church songs. These and 'Granny' attracts multitudes to hear them sing."

[312] Famed Artists Appear in Two-Day Singers, Musicians' Convention. 1943, Oct 29. Pomona Progress Bulletin. "R. E. Davis, Upland, president of the convention, will be master of ceremonies. He was one of the original Stamps Quartet when it traveled out of Dallas, and which sang on Chautauqua programs featuring William Jennings Bryan, Congressman Upshaw, and r. Caleb A. Ridley."

[313] Radio gospel Singers in Nazarene Revival Here: Jack and Granny. 1936, Dec 3. Grandfield Enterprise. "Jack and Granny, gospel radio singers have traveled all over America and on foreign soil singing the gospel. They have been associated with such religious celebrities as Dr. John Roach Straton, former pastor of the Calvary Baptist Church, New York, Dr. Caleb A. Riley, former pastor of the Central Baptist Church, Atlanta, Georgia, Billy Sunday, and several others."

[314] Open Revival Wednesday Night. 1937, Feb 23. Chickasha Daily Express. "For two years he [Roy Davis] served as one of the national directors of the Fundamentalists of the world.

[315] Paul Rader. "He served as President of the Christian and Missionary Alliance from 1921-23."

[316] Barnes, Roscoe III. 2018, Dec 31. Reading with F. F. Bosworth. Accessed 2022, Dec 28 from http://roscoereporting.blogspot.com/2018/12/. "Bosworth's magazine also featured the writings of his wife, Florence, and his brother, B.B. Bosworth. Other writers included Evangelist A.G. Jeffries, Harry Hodge, C.C. Fitch, Rev. William T. MacArthur, Rev. Herbert Dyke, Rev. P. Gavin Duffy, Bishop Charles H. Brent, James Moore Hickson, Carrie Judd Montgomery, Rev. J. P. Roberts, Mary Lowe Dickinson, Rev. W. J. Bennett,

the early years of the healing revivals. Bosworth was also a member of the Christian and Missionary Alliance, and he wrote articles for Winrod's magazine.[317]

In Jeffersonville, Davis totally abandoned every semblance of his Baptist past. Services were advertised as *old-time Pentecostal religion.*[318] Not just any Pentecostal religion — Davis specifically and strategically posed as the Indiana-style Jesus-only Pentecostal made famous by black Pentecostal leader G. T. Haywood. Davis advertised his services with the motto, *"The Common People's Church. One creed, the Bible. One God, Jesus."*[319] He invited the curious to attend with sermon titles such as *"What is the Pentecostal Religion, and Why Have It?"*[320] The strategy worked, at least while Davis continued to evade government officials. Pentecostalism became so popular in Jeffersonville that multiple Pentecostal churches were established, one of which was led by Roy's brother Dan Davis.

Dan S. Davis was also deeply involved with Roy's (and the Klan's) initiative to spread Pentecostalism in Southern Indiana. Shortly after he, Roy, and W. L. Davis launched the Pentecostal Baptist Church of God sect with a Pentecostal Revival, Dan opened the doors to his "First Pentecostal Church".[321] While Davis won converts to his Pentecostal sect, Dan advertised that his church was *"not affiliated in any way with the Pentecostal Baptist Church"*,[322] but advertised that *"true Pentecost is here to stay."*[323] Dan's Pentecostal church also purchased an arbor[324] on Eighth and Graham streets, and held Pentecostal revivals at the arbor and meeting hall on the

---

Ethel E. Tulloch, E. West, Charles H. Usher, John Harris, Fannie J. Rowe, J. Albert Libby and Dr. Gerald B. Winrod."

[317] Paul Rader. Accessed 2022, Dec 31 from https://christianhof.org/rader/.

[318] First Pentecostal Baptist. 1933, Feb 11. Jeffersonville Evening News.

[319] First Pentecostal Baptist. 1932, Dec 17. Jeffersonville Evening News."

[320] First Pentecostal Baptist. 1933, Feb 18. Jeffersonville Evening News.

[321] First Pentecostal Church. 1932, January 15. Jeffersonville Evening News.

[322] First Pentecostal Church. 1932, January 15. Jeffersonville Evening News.

[323] Baptized Church of God Pentecostal. 1933, Jul 1. Jeffersonville Evening News.

[324] Baptized Church of God Pentecostal. 1933, Jun 24. Jeffersonville Evening News. "we have decided to postpone construction of our arbor at Eighth and Graham.

grounds.[325] This arbor and hall would become a significant part of Indiana's Pentecostal history just a few years later, but Dan himself would fade from public view. In the late 1930s, Dan was arrested on charges of criminal conspiracy[326] for misleading donors contributing to the "Hope Rescue Mission" of the Bethel Baptist Church in Louisville.[327] Dan started collecting money for the "Bethel Rescue Mission", and donors who mistakenly thought they were giving money to the Bethel Baptist Church fund were surprised to learn that they were donating to Dan Davis's (and likely Roy's) Pentecostal operation(s).

Of the people in Southern Indiana that would be caught with Davis's wide-sweeping Pentecostal net, however, none would become as interesting as Jeffersonville native and Pentecostal leader William Branham. It was through Branham that the Pentecostal Baptist Church movement would spread throughout the world under many names and splinter into many sects and movements, from the "Latter Rain Message"[328,] to the Shepherding[329] and Word of Faith Movements,[330] to various splinter groups that simply called themselves "The Message".[331]

---

[325] Baptized Church of God Pentecostal. 1933, Jul 8. Jeffersonville Evening News. "every night at 8th and Graham streets, plenty of safe parking anywhere on the lot, all services will be held at the arbor except Thursday morning which will meet at the hall."

[326] Minister Arrested. 1939, Mar 13. The Courier Journal. "Dan Davis, a minister of 510 W. Main, New Albany, was arrested at 8:10 p.m. Sunday at the Bethel Mission, 421 E. Jefferson, on a charge of criminal conspiracy concerning solicitation of funds for charity. He was named in a criminal Court bench warrant.

[327] The Point of View. 1939, Dec 21. Courier Journal

[328] ex: Latter Rain Message. 1952, Feb 23. Tampa Bay Times.

[329] Wilhelm, Todd. 2015, Dec 26. Is 9Marks the New Shepherding Movement? Accessed 2022, Apr 24 from https://thouartheman.org/2015/12/26/is-9marks-the-new-shepherding-movement/. "In the early 1970s, four well-known charismatic leaders responded to a moral failure among charismatics in south Florida. Bob Mumford, Derek Prince, Don Basham, and Charles Simpson felt a need for personal accountability and covenanted together for this purpose, submitting their lives and ministries to one another. Ern Baxter, who had ministered with William Branham, was later added to the group and they became known as the "Ft. Lauderdale Five." They formed Christian Growth Ministries in 1974, and in the movement that they began, the accountability they shared became an emphasis that all believers should submit to a "shepherd" in order to be discipled in the Christian life. Their prominence helped gain wide acceptance for

92

their teaching, which included what was felt to be correctives to the charismatic movement at the time."

[330] What is Branhamism? Accessed 2022, Apr 24 from https://www.gotquestions.org/Branhamism.html. "The teachings of William Branham are a bit jumbled and contradictory and difficult to categorize. But some of the most controversial doctrines are as follows: modalism (God exists as only one Person but reveals Himself in different modes), baptism in the name of Jesus only (believers baptized using the Trinitarian formula must be re-baptized), the serpent seed doctrine (Eve's sin in the Garden was having sex with the snake), annihilationism (hell is not a place of everlasting punishment), Word Faith (sometimes dubbed "name it and claim it"), the idea that the zodiac and the Egyptian pyramids are equal to written Scripture, and of course his own exalted place in the plan of God and the history of the church along with his exaggerated claims to miraculous revelation and healing abilities."

[331] The Message. Accessed 2022, Apr 24 from https://freedomofmind.com/group-information-resource/the-message/. "The Message," otherwise referred to as "Branhamism," "Branhamites," "Bride Churches," "Evening Light Churches," or "Spoken Word" are collectively describing the worldwide cult following of William Marrion Branham from Jeffersonville, Indiana. With the exception of the more extremist sects, most consider Voice of God Recordings in Jeffersonville Indiana to be the cult headquarters. "The Message," is a Pentecostal-style doomsday cult which believed (until 1978) that the year 1977 was the time of Armageddon. The cult leader held joint campaigns with Jim Jones of Jonestown, Guyana, and some believe the events leading to 1978 massacre are related to his influence by William Branham.

CHAPTER 8

C. I. SCOFIELD

❖

"The way Scofield got our money — and he plucked $2,000 of mine — was by intimating that it was needed by Senator Ingalls, who would see that it was paid. We knew that Ingalls was good, and we supposed that on account of his official position, he did not care to be known in a money-borrowing transaction and was doing the business through a friend"
- A Victim

Of all the men who influenced American Christianity during the birth of Pentecostalism, none were so widely respected as C. I. Scofield. The Scofield Reference Bible published in 1909 quickly became the preferred study guide to the Christian Bible for fundamentalist Christianity. Even still today, it is widely used by the Pentecostal-Holiness sects as a tool for "understanding" the Queen's English of the King James Version translation of the Bible. The study notes, largely copied from the works of John Darby, suggested that the Seven Churches in Asia Minor mentioned in the Book of Revelation were instead *"Church Ages"*, or *"Dispensations"*. With each supporter of Dispensationalist Theology came the notion that the current "dispensation" was to be the last, or seventh — making it the preferred theology for many doomsday cults. Darby's theology was also a fundamental building block for the British Israel doctrine.

Since it was first published in 1909, the Scofield Reference

Bible has made uncompromising Zionists out of tens of millions of Americans. When John Hagee, the founder of Christians United for Israel (CUFI), said that "50 million evangelical bible-believing Christians unite with five million American Jews standing together on behalf of Israel," it was the Scofield Bible that he was talking about. [332]

The Scofield Reference Bible was heavily advertised among Christian Fundamentalist, Pentecostal,[333] and Latter Rain sects. Scofield's reference notes focused heavily upon dispensationalism theology and were often quoted in sermons and literature for these sects, especially for those advertising angelic visitations for the current "dispensation".[334] According to Scofield, "angels" were to come in "human form", giving credence to William Branham and other Post-WWII healing revivalists who claimed to have been visited by "angels". Cyrus Ingerson (C.I.) Scofield, the author of the Scofield Reference Bible, had quite a colorful background.

C. I. Scofield was a probate attorney in Kansas[335] who served under the Republican Ticket as Representative of the 8th District for President Ulysses S. Grant[336] and later as United States Attorney for Kansas.[337] Scofield's wife was one of the heirs of Frenchman Regis Loisel, whose heirs were permitted to select 38,000 acres of land in Kansas upon his death. After Loisel died, Scofield (through his wife) became a significant landowner in

---

[332] Cathail, Maidhc Ó. The Scofield Bible—The Book That Made Zionists of America's Evangelical Christians. Washington Report on Middle East Affairs, October 2015

[333] An Unparalleled Bible Opportunity. 1917, May 26. Pentecostal Evangel.

[334] ex. Bosworth, F. F. 1949, Dec. Gifts of Healing Plus: An Angel Appears. The Voice of Healing. "On Page 1291 of the Scofield Bible, Dr. C. I. Scofield, D.D. in his footnote on Angels says, 'Though angels are spirits (Psa. 104: 4; Heb. 1:14), power is given to them to become visible in the semblance of human form."

[335] Notice. 1879, Feb 10. Marshall County News. "Cyrus I. Scofield, Administrator de homis no of the estate of Isaac T. Greene, deceased."

[336] Republican Ticket. 1872, Oct 25. Courier-Tribune. "For Representative 8th District, Cyrus I. Scofield."

[337] Telegraphic Summary: Washington. 1873, Mar 20. Chicago Evening Post. "Cyrus I. Scofield, United States Attorney for Kansas."

Kansas.[338]   Scofield moved to Kansas, was appointed to the legislature, and became instrumental in helping elect United States Senator John J. Ingalls. Ingalls jointly produced the constitution under which Kansas now functions.[339]   Ingalls was both Mrs. Scofield's attorney and a direct heir of Loisel.[340]

Together with Ingalls,[341] Scofield devised a railroad scam that went largely unreported by its victims. Thousands of dollars were invested by several prominent Republicans — men whose political careers would have suffered had the public known of their involvement. One victim admitted that *"The way Scofield got our money — and he plucked $2,000 of mine — was by intimating that it was needed by Senator Ingalls, who would see that it was paid. We knew that Ingalls was good, and we supposed that on account of his official position, he did not care to be known in a money-borrowing transaction and was doing the business through a friend"*[342] As a

---

[338] Canfield, Joseph M. 1988. The Incredible Scofield and His Book. "He was drawn to Kansas by reason of the fact that his wife was one of the heirs of Regis Loisel, the intrepid Frenchman whose descendants were permitted to select 38,000 acres of land in Nemaha and other Kansas counties in lieu of a grant of which Loisel had held the title at the date of his death."

[339] John J. Ingalls. Accessed 2023, Feb 23 from https://www.kshs.org/kansapedia/john-james-ingalls/12095. "Ingalls was a member of the 1859 Wyandotte Constitutional Convention, which produced the constitution under which Kansas now functions."

[340] Canfield, Joseph M. 1988. The Incredible Scofield and His Book. "Scofield landed in Nemaha County in 1872, just in time to be nominated on the Republican ticket for member of the legislature. He was elected, and though ostensibly a supporter of Senator Pomeroy, he became largely instrumental in causing the election of Ingalls. Indeed, he was recognized as one of the foremost leaders in the Ingalls camp and by some as Ingall's personal representative, and in reward for his services he was made United States district attorney for the state. But he did not hold this office long. He was ousted in disgrace on account of some shady financial transactions which left him indebted in a number of thousands to a score of prominent Republicans.

[341] Letters to the Editor: Scofield Bible Had Big Effect on United States; Take Action to Change Federal Government. 2013, Feb 7. Accessed 2023, Feb 23 from https://www.chronline.com/stories/letters-to-the-editor-scofield-bible-had-big-effect-on-united-states-take-action-to-change,110269.

[342] Canfield, Joseph M. 1988. The Incredible Scofield and His Book. "Pulling strings both in Kansas and with his compatriots back east, Ingalls assisted Scofield in gaining admission to the bar, and procured his appointment as federal attorney for Kansas.

result, Scofield's political career was short-lived. Scofield was forced to resign from federal office, and he fled the state to Kansas to St. Louis[343] where he continued swindling people out of money and was forced to flee.

In October 1878, Scofield was finally apprehended on charges of forging the name of Emeline E. Papin, his sister,[344] as an endorser on a promissory note for $900. He had collected that amount from Dr. J. H. McLean, and a warrant was issued for Scofield's arrest.[345] According to officials, this was not the only warrant for forgery against Scofield; he was also wanted in the State of Illinois for forgery against one William Shepherd in the amount of $325.[346] Scofield was eventually apprehended in Horicon, Wisconsin,[347] and was jailed for the crimes.[348]

Scofield disappeared from St. Louis, and private detectives were employed to hunt him up, but they failed to find him till last Monday, when he was arrested in Horicon, Wis. Scofield

These two became partners in a railroad scam, which led to Scofield serving time for criminal forgery."

[343] Canfield, Joseph M. 1988. The Incredible Scofield and His Book. "In due time, however, the shady nature of Scofield's financial transactions became known to Ingalls and the money lenders and then followed an explosion which compelled Scofield to resign his federal office and leave the state. From Kansas he went to St. Louis, and, shortly after his arrival there, he was lodged in jail on a charge of forgery, preferred by his own sister."

[344] Canfield, Joseph M. 1988. The Incredible Scofield and His Book. "shortly after his arrival there, he was lodged in jail on a charge of forgery, preferred by his own sister."

[345] Gone for Cyrus Scofield. 1878, Oct 3. St. Louis Globe-Democrat. "On the 5th of last April, Dr. J. H. McLean swore out a warrant charging Scofield with forgery in the third degree. It would appear from the complaint that Scofield forged the name of Emeline E. Papin, as indorser on a promissory note for $900, and obtained this amount from the doctor.

[346] Gone for Cyrus Scofield. 1878, Oct 3. St. Louis Globe-Democrat. "William Shepherd, 209 Market Street, is the one who swears out this second warrant, which alleges that the same name was again forged on a note for $325, the date being June 19, 1877."

[347] An Ex-Kansas Official Comes to Grief. 1878, Oct 10. Wyndott Herald. "Cyrus I. Scofield was arrested a few days ago at Horicon, Wisconsin, and taken to St. Louis on a charge of forgery."

[348] Caught and Jugged, A Former U. S. Attorney of Kansas in Jail. 1878, Oct 4. Topeka State Journal.

was one of the slickest fellows we ever knew. His election to the Legislature from Seneca was the shrewdest political dodge we ever saw. He was highly educated, well-read, and had much natural ability; but his propensity for "dead-beating" every friend he had overpowered everything. It is a wonder he was not in the penitentiary long ago.[349] - Courier-Tribune.

While incarcerated for forgery, Scofield began claiming to have been "born again" and converted to the Congregational Church. A band of female Congressional missionaries began visiting Scofield in jail,[350] one of which apparently became Scofield's mistress. Scofield abandoned his first wife and two daughters for the woman, later abandoned her, and married another woman.[351] The "Christian" conversion story, however, continued as Scofield entered the Congregational ministry and started pastoring a church in Dallas. The church was so successful that it became one of the wealthiest and most aristocratic church organizations in the State of Texas.[352]

In 1888, Scofield printed *Rightly Dividing the Word of Truth* as a study guide for teaching classes on dispensational theology. Scofield also taught Darby's "Rapture Theology", which combined with dispensationalism to become a core teaching in Pentecostalism. As interest grew for Scofield's doctrinal teaching, he gained enough recognition in the religious community to

---

[349] Cyrus I. Scofield. 1978, Oct 11. Courier Tribune.

[350] Canfield, Joseph M. 1988. The Incredible Scofield and His Book. "While in jail he had been visited by a band of Christian women who prayed with him and worked his conversion"

[351] Letters to the Editor: Scofield Bible Had Big Effect on United States; Take Action to Change Federal Government. 2013, Feb 7. Accessed 2023, Feb 23 from https://www.chronline.com/stories/letters-to-the-editor-scofield-bible-had-big-effect-on-united-states-take-action-to-change,110269. "Upon his release from prison, now as a professing 'born again' Christian, Scofield deserted his first wife and two daughters and took as his mistress a young girl from the St. Louis Flower Mission. He later abandoned her for another woman, whom he eventually married."

[352] Canfield, Joseph M. 1988. The Incredible Scofield and His Book. "upon his release he entered the Congregational ministry. His first pastorate was at Dallas, Tex., where he built up one of the wealthiest and most aristocratic church organizations in the state."

become head of the Southwestern School of the Bible in Dallas, the forerunner of the Dallas Theological Seminary.[353]

Finding great financial success in religion, Scofield quickly became a recognized expositor of the Bible. When approached for payment for debts accumulated in Kansas, however, Scofield continued to declare himself to be poor and unable to pay.[354] Meanwhile, Scofield began printing (and charging large sums of money for) all sorts of religious materials, from various tracts and volumes of his sermons and/or sermon notes, and Bible studies. His success attracted the attention of famed evangelist Dwight Moody, and Scofield suddenly found himself on the board of Moody's Northfield Bible School, and pastor of the Northfield Congregational Church.[355]

Many of Scofield's study notes, which were later converted into the Scofield Reference Bible, were directly copied, or paraphrased from the writings of dispensationalist John Darby. Interestingly, Darby made seven trips to the United States and Canada to promote his dispensational theology, a few of which included visits to St. Louis that coincide with Scofield's time there.[356] Regardless of the source of his theology, and without any

---

[353] The Gospel Truth: Analyzing Scofield. Accessed 2023, Feb 23 from https://www.gospeltruth.net/scofield.htm. "During this time, Scofield was the head of Southwestern School of the Bible in Dallas, the forerunner of the Dallas Theological Seminary. This school is now a major center for spreading Scofield's views."

[354] Canfield, Joseph M. 1988. The Incredible Scofield and His Book. "When approached by his Kansas creditors Parson Scofield declares that he is poor and unable to pay, but has never failed to do the right and easy thing by renewing his notes."

[355] Canfield, Joseph M. 1988. The Incredible Scofield and His Book. "Almost at once Scofield became a noted expositor of the Bible, and, after he had attracted the attention of Evangelist Moody, he was given the chair of Bible history in Moody's Northfield Bible school, as well as the pastorate of the Northfield Congregational church. He became the author of a number of tracts and volumes of sermons, and under his name are now printed regular issues of Bible lessons and studies."

[356] Sizer, Stephen. Referenced from Cyrus Ingerson Scofield: Charlatan and Heretic. Ernest Sandeen, The Roots of Fundamentalism British & American Millenarianism 1800-1930 (Chicago, University Chicago Press, 1970), pp. 74-75. "Brookes sympathized with J. N. Darby's dispensational views of a failing Church, corrupt and beyond hope, but it is known they met during five visits Darby made to St Louis between 1864-186535 and again between 1872-1877"

sort of theological training or real Christian scholarship, Scofield was suddenly a respected and prolific writer of Christian theology that strongly resembled the works of Darby. The influence may have come through Scofield's close ties to Rev. James H. Brooks of the Walnut Street Presbyterian Church; Brooks was a student of Darby's and had been in personal contact with Darby when he passed through St. Louis.[357]

Buried in Scofield's (and Darby's) theology was the notion that a literal Jewish kingdom would be restored for a millennium in the last days.[358] This presented a problem in early American Christianity; very few American Christian leaders wanted to be governed by a literal kingdom of Jews. It also presented a geographical problem; the Nation of Israel would not form until 1948, and it was unclear where, exactly, this Jewish Kingdom would form. Worse, according to Scofield's notes, the term Jewish Kingdom would be comprised of the "Jewish Remnant" who "preached the Gospel of the Kingdom to all nations during the tribulation" — meaning that those who would consider themselves to be the "Lost Tribes of Israel" could force their way into the Kingdom as the "remnant".

This judgment is to be distinguished from the judgment of the great white throne. Here there is no resurrection; the persons judged are living nations; no books are opened; three classes are present, sheep, goats, brethren; the time is at the return of

---

[357] Canfield, Joseph M. 1988. The Incredible Scofield and His Book. "The unseemly haste to get Scofield's forgery cases off the court dockets without fair adjudication was a prelude to his entry into this new role as a Christian worker. For the next several years, his life in Christian service was under the aegis of Rev. James H. Brookes, pastor of the Walnut Street Presbyterian Church. Brookes had accepted a prophetic view remarkably close to that of the Plymouth Brethren and Brethren leader John Darby. It has been claimed that Brookes and Darby had been in personal contact when Darby passed through St. Louis either in 1877 or on earlier trips."

[358] The Gospel Truth: Analyzing Scofield. Accessed 2023, Feb 23 from https://www.gospeltruth.net/scofield.htm. "This Scofield teaching is concerned with a literal Jewish kingdom to last for a millennium. It was first brought into the early church by some Jews who still could not give up the hope taught to them by the scribes and Pharisees."

Christ (v. 31); and the scene is on earth. All these particulars are in contrast with rev. 20. 11-15. The test in this judgment is the treatment accorded by the nations to those whom Christ here calls "my brethren." These "brethren" are the Jewish Remnant who will have preached the Gospel of the kingdom to all nations during the tribulation.[359]

Scofield's widely popular Reference Bible, books, and tracts were open fields planting seeds for the framework of British Israelism to be adopted among Church leaders in the United States. Combined with the lack of a visible "Israel" for which to target this doctrine, fundamentalist Christians were able to convince their listeners that they, as American Christians, could be the "brethren" from Scofield's notes and therefore part of the Jewish Kingdom. This theology would become disastrous after the holocaust when the Jewish State was formed; as British Israelism merged with white supremacy, the *real Jews* were scorned by the *adopted Jews*.

During the worst months of World War I, Scofield published an updated edition of the Scofield Reference Bible linking key passages of the Bible to world events. Christian leaders across the nation were suddenly able to link vague, symbolic words and phrases from books of prophecy in the Old Testament and Revelation to current world events. The names "Gog" and "Magog" from the Book of Zechariah, for example, were suddenly associated with Moscow and Tobolsk.

That the primary reference is to the northern (European) powers, headed up by Russia, all agree. The whole passage should be read in connection with Zech. 12. 1-4; 14. 1-9; Mat. 24. 14-30; rev. 14. 14-20; 19. 17-21. 'Gog' is the prince, 'Magog.' his land. The reference to Meshech and Tubal (Moscow and Tobolsk) is a clear mark of identification. Russia and the northern powers have been the latest

---

[359] Scofield, C.I. 1917. Scofield Reference Bible

persecutors of dispersed Israel, and it is congruous both with divine justice and with the covenants (e.g., Gen. 15. 18, note; Deut. 30. 3, note) that destruction should fall at the climax of the last mad attempt to exterminate the remnant of Israel in Jerusalem. The whole prophecy belongs to the yet future 'day of Jehovah' (Isa. 2. 10-22; rev. 19. 11-21), and to the battle of Armageddon (rev. 16. 14; 19. 19, note), but includes also the final revolt of the nations at the close of the kingdom-age.[360]

Scofield's strategy, which was likely a strategy involving key figures among the politicians that he was connected to, was brilliant. Not only had Scofield weaponized religion in his books, classes, and sermons, he had weaponized the Bible itself for current political agendas. Every man, woman, and child who owned the Scofield Reference Bible could easily turn the pages of their Bibles to watch it come alive during key moments in World War I, World War II, and other current events. As the political landscape changed over time, new versions of the Scofield Reference Bible could be published with updated political agendas.

The same footnote in the 1984 version, for example, changed dramatically with the absence of global conflict. Reference to Tobolsk was completely removed, while the *"final revolt of the nations at the close of the kingdom-age"* was simplified to *"the yet future day of the Lord"*.

The reference is to the powers in the north of Europe, headed by Russia. The whole passage should be read in connection with Zech. 12. 1-4; 14. 1-9; Mat. 24. 14-30; rev. 14. 14-20; 19. 17-21. Gog is probably the prince; Magog, his land. Russia and the northern powers have long been the persecutors of dispersed Israel, and it is congruous both with divine justice and the covenants of God that destruction shall fall in connection with the attempt to exterminate the

---

[360] Scofield, C.I. 1917. Scofield Reference Bible

remnant of Israel in Jerusalem. The entire prophecy belongs to the yet future day of the Lord.[361]

During the early years of its publication, Scofield improved race relations to some extent. Post-Civil War Dallas Jews achieved a certain degree of "whiteness", at least for a period of time.[362] Shortly after the Ku Klux Klan was revived in 1915, however, Scofield set out to create what would be the best-selling edition of the Scofield Bible, the 1917 edition. Even abroad, the 1917 Scofield Reference Bible is[363] *"consistently the best-selling edition of the Scofield Bible."* Some of those notes seemed to attack the Jewish "merchant princes" in Dallas and other large cities by painting the picture of separating the Jews after the millennium, resulting in antisemitism for Jews in Dallas[364] — a theme that would soon spread throughout the United States and Canada. Scofield had successfully used Anglo-Irish John Darby's Christian Zionist works to radicalize a nation to believe that the End of Days prophecies of the Bible were being fulfilled with current events, and over time, white supremacists would interpret this to suggest that the Bible prophets had described an End of Days race war.

---

[361] Scofield, C.I. 1984. Scofield Reference Bible

[362] Phillips, Michael. 2010. White Metropolis: Race, Ethnicity, and Religion in Dallas, 1841-2001

[363] R. Todd Mangum and Mark S. Sweetnam, The Scofield Bible: Its History and Impact on the Evangelical Church (Colorado Springs: Paternoster Publishing, 2009)

[364] Phillips, Michael. 2010. White Metropolis: Race, Ethnicity, and Religion in Dallas, 1841-2001. "To some Dallas Gentile elites, Jewish workers would remain Semitic aliens, carrying the non-Anglo-Saxon toxin of socialism. Jewish elites would find themselves suspected as disloyal by the Gentiles and attacked by leftists within their community. Scofield had argued for the separateness of Jews after the millennium, but the city's Jewish community would remain outsiders in this world. For Dallas Jews, separate would not mean equal."

CHAPTER 9

THE ANGELUS TEMPLE

❖

"After being duly and regularly sworn under oath, falsely, wickedly, maliciously and with intent to carry out the purpose of said conspiracy, swear that she (McPherson) had been kidnaped, and described the alleged kidnapers as 'Rose' and 'Steve.'" - Aimee Semple McPherson Criminal Conspiracy Complaint

The same month that Pentecostal Bishop G. T. Haywood published his *Victim of the Flaming Sword* tract in Indiana, and during the same time that Col. William Joseph Simmons and Roy E. Davis would have begun plotting their Knights of the Flaming Sword strategy, Foursquare Pentecostal leader Aimee Semple McPherson opened the doors to her massive Angelus Temple[365] in Los Angeles. It was the same year that Daniel Speicher of the Indiana Holiness Association purchased controlling interest in the

---

[365] Marshall, Colin. 2017, May 17. Los Angeles in Buildings: The Angelus Temple". Accessed 2022, Dec 23 from https://www.kcet.org/shows/lost-la/los-angeles-in-buildings-the-angelus-temple. "the Angelus Temple comes with not just greater architectural interest than its big-box descendants, but a compelling personality behind it as well. The newly built – and, for the time, extravagantly scaled – house of worship opened its doors on New Year's Day 1923, owing to the tireless efforts of rural Ontario-born celebrity preacher Aimee Semple McPherson, not just a towering figure in the history of Pentecostal evangelism, but one of the most unlikely urbanists in the history of Los Angeles."

Cadle Tabernacle[366] in Indianapolis and the Tabernacle began to shift to become the Indiana Klan's headquarters. The Angelus Temple opened its doors on New Years' Day, 1923.

Interestingly, 1923 was also the same year that the Hollywood sign was erected. The world-famous iconic white letters in the Hollywood hills were first created as an advertisement for "Hollywoodland", a local real estate development.[367] It was also the same year that Bel Air was founded in the foothills of the Santa Monica Mountains. A young Walt Disney, who had arrived in Los Angeles with only $40 in his pocket, would have seen the new sign in its original glory.

Regarding the agenda of Roy Davis, William Upshaw, and William Branham, 1923 was an important year for the anti-civil rights agenda. In 1923, Texas legislature passed a law blocking people with black skin from participating in the Democratic primary.[368] Nationally, the Klan's agenda against racial integration of school systems was being strategically architected and implemented. In North Carolina, for example, the larger counties began constructing public high schools for African Americans to

---

[366] Holiness Get Big Tabernacle. 1923, Jun 22. Muncie Evening Press. "With the purchase yesterday at Indianapolis of the Cadle Tabernacle from Howard Cadle, Daniel L. Speicher, president of the Indiana Holiness Association at Beulah Park, and Walter Hansing, secretary of the Holiness Association, came into possession of one of the largest religious structure [sig] in the United States."

[367] Historical Timeline of Los Angeles. 2022, Dec 31. Accessed 2022, Dec 31 from https://www.discoverlosangeles.com/things-to-do/historical-timeline-of-los-angeles. "Originally created in 1923 as an advertisement for a local real estate development called "Hollywoodland," the Hollywood Sign has become a world-famous icon of Los Angeles. {...} A young cartoonist named Walt Disney arrives in Los Angeles with $40 in his pocket."

[368] The Civil Rights Act of 1964: A Long Struggle for Freedom The Segregation Era (1900-1939). Accessed 2022, Dec 31 from https://www.loc.gov/exhibits/civil-rights-act/segregation-era.html. "In 1923 the Texas legislature passed a law that barred blacks from participating in the Democratic primary. Because the Democratic Party was the dominant political party in Texas, black voters were therefore denied participation in the electoral process. "

separate them from white students. New black-only schools opened in Mecklenburg, Durham, Forsyth, Guilford, and Wake Counties.[369]

Compared to the Cadle Tabernacle, which was very large for its time, the Angelus Temple was even more massive and impressive. The Cadle Tabernacle held over two thousand more people, but the Angelus Temple building itself was an enormous sight to behold. The building resembled the ancient temples of Rome in design on the outside, and Parisian Opera House on the inside. It could accommodate as many as 7,500 worshippers at capacity, and with its 125-foot sky-and-cloud-painted concrete dome, was touted as the largest on the continent.[370] Its 250-foot radio tower was highly effective in the religious and political influence of Los Angeles; those who didn't attend could listen to broadcasts on the radio. Combined with its outreach and missionary programs, Angelus Temple was by far the most influential church in Los Angeles and its surrounding cities for its time. The Angelus Temple school trained as many as five hundred evangelists each year, sending an average of over forty new evangelists to the field each month. Angelus Temple quickly became the first true megachurch. It attracted over forty million

---

[369] Wadelington, Flora Hatley. Segregation in the 1920s. Accessed 2022, Dec 31 from https://www.ncpedia.org/history/20th-Century/segregation-1920s. "Public elementary schools for African Americans were built in 1910, and in 1918 the first public secondary school for African Americans was established. Most such high schools were limited to only one or two years. Between 1923 and 1929, public high schools for African Americans were built in larger counties such as Mecklenburg, Durham, Forsyth, Guilford, and Wake. Second Ward High School in Charlotte opened in 1923, and students traveled from every direction to attend."

[370] Marshall, Colin. 2017, May 17. Los Angeles in Buildings: The Angelus Temple". Accessed 2022, Dec 23 from https://www.kcet.org/shows/lost-la/los-angeles-in-buildings-the-angelus-temple. "The Angelus Temple". The result struck one visiting preacher as "half Roman Coliseum, half like a Parisian opera house," and, at a cost of $1.5 million, had every feature a church of the day could need and then some: 5,300 seats (though the building would often accommodate up to 7,500 worshipers); stained-glass windows depicting Biblical scenes; a 125-foot, sky-and-cloud-painted concrete dome touted as the largest on the continent; classrooms used for the training of 500 evangelists a year; a watchtower used for prayer at all hours; a baptismal tank refilled by a real stream and waterfall; a section dedicated specifically to faith healing; a separate room just for speaking in tongues; and no fewer than 25 exits, so as to avoid the kind of stampedes she'd too often seen at overheated revival meetings before."

visitors during its first seven years of operation.[371]   In the Pentecostal and Charismatic circles, Angelus Temple meetings were groundbreaking in presentation style. McPherson's theatrical performances of Pentecostalism, in many ways, became the prototype for the televangelists of the future. some of whom surpassed her own ministry during her lifetime.[372]

Following the pattern of John Alexander Dowie, McPherson rose to almost overnight fame through a series of "faith healing" revivals in the United States. Though many fraudulent claims were identified during her healing ministry — in some cases doing more harm than good[373] — she was able to convince others of her self-proclaimed title of "miracle woman". Some of the alleged miracles, such as the case of Henry Schaeffer, resulted in death.[374] Eventually, McPherson migrated to Los Angeles to the large concentration of Pentecostals influenced by Azusa Street. Also following the pattern of Dowie, McPherson used the power of controversy to attract a following and eventually create her own cult of personality.[375]

---

[371] Dowd, Katie. 2020, Dec 11. How America's most famous preacher made a fake megachurch in Tahoe. Accessed 2022, Dec 23 from https://www.sfgate.com/renotahoe/article/famous-preacher-America-Aimee-Semple-McPherson-15632095.php. "Her Angelus Temple in Echo Park became America's first true megachurch, drawing 40 million visitors in its first seven years according to church records."

[372] Dowd, Katie. 2020, Dec 11. How America's most famous preacher made a fake megachurch in Tahoe. Accessed 2022, Dec 23 from https://www.sfgate.com/renotahoe/article/famous-preacher-America-Aimee-Semple-McPherson-15632095.php. In 1944, now overtaken by a wave of proto-televangelists she'd laid the foundation for, Sister Aimee went on tour to revive her fame. After a sermon at the Oakland Auditorium on Sept. 26, she returned to her 10th-floor room at the Leamington Hotel on 1814 Franklin Street. In the morning, her son Rolf went to wake her. She was dead, killed by an accidental overdose of sleeping pills.

[373] ex: Fresno Finds 'Miracle' Claims are Unfounded: Instead, Investigations Are Being Made into Cases in Which It Is Alleged Harm Resulted from "Healings" by Mrs. Aimee Semple McPherson". 1922, Feb 16. Sacramento Bee.

[374] Sacramentan Healed by Miracle Woman Dies: Henry Schaeffer Passes Away in Stockton Hospital with Exhaustion from Raving over Mrs. Aimee McPherson. 1922, Mar 1. Sacramento Bee.

[375] Dowd, Katie. 2020, Dec 11. How America's most famous preacher made a fake megachurch in Tahoe. Accessed 2022, Dec 23 from

Many of the men and women responsible for the spreading of William Branham's ministry in the Post WWII healing revivals were either trained by, affiliated with, or working for the Angelus Temple. LeRoy Kopp, who promoted William Branham's ministry through the video "20th Century Prophet", was the vice chairman of the Angelus Temple Evangelists.[376] Herrick Holt, president of the Sharon Orphanage, from which the Latter Rain movement promoted and spread William Branham's ministry, was a minister trained by the Foursquare Church.[377] And McPherson, through the power of the Angelus Temple, funded the Sharon Orphanage and Schools.[378]

In a covert strategy similar to that of William Branham, who pretended to support racial equality while introducing the very racist Christian Identity doctrine to the masses, McPherson initially had the public appearance of racial equality. Behind the scenes, her approach was mixed with not-so-obvious support and mentoring of white supremacy. It was highly effective; to her cult of personality, McPherson was recognized for *leading efforts* toward racial equality. McPherson apparently recruited a black minister to baptize her daughter Roberta to symbolize her support of all

---

https://www.sfgate.com/renotahoe/article/famous-preacher-America-Aimee-Semple-McPherson-15632095.php. "Sister Aimee was once one of America's most captivating public figures, a charismatic young woman with a calling to preach the word of God. And much like the characters of today's TV shows, controversy followed McPherson wherever she went. McPherson rose to fame in the early 1920s with a series of faith 'healings' around the nation. Armed with a few miracles under her belt, she moved to — where else? — Los Angeles to put down roots. Just as the city started to churn out Hollywood celebrities, the Canadian-born preacher was one of the first to garner around-the-clock tabloid fame. "

[376] Misc. News. 1936, Oct 22. Fairview Enterprise. "Rev. LeRoy Kopp, formerly of Fairview is now vice chairman of the Angelus Temple Evangelists Bureau. He is now on a tour of churches of the denomination in the east and middle west."

[377] Orphanage Scheme Under Way at North Battleford. 1943, Oct 30. Star Phoenix. An orphanage scheme, involving a total anticipated expenditure of a quarter of a million dollars is under way at North Battleford. The city council has already assured Rev. H. Holt, pastor of the Four-Square Gospel Church, one of the prime movers in the plan, that 34 acres of city-owned property will be made available for orphanage purposes."

[378] Foursquare Heads Named. 1943, Aug 18. The Province. "Aimee Semple McPherson and Giles N. Knight, both here from Los Angeles ... Other Canadian provincial superintendents appointed were Rev. Herrick Holt, North Battleford."

races.[379]   Also, in what appeared to have been a staged event, McPherson de-converted two hundred members of the Ku Klux Klan during one single sermon. The group entered Angelus Temple in white robes, but after hearing McPherson's sermon, left in the middle of the service, disrobed, and re-entered the church in the suits beneath the robes.[380]   In 1922, however, McPherson was not so secretive in her support of the Klan. She addressed an assembled delegation of Klan members at town hall — an appeal that apparently paid off just a few years later during her infamous kidnapping plot.

In 1926, Aimee Semple McPherson faced felony charges of criminal conspiracy for staging her own kidnapping and paying others to mislead government officials. She faced a maximum sentence of forty-two years in prison for the crime.[381]   In a highly publicized trial, readers from coast to coast learned how McPherson's secretary, Elizabeth Schaffer, spread the news that McPherson had drowned in the Pacific off of Santa Monica.[382]

---

[379] Religious Worship and American Race Relations (interview). PBS. Accessed 2022, Dec 23 from https://www.pbs.org/wgbh/americanexperience/features/sister-religious-worship-and-american-race-relations/ "During her revivals in the South Aimee was so interested in racial reconciliation and working with all people that she actually recruited an African American minister to baptize her daughter Roberta in one of the local rivers... this really becomes a symbol of Aimee's effort to work with all people, of all races, creeds, cultures, and classes."

[380] Wolfgram, Christina. 2013. How an L.A. Nun Took on the K.K.K. (Podcast). Accessed 2022, Dec 25 from https://www.lamag.com/citythinkblog/podcast-preview-how-an-la-nun-took-on-the-kkk/. "In this exclusive clip, Jackie Miller, historian at the Parsonage of Sister Aimee Semple McPherson, recalls a time when 200 members of the K.K.K. showed up at Angelus Temple clothed in their white robes. Her aim was to preach the gospel without offending anyone, and according to Miller, all 200 clansmen left in the middle of the service, disrobed, and reentered the church in the suits they donned underneath."

[381] The People vs. Aimee Semple McPherson, et al., Case CR 29181, January 10, 1927; Superior Court of Los Angeles County, County records and Archives

[382] Here Are Highlights of Aimee's Dramatic Life. 1926, Jun 23. Oakland Tribune. "Aimee McPherson, accompanied by her secretary, Miss Elizabeth Schaffer, drive to Santa Monica to go swimming. Mrs. McPherson disappears while alone on the beach and Miss Schaffer spreads an alarm that woman evangelist has drowned. No one could be found who saw Mrs. McPherson actually enter the water. An alarm was sounded, and forces began to search the beach for some trace of the missing woman. Her mother, Mrs. Minnie Kennedy, was notified at Angelus Temple and started for the beach district with scores of volunteers to hunt for the body of the missing pastor in the water".

McPherson's mother, Minnie Kennedy, later declared that McPherson did not drown, but had instead been killed by gangsters angered by McPherson's position against the re-opening of the Venice dance halls.[383] She was not kidnapped, however, and had not drowned. Instead, McPherson had traveled to a vacation resort in Monterey County named Carmel-by-the-Sea with Kenneth Ormiston.[384] After a few weeks of what appears to have been a romantic tryst, McPherson reappeared in Los Angeles, claiming to have been kidnapped by two people named "Rose and Steve".[385] She went so far as to re-enact her alleged kidnapping for Los Angeles investigators. She and city officials retraced her steps in Venice — not telling them that she was not there during her mysterious absence and was instead at the vacation resort.[386]

McPherson's kidnapping case was sent to the Grand Jury, and her defense team faced an impossible mound of evidence against her. No doubt the entire jury pool leaned towards the

---

[383] Here Are Highlights of Aimee's Dramatic Life. 1926, Jun 23. Oakland Tribune. "Mother Kennedy declared her belief that Aimee McPherson did not drown but was killed by gangsters whose enmity she aroused by fighting against the re-opening of the Venice dance halls."

[384] Text of Conspiracy Complaint in McPherson Case. 1926, Sep 18. Daily News. "he had voluntarily and with intent to carry out the purpose of the criminal conspiracy absented herself from her usual habitation at the city of Los Angeles, and from the 19th day of May, up to and including the 29th day of May, 1926, resided and remained concealed and disguised with goggles and other devices and contrivances at Carmel-by the Sea, from which place she departed with Kenneth G. Ormiston, one of the conspirators herein named, with the full knowledge, acquiescence and consent of Minnie Kennedy"

[385] Text of Conspiracy Complaint in McPherson Case. 1926, Sep 18. Daily News. "after being duly and regularly sworn under oath, falsely, wickedly, maliciously and with intent to carry out the purpose of said conspiracy, swear that she had been kidnaped, and described the alleged kidnapers as "Rose" and "Steve," and falsely and wickedly represented and pretended that they had kidnaped her, and that they had held her captive from the 18th day of May up to and including the time when she appeared in a spectacular manner behind the slaughter house; well knowing that said fact was false and untrue, and made for the purpose of concealing her true whereabouts during that time, and made for the purpose of deceiving the grand jury of Los Angeles county"

[386] Aimee Will Act Kidnaping to Aid Hunt of Sleuths. 1926, Jun 27. Oakland Tribune. "The 'kidnaping' of Aimee Semple McPherson is to be re-enacted at Venice early next week at the evangelist's request. Mrs. McPherson told Los Angeles investigators on her return here today that she was desirous of retracing her movements on the afternoon of May 18 to aid in running down the alleged abductors, and the officers agreed."

prosecution. Newspapers had funded an estimated $500,000 investigation into her claims, and the whole nation was aware of what had happened.[387] It was unlikely that a single person in the Los Angeles area did not know that McPherson had escaped with her lover to a vacation resort and came back to Los Angeles pretending to be kidnapped to cover her tracks. In fact, with McPherson's national fame, it would have been difficult to find a person in the United States who had not heard about the case.

McPherson brilliantly weaponized her sermons against the court system and jury pool, insinuating that she was the target of a Roman Catholic plot, and began appealing to the Ku Klux Klan for assistance.[388] Her sermons began to speak of an impending invasion by the "alien religion" of Los Angeles, claimed that investigators and prosecuting attorneys were part of that religion, and blamed it on the "un-American" culture. McPherson's sermons targeted Southern and Eastern European immigrants who were changing the culture of America, and the Klan sympathized with her impossible dilemma. Eventually, McPherson claimed, it would result in America's downfall.

Not long after, key figures in the case against her were "suicided". Such was the case of one A. M. Waters, mentioned in association with her alleged kidnapping plot, who took his own life with poison. Only a few months before his death, Waters had told city officials that he was attacked by unknown assailants.[389] Whether or not his killing was at the hands of Klan operatives,

---

[387] Epstein, Daniel Mark. 1993. Sister Aimee: The Life of Aimee Semple McPherson. p289
[388] Gordon, Linda. 2017. The Second Coming of the KKK. "Evangelist Aimee Semple McPherson similarly endorsed the Klan in her tirades against Japanese Americans – she labeled them Satan's saboteurs – and depended on its support. In 1926, after she was charged with faking her own kidnapping, presumably to collect a ransom, rumors circulated that she had actually been off on a tryst with her lover."
[389] Hoax Figure Kills Himself: A. M. Waters, Mentioned in Msr. Sielaff's Notebook, Takes Own Life with Poison. "A new and unexpected mystery was injected into the Aimee Semple McPherson case yesterday when A. M. Waters, 871 South New Hampshire Avenue, whose name was found in a notebook in possession of Mrs. Lorraine Wiseman-Sielaff at the time of her arrest, committed suicide by drinking poison. Waters, whose assertion that he was a retired physician was attacked when he was arrested on a larceny charge several months ago."

knowing that the Invisible Army supported McPherson would have been a strong deterrent for any other witnesses who took the stand. Several key witnesses in the case changed their testimonies,[390] resulting in the case against McPherson being dismissed.

At the height of her fame in 1928, McPherson was caught in a get-rich-quick scheme in which she sold non-existent lots of property in a fictional "Tahoe Cedars" neighborhood adjacent to a new Foursquare temple to be erected on the banks of Lake Tahoe. It was advertised in a pamphlet depicting her in a sailor suit on the lake with the caption "Vacation with Sister".[391] McPherson fraudulently claimed that the non-existent neighborhood was the centerpiece of her "new ministry" and began peddling them to her own converts. When certain members of her sect learned that this "neighborhood" was instead plots of undeveloped land,[392] the Los Angeles District Attorney opened a criminal investigation.[393] It was

---

[390] Epstein, Daniel Mark. 1993. Sister Aimee: The Life of Aimee Semple McPherson. p312-313

[391] Dowd, Katie. 2020, Dec 11. How America's most famous preacher made a fake megachurch in Tahoe. Accessed 2022, Dec 23 from https://www.sfgate.com/renotahoe/article/famous-preacher-America-Aimee-Semple-McPherson-15632095.php. "At the zenith of her fame, McPherson, then 37, announced a new branch of her temple on the banks of Lake Tahoe. The summer of 1928 would bring her 'headquarters' to Tahoe Pines, the Associated Press reported. The alpine setting would host a brand-new temple, a religious summer camp and lodgings for parishioners. Sister Aimee advertised the Tahoe expansion heavily, mentioning it in sermons and circulating a pamphlet depicting her in a sailor suit on the lake. 'Vacation With Sister?' it asked, going on to extol the virtues of scenic surroundings."

[392] Dowd, Katie. 2020, Dec 11. How America's most famous preacher made a fake megachurch in Tahoe. Accessed 2022, Dec 23 from https://www.sfgate.com/renotahoe/article/famous-preacher-America-Aimee-Semple-McPherson-15632095.php. "In August, the first of several lawsuits was filed. It alleged that McPherson's ambitious Tahoe headquarters was nothing more than a get-rich-quick scheme. The lawsuit outlined the fraud allegations: Sister Aimee and three Tahoe real estate agents teamed up to create a fictional 'Tahoe Cedars' neighborhood adjacent to a new temple. Using her influence, she would fraudulently claim the neighborhood was the centerpiece of her new ministry and sell lots to her congregation. The suit said McPherson promised a vibrant religious center. Instead, there was nothing but forest and dirt.

[393] Dowd, Katie. 2020, Dec 11. How America's most famous preacher made a fake megachurch in Tahoe. Accessed 2022, Dec 23 from

then learned that real estate agents were giving McPherson a ten percent cut of any lot sold, with nine hundred lots allegedly available. Damages were estimated at $150,000,[394] which in today's money, is over 2.6 million dollars.[395]

Interestingly, Aimee Semple McPherson died of a medication overdose in September of 1944 by a medicine that had not been prescribed to her. It was at the same time that Roy E. Davis began mounting his charge against the City of Los Angeles for a criminal trial in Los Angeles after defrauding donors for his orphanage scheme to fund the Klan.[396] Semple's wavering position towards the Ku Klux Klan agenda would have been perceived as a threat to the White Knights, and some people speculated that she might have been poisoned. An inquest was ordered for October 6, 1944, to rule out foul play.[397] In the end, her death was ruled to be the consequence of an overdose of sleeping pills.[398]

Regardless of her cause of death and questions about Klan-related foul play, McPherson's Angelus Temple in Los Angeles would play a fundamental role in the Klan's weaponization of religion through key religious figures influenced by McPherson's ministry. Her heated statements about the "alien religion"

---

https://www.sfgate.com/renotahoe/article/famous-preacher-America-Aimee-Semple-McPherson-15632095.php. "Things got worse for McPherson when the Los Angeles District Attorney announced he too was investigating the reported fraud. The D.A.'s office took a hard look into the Echo Park Evangelistic Association, the holding company for the temple's properties, to see if any financial misdeeds occurred."

[394] Dowd, Katie. 2020, Dec 11. How America's most famous preacher made a fake megachurch in Tahoe. Accessed 2022, Dec 23 from https://www.sfgate.com/renotahoe/article/famous-preacher-America-Aimee-Semple-McPherson-15632095.php. "The three real estate agents would allegedly give McPherson a 10% cut of any lot sold, and with 900 lots available that quickly added up to big money. The lawsuits asked for $150,000 in damages (almost $2.3 million today); all the plaintiffs were members of the Angelus Temple."

[395] $150,000 in 1928 is worth $2,611,500 today. Accessed 2022, Dec 23 from https://www.in2013dollars.com/us/inflation/1928?amount=150000.

[396] Upland Pastor, Acquitted of Theft Charges, Sues Police Chief, 21 Others for Half Million. 1944, Sep 12. San Bernardino County.

[397] Funeral Services Will Not Be Held Until Oct 9. 1944, Sept 30. Times-Herald.

[398] L.A. Times, Aimee Semple McPherson Dies Suddenly in Oakland, latimes.com, USA, September 28, 1944

associated with the "downfall" of the nation became a theme in the Latter Rain revivals — not only with politics but also with regards to religion. This was especially true when one considers the impact of British Israelism on Angelus Temple.

McPherson was an early proponent of the British Israelism doctrine.[399] British Israelism, or "Anglo-Israelism", was a pseudo historical and pseudo religious notion that the people of Great Britain are *"genetically, racially, and linguistically the direct descendants"*[400] of the Ten Lost Tribes of ancient Israel. It was the foundation for the Christian Identity Doctrine used by white supremacists, which emerged in the United States in the 1920s and 1930s, to weaponize religion against people with black skin. McPherson apparently came in contact with the doctrine through Charles Fox Parham, who taught the British Israel theology to Angelus Temple.[401] According to the Christian Identity doctrine, people with black skin were descendants of Ham, the son of Noah, who was cursed. Adherents of Christian Identity believed that the alleged "curse of black skin" was directly related to a sexual union between Eve and the serpent from the Garden of Eden to produce Cain. This sexual union introduced an "evil bloodline" into the world, and theologians for the racist doctrine traced the lineage of Cain past the Great Flood through Ham, to Nimrod in Babylon, and all the way down to Judas Iscariot. Finally, according to the racist theologians, the curse came to the African Americans in the United States. They believed it to be a *"mongrel race"*.[402] Combined with

---

[399] Williams, Joseph. 2021, Jan 20. Pentecostals, Israel, and the Prophetic Politics of Dominion. "As with early Pentecostal proponents of British Israelism, the ministry of Aimee Semple McPherson points to a more complicated picture regarding early Pentecostal engagement with politics. See Matthew Avery Sutton, Aimee Semple McPherson and the Resurrection of Christian America (Cambridge, MA: Harvard University Press, 2007)."

[400] Brackney, William H. 2012, May 3. Historical Dictionary of Radical Christianity. Scarecrow Press. pp. 61-62.

[401] Barkun, Michael. 1997. Religion and the Racist Right: The Origins of the Christian Identity Movement. UNC Press Books. p. 68

[402] Branham, William. An Exposition of The Seven Church Ages. "The Smyrnaean church had drifted far from the original. It had become a hybrid. It had hybridized itself the way Eve did. You know that a hybrid is what comes of two species mixing. The result is no

the predictions made in the notes of the Scofield Reference Bible, the mixture of doctrine and propaganda suggested that people with black skin were the enemy.

One of the most outspoken ministers spreading the Christian Identity Doctrine entered the ministry as a student at the Angelus Temple Bible School while McPherson was alive[403] and while LeRoy Kopp was the Vice Chairman of the Angelus Temple Evangelists.[404] Rev. Wesley A. Swift was one of the original leaders in Christian Identity and formulated the version of the doctrine that William Branham would eventually propagate through the Latter Rain revivals disguised under the name "Serpent's Seed". Through Swift, everyone from Southern Baptist ministers to Pentecostal revivalists would be indoctrinated to believe that war would soon break out in the United States, directed by the Catholic Church, and executed by the "Seed of the Serpent" who were not born with white skin).

---

longer pure like the original. It is mongrel. Well, when Eve allowed the beast to mingle his seed with hers, she produced a creature called Cain that wasn't pure human. He was of the WICKED ONE. Notice how different he was from Abel. Notice how different he was from Seth. He hated God and would not obey the Word and persecuted and killed the righteous. He set himself up above the Word of God."

[403] Husband Routs Kidnaping Band. 1932, Dec 14. Los Angeles Times. "Wesley A. Swift, 19, a student at the Angelus Temple Bible School"

[404] Misc. News. 1936, Oct 22. Fairview Enterprise. "Rev. LeRoy Kopp, formerly of Fairview is now vice chairman of the Angelus Temple Evangelists

CHAPTER 10

THE GREAT SEDITION TRIAL OF 1944

❖

"People, we're living in the end time. How many of you people has heard years ago down here when they was going to have me arrested down here for preaching on that 'mark of the beast'? When I said that Mussolini, when he first come in power twenty-some-odd years ago, I said, 'If Mussolini ever goes towards Ethiopia, mark this down, there will never be peace till Jesus Christ comes.'" - William Branham

As Aimee Semple McPherson was rising to fame through the Angelus Temple in Los Angeles and shortly before her kidnapping hoax, an even bigger hoax was being propagated through the United States, one that originated in Kansas where Scofield and Parham had left their marks. Wichita, Kansas native Gerald Burton Winrod, nicknamed *"The Jayhawk Nazi"*[405] and "The Kansas Hitler"[406] founded "The Defenders of the Christian Faith", a

---

[405] The Winrod Legacy of Hate. Anti-Defamation League. Accessed 2022, Dec 26 from https://www.adl.org/sites/default/files/documents/assets/pdf/combating-hate/The-Winrod-Legacy-of-Hate.pdf. "Gordon Winrod, now in his late 60s, who has declared that "Not Jew-wise, the American citizenry always gets Jewed," is the current patriarch of the Winrod clan. His father was the late Rev. Gerald B. Winrod of Wichita, Kansas, a propagandist so notorious for his pro-Nazism and anti-Semitism in the 1930s and 1940s. that he earned himself the sobriquet of the "Jayhawk Nazi," ("Jayhawk" is a nickname for a Kansas native.)"

[406] Protection Sought by 'Kansas Hitler'. 1940, May 29. San Bernardino County Sun. "Mrs. Gerald Winrod today appealed for police protection for her husband, the Rev. Gerald

fundamentalist Christian-fascist organization.[407]   Winrod held several meetings and revivals spreading Christian fundamentalism mixed with white supremacy, some of which were youth rallies in collaboration with McPherson.[408]   Those rallies were also at the same time that William Branham and Roy E. Davis were invading Indiana Pentecostalism under the disguise of the Pentecostal Baptist Church of God.

Winrod was an avowed anti-Semitic and anti-Catholic, and a strong supporter of the British Israelism theology. Winrod was so zealous that in 1935, he published a book entitled *The Truth About the Protocols* proclaiming the veracity of a Russian fabricated antisemitic text describing the Jewish plan for global domination entitled *The Protocols of the Elders of Zion*.[409]   Winrod's church offered the fabricated text along with several other virulently antisemitic books describing *The Jewish Assault on Christianity*, including a book he had written by that name.[410]

Winrod, who was called the 'Kansas Hitler' when he was candidate for the U. S. senate in 1938. She said he feared violence but did not explain what source."

[407] Fine, Morris. Review of the Year. Accessed 2022, Dec 26 from https://ajcarchives.org/AJC_DATA/Files/1939_1940_4_YRUS.pdf. "The past year has also seen some expansion in the activities of such notorious Jew-baiters as William Dudley Pelley, National Commander of the Silver Shirts, and Gerald B. Winrod, Kansas Fundamentalist preacher and leader of the Defenders of the Christian Faith. Pelley was extremely active during the year in the publication and dissemination of anti-Jewish propaganda. Winrod, who during his unsuccessful Gubernatorial campaign in 1938 (See Vol. 40, p. 120) had attempted to gloss over his previous anti-Semitic and anti-Catholic record, once again resumed his Jew-baiting attacks."

[408] Sutton, Matthew Avery. 2007. Aimee Semple McPherson and the Resurrection of Christian America Aimee Semple McPherson and the Resurrection of Christ. "Excerpts from his magazine, the Defender, often appeared in Bridal Call and Crusader columns on biblical prophecy and contemporary events, and he and McPherson worked together in the 1930s at youth rallies focused on fundamentalism."

[409] Winrod, Gerald B. WorldCat Identities. Accessed 2022, Dec 26 from https://worldcat.org/identities/lccn-n83065962. "9 editions published between 1935 and 1978 in English and held by 31 WorldCat member libraries worldwide."

[410] The Winrod Legacy of Hate. Anti-Defamation League. Accessed 2022, Dec 26 from https://www.adl.org/sites/default/files/documents/assets/pdf/combating-hate/The-Winrod-Legacy-of-Hate.pdf. "The Winrod Letter and Our Savior's church have offered for sale a number of virulently anti-Semitic books including The Protocols of the Learned Elders of Zion, The Talmud Unmasked, Jewish Ritual Murder, and The International Jew. Also offered are books by Winrod's late father, Gerald B. Winrod, such as The Jewish

In *The Jewish Assault on Christianity*, Winrod claimed that the Christian Church had been invaded by Communism at the hands of Russia.

> *The Same forces which crucified Christ nineteen hundred years ago are today trying to crucify His Church. Many Christian leaders have not yet realized it, but Christianity is in the grip of a life and death struggle at the present time. International Jewish Communism, which has already undermined all nations, firmly expects to exterminate all Christians. What the Cause of Christ has endured in Russia the past eighteen years, surpasses its suffering at the hands of bloody Nero. One of the purposes of the present treatise is to show that this conspiracy is not of recent origin. {...} Will the Church be able to demonstrate sufficient power to triumph over its foes in the present crisis, or has it become so weakened by apostasy and pernicious teachings that it will have to be drenched in its own blood before it can be brought to its senses?*

In the late 1940s and 1950s, Winrod's theology would become a theme in the Latter Rain and Voice of Healing revivals that would unite to form the Post WWII healing revival. William Branham, leader of the revival, convinced the masses that Communism was invading the Church in opposition to his brand of Divine Healing,[411] and that, as a result, Christian Churches (not the churches in his cult of personality and affiliates) had become

---

Assault on Christianity published in 1935. Moreover, Winrod's Our Savior's Church has been the source of anti-Semitic tracts such as "Freemasonry: Jewish Front" and "Wake-up America." The latter tract alleged that Jews "started Communism," "control the money," "publish and distribute all pornography" "make the money off all liquor, dope and wars," and "control all politics by the power of money."

[411] Branham, William. 1949, Dec 25. The Deity of Jesus Christ. "I see the great red lights, of communism, swaying around over the earth. I see the formal churches taking their standard against Your Church, trying to condemn them, saying, "Divine healing is wrong. It's a bunch of fanaticism." A bill in our own White House, to close It down."

apostate.[412]   Winrod frequently attacked the Federation of Churches, claiming that the group had rejected the doctrine of the virgin birth of Christ,[413] both of which also were themes used in Branham's revivals.[414] [415] Winrod preached throughout the country in the late 1920s appearing in everything from conventions for the Christian and Missionary Alliance to small churches. In those events, Winrod claimed that there was a Biblical connection between Fascist Benito Mussolini and the return of Christ at the End of Days.[416]   Interestingly, William Branham initially shared Winrod's position and claimed to have almost been arrested for it.[417] This is particularly of interest when one considers the Great

---

[412] Branham, William. 1949, Dec 25. The Deity of Jesus Christ. "I see the great red lights, of communism, swaying around over the earth. I see the formal churches taking their standard against Your Church, trying to condemn them, saying, "Divine healing is wrong. It's a bunch of fanaticism." A bill in our own White House, to close It down."

[413] Fess Up, Rev. Winrod! 1938, Aug 1. Red Bluff Tehama County Daily News. "Winrod attacks the Federal Council of Churches, of which, in Kansas, the Methodists, the Presbyterians, the Baptists, the Christians are members. He even declared in his own paper, over his own signature, that the modern churches represented by the Federal Council were trying to prove 'Jesus a bastard' - These are Winrod's own words. His defense is that he hates the evils of communism in Russia."

[414] Branham, William. 1957, January 14. The Infallible Proof of The Resurrection (57-0114). "Now, that's an infallible proof through skeptics, and—and infidels, and other religious people, and social preachers, who preach the social gospel and so forth, that deny the virgin birth and the resurrection. To me, that takes the very foundation from under Christianity."

[415] Branham, William. 1963, December 1. Just Once More, Lord (63-1201E). "This Jezebel system, now blind spiritually, I'm saying, to the Word of God, joining themselves right into the Council of Churches. Everything, our great evangelical teaching, we have to forfeit that, to be an organization. Cause, all organizations that isn't in this Council of Churches, I got the paper on it, that even if your church is not in this Council of Churches, in time of trouble, they can use your church to store ammunition or anything they want to. And if any man is caught having a prayer for anybody, outside of affiliating with this Council of Churches, can be shot, as a federal offense."

[416] Oswald-Smith. 1928, Mar 24. Los Angeles Evening Express. "Rev. Gerald B. Winrod of Wichita, Kansas, orator, editor, author, will speak each afternoon and evening on startling subjects of thrilling interest. Tomorrow, 2:30 p. m. his subject will be: 'Mussolini and the Second Coming of Christ."

[417] Branham, William. 1953, Mar 26. Israel and the Church #2. "People, we're living in the end time. How many of you people has heard years ago down here when they was going to have me arrested down here for preaching on that "mark of the beast"? When I said that Mussolini, when he first come in power twenty-some-odd years ago, I said, "If Mussolini ever goes towards Ethiopia, mark this down, there will never be peace till

119

Sedition Trial of 1944 and its origins, as well as Winrod's many connections to William Branham through other key religious figures.

Winrod was well connected to key players who worked directly with William Branham or who were fundamental to his origination in the healing revivals. In 1932 when Branham promoter,[418] Klan member,[419] and former congressman William D. Upshaw ran for the Presidential election under the Prohibition Party ticket, Winrod actively campaigned for Upshaw in New York and Pennsylvania.[420] Of Gerald Winrod, Upshaw stated, "*Gerald B. Winrod, the 'Cyclone of Kansas,' is a dynamo of sanctified energy. He is a great thinker, patriot, crusader, defender of the faith, and pulpit statesman. It is an education to hear him.*"[421] Upshaw's campaign convention was held at the Cadle Tabernacle in Indianapolis, which was also the headquarters for the Indiana sect of the Ku

---

Jesus Christ comes." And I said, "There'll be three great isms, Communism, Fascism, and Nazism." And I said, "They'll wind up in one ism, and that one ism will dominate the world and will burn the Vatican City." You remember me saying that years and years and years ago. "

[418] Ex-Rep. Upshaw Discards Crutches After 59 Years. 1951, February 19. The Los Angeles Times. "And then in the temple last Feb 8, on what he said was the 66th anniversary of his injury, he had walked up to the pulpit where the Rev. William Branham was holding revival services."

[419] Norfolk Chief of Police Said to Be Member Ku Klux. 1921, Oct 12. Durham Morning Herald. "Upshaw a member. Information Gained from Newsletters Sent from Klan Headquarters"

[420] Beale, Barbara Jean. 1989. Gerald Burton Winrod: Defender of Christianity and Democracy in the United States. Accessed 2022, Dec 26 from https://soar.wichita.edu/bitstream/handle/10057/24253/t1994_Beale.pdf. Winrod actively campaigned for Upshaw in New York and Pennsylvania because both Hoover and Roosevelt had the support of the states to win. Winrod hoped Upshaw could wrest these essential votes from the two major presidential candidates. Although Winrod quietly admitted that Upshaw had a very slim chance of winning, he anticipated that Upshaw's campaign might throw the election into the House of Representatives.

[421] Noted Speaker Coming to Local Baptist Church. 1933, Feb 3. Redondo Reflex.

Klux Klan[422] founded by Branham's close associate E. Howard Cadle.[423]

These connections were further solidified through the World's Christian Fundamental Association (WCFA), of which Gerald Winrod[424] and William Branham's mentor Roy E. Davis[425] were both directors. Paul Rader, author, and composer of the "Only Believe" theme song used in Branham's revivals, was also a member.[426] Davis toured the country for three years with John Roach Straton,[427] and Straton often submitted articles to Winrod's "Defender" publication.[428]

Winrod was also well-connected to the Pentecostal community. Though initially an independent evangelist and publisher of *The Defender*, a fundamentalist newsletter, Winrod partnered with Juan Francisco Rodriguez Rivera, a Christian and

---

[422] Rice, Tom. 2016. White Robes, Silver Screens: Movies and the Making of the Ku Klux Klan. "Noting the 'very appropriate' sign outside the building - 'The Traitors within' - it commented that 'the Cadle Tabernacle, being a Klan headquarters is the natural home of traitors.'"

[423] Branham, William. 1953, Dec 13. What Think Ye of Christ. "What if I could call this morning…What if I could go call E. Howard Cadle, an old friend of mine with the Cadle Tabernacle."

[424] Beale, Barbara Jean. 1989. Gerald Burton Winrod: Defender of Christianity and Democracy in the United States. Accessed 2022, Dec 26 from https://soar.wichita.edu/bitstream/handle/10057/24253/t1994_Beale.pdf. "although he was not as well-known as the others, Gerald Winrod served on the original board of directors."

[425] Open Revival Wednesday Night. 1937, Feb 23. Chickasha Daily Express. "For two years he [Roy Davis] served as one of the national directors of the Fundamentalists of the world.

[426] Beale, Barbara Jean. 1989. Gerald Burton Winrod: Defender of Christianity and Democracy in the United States. Accessed 2022, Dec 26 from https://soar.wichita.edu/bitstream/handle/10057/24253/t1994_Beale.pdf. "Paul Rader of the Moody Bible Institute of Chicago"

[427] Open Revival Wednesday Night. 1937, Feb 23. Chickasha Daily Express. "of which the late Dr. John Roach Stratton [sig], former pastor of the Calvary Baptist Church, New York City. He was associated with Dr. Stratton [sig] in bible conferences for a period of three years."

[428] Beale, Barbara Jean. 1989. Gerald Burton Winrod: Defender of Christianity and Democracy in the United States. Accessed 2022, Dec 26 from https://soar.wichita.edu/bitstream/handle/10057/24253/t1994_Beale.pdf. "John Roach Stanton [sig] and Paul Rood of the Bryan Bible Institute also submitted articles for the Defender."

Missionary Alliance minister. Together, the two started a missionary program, attracting many converts to "Defenders of the Faith", a full-fledged Pentecostal denomination.[429]   Many key figures in the healing revival were both connected to the Christian and Missionary Alliance and strongly influenced by John Alexander Dowie, including F. F. Bosworth, Paul Rader, A. B. Simpson, and Russel Kelso Carter. Winrod wrote articles for Bosworth's "Exploits of Faith" magazine,[430] and toured with Paul Rader. Rader was a close relative of Rev. Ralph Rader of Jeffersonville, Indiana, who initially partnered with William Branham and Roy Davis for healing revivals before planting Davis's Jeffersonville church. Rader and Winrod held conferences at the Cadle Tabernacle[431] (Indiana Klan headquarters),[432] and Rader was a member of Winrod's "Defenders of the Christian Faith".[433]

---

[429]   Spanish   Speaking   Pentecostals.   Accessed   2022,   Dec   26   from https://www.encyclopedia.com/religion/encyclopedias-almanacs-transcripts-and-maps/spanish-speaking-pentecostals-0. "The Defenders of the Faith was neither intended to be a church-forming organization nor meant to be associated with Pentecostalism. In 1931, however, Gerald Winrod went to Puerto Rico to hold a series of missionary conferences. There he met Juan Francisco Rodriguez Rivera, a minister with the Christian and Missionary Alliance. Winrod decided to begin a missionary program and placed Rodriguez in charge. A center was opened in Arecibo, and El Defensor Hispano was begun as a Spanish edition of The Defender. Rodriguez's congregation became the first of the new movement. In 1932 Rodriguez accompanied Francisco Olazabal, founder of the Concilio Olazabal de Iglesias Latino Americano, on an evangelistic tour of Puerto Rico. The Defenders of the Faith received many members as a result of the crusade and emerged as a full-fledged Pentecostal denomination."

[430] Barnes, Roscoe III. 2018, Dec 31. Reading with F. F. Bosworth. Accessed 2022, Dec 28 from   http://roscoereporting.blogspot.com/2018/12/.   "Bosworth's   magazine   also featured the writings of his wife, Florence, and his brother, B.B. Bosworth. Other writers included Evangelist A.G. Jeffries, Harry Hodge, C.C. Fitch, Rev. William T. MacArthur, Rev. Herbert Dyke, Rev. P. Gavin Duffy, Bishop Charles H. Brent, James Moore Hickson, Carrie Judd Montgomery, Rev. J. P. Roberts, Mary Lowe Dickinson, Rev. W. J. Bennett, Ethel E. Tulloch, E. West, Charles H. Usher, John Harris, Fannie J. Rowe, J. Albert Libby and Dr. Gerald B. Winrod."

[431] An Intellectual and Religious Treat! 1929, Feb 2. Indianapolis Times. (Paul Rader and Gerald B. Winrod Pictured).

[432] An Intellectual and Religious Treat! 1929, Feb 2. Indianapolis Times. (Paul Rader and Gerald B. Winrod Pictured).

[433] Chicago Gospel Tabernacle World Defenders' Convention. 1930, May 17. Chicago Tribune. "Gerald R. Winrod: 'The Church and its Parasites' {...} Paul Rader"

Winrod described the world conflict as the result of prophecy and claimed that 1933 was the climax of that prophecy in sermons with titles such as "The Jew, Mussolini, and 1933 in Prophecy".[434] Winrod claimed that Mussolini was the Antichrist and had silently been infiltrating the United States politics and religion. William Branham mentioned almost being arrested for making similar statements. This appears to have been the reason for Branham's trouble with law enforcement, but also appears to have been the origin for Branham's Mussolini prediction mentioned in his alleged 1933 prophecies for which he would become famous. In May of 1955, Branham introduced a new claim in his stage persona in which he was supposed to have had a vision in 1933 of Mussolini rising into power.[435]

Winrod's End of Days theology used the framework of Dispensationalism described in Clarence Larkin's book, *Dispensational Truth*. *Dispensational Truth* was also the source of William Branham's "Church Age Theology",[436] though Branham claimed to have received Larkin's published information as a "divine revelation from God".[437] The supposed revelation was also

---

[434] Dr. Winrod Giving Sermon Series Here. 1933, Feb 10. Rodondo Reflex. "Dr. Gerald B. Winrod, the 'Kansas Cyclone', one of America's foremost crusaders and an outstanding Christian statesman, is giving a series of evangelistic sermons this week at the First Baptist church of Redondo Beach. His first address was delivered before a packed house last Sunday evening. The series will conclude next Sunday evening when he speaks on 'The Jew, Mussolini, and 1933 in Prophecy.'"

[435] Branham, William. 1955, May 1. The Faith That Was Once Delivered to the Saints. "And now, Jude speaking after thirty-three years, just think of how…What we need today, I believe, first is some good old fashion persecution to run us together. We find out that when the church is really persecuted…I believe that God is permitting communism to hit the land. I believe I can sensibly prove that by the Bible, that God promised that up into those isms, as communism years ago, when they first got out that N.R.A. I…Now, you remember that. And when Mussolini had first come in power, one morning by a vision…Now, it's written on old paper, laying at the house today, dated way back in 1933–'32 or '33."

[436] Seven Church Ages. Accessed 2023, Mar 5 from https://provetheclaims.wixsite.com/home/seven-church-age-teachings. "Branham also used and relied significantly on Clarence Larkin's, 1909 'Dispensational Truth' publication when formulating his "Seven Church Age" teachings."

[437] Branham, William. 1964, Jan 12. Shalom. "Did any of you see the paper where they took the pictures of the moon? I have it here. If it ain't a perfect image, leaving out the

closely aligned with the Scofield Reference Bible. Before Branham's alleged 1933 vision, Winrod was already holding talks and publishing literature that expounded upon Larkin's *Dispensational Truth*.[438]

Winrod was violently opposed to President Franklin D. Roosevelt, and in 1937, as world conflict was building to WWII, he spread propaganda claiming that Roosevelt and the Supreme Court were being controlled by *"both Moscow and Rome"*.[439] This, too, was a theme in Branham's revivals.[440] Branham often described Roosevelt as having run a *"dictatorship"* in sermons with titles such as *The Invasion of the United States*.[441]

Following the pattern of John Alexander Dowie, Winrod frequently mixed politics and religion, and he used his religious influence to sway American votes. He often exercised that power over elected officials to breed discontent.

WEAKENING THE REPUBLIC

By Dr. Gerald B. Winrod.

If, in the present crisis, the American people prove themselves

---

seventh age which is not yet, exactly the way I drawed by the Holy Spirit, the Church Ages."

[438] Gerald B. Winrod. 1928, May 16. The Pomona Progress Bulletin. "His afternoon lectures will start at 3:30 o'clock with the first one Sunday afternoon on the subject of 'Science and Religion' The only other afternoon address will be given on the following Sunday on 'Dispensational Truth.'"

[439] Judicial Bill Is Signed by Roosevelt. 1937, Mar 2. Pasadena Post. "The letter, carrying the salutation 'Dear Christian Friend' and signed 'Yours in Christ, Gerald B. Wlnrod,' was forwarded to Robinson by Theo Hahn of Alma, Neb., who received it from Wichita, Kan. It asserted that the President's Supreme Court proposed was supported by 'both Moscow and Rome.' It added that if the President 'succeeds in usurping powers of the court the Constitution will become a dead letter."

[440] Branham, William. 1954, May 15. Questions and Answers. "And according to the Word of God, it was supposed to be controlled by a single man, one man. And that man was to be in a church that was set on seven hills in Rome, according to the Bible."

[441] Branham, William. 1954, May 9. The Invasion of the United States. "But let me tell you, when Mr. Roosevelt...The man is dead. Let him rest; I trust he is. Come in, and run in three or four terms, and taken over, just a preliminary dictatorship."

unworthy of the advantages handed down by their fathers, they will become the greatest set of fools the world has ever known.

History shows that only a sound form of government can produce harmony, happiness, and prosperity. These are days when Americans should carefully compare their governmental philosophy, as established in 1787, with those existing in other parts of the world.

The inroads which are being made upon our Republic, from alien sources may serve to make extreme isolation necessary, in order to preserve the integrity of our system. During the many years that constitutional government was held sacred and inviolate, we become the envy of the whole world. Our social, spiritual, and economic development was phenomenal {...} The heads of such governmental groups are always appointed by the President. They are NOT chosen by the people. For instance, not one member of the Britain Trustees was elected to the public offense, and yet from this source, there has come a constant stream of radical, Socialistic legislative measures for "five long years."

This system of appointment, which began back in the days of Woodrow Wilson, has grown to monstrous proportions. It is usurping the duties of the Congress. It is putting abnormal powers in the hands of the Executive. It has made government by bureaucracy possible. It is contributing scandalously to political corruption. It is placing an unbearable tax burden upon the private citizens. It is placing instruments of power in private hands, which if continued will result in the dissolution of the Republic and bring about a dictatorship of the Fascist order.

Gerald Winrod was part of a much larger combination of men, women, and organizations that saw revolution as inevitable, and he saw himself as the *"nominal head of the country when the revolution comes".[442]* He arranged for his wife to be moved to a secret location when the government began to close in, but she refused and ultimately divorced him. Not long after the divorce, Winrod was indicted and eventually found himself incarcerated for criminal conspiracy. The case went before a Federal Grand Jury naming individuals and groups collectively working together to strategically and systematically destroy the morale of the United States Military.[443] The case was covered in newspapers across the nation as the biggest sedition trial of war in 1943,[444] later to be named by historians as The Great Sedition Trial of 1944.[445] Winrod fled the state of California with the FBI close on his heels.[446] He was eventually caught and held for trial.

During the months leading up to the trial, retired United States Army captain John H. Schmidt, who was under subpoena to testify as a government witness, died. According to his wife, Alice, the death was the result of poisoning. He was fine when dining out with her on Friday evening, but he was dead by Monday morning. Dr. Stanley McCool, who had been treating Schmidt, stated that the death resulted from natural causes, but he refused to sign the death certificate.[447]

---

[442] Woman Divorces Alleged Pro-Nazi. 1940, Jun 20. Los Angeles Times. "Mrs. Winrod testified her husband expected to be the 'nominal head of the country when the revolution comes,' and added he 'wanted to take me to a secret hideout so I would be protected when the government should close in on him.'"

[443] Jury Indicts 27 Trying to Break Morale of Army. 1942, Jul 23. Long Beach Press Telegram. "These men were named defendants: Gerald B. Winrod of Wichita, Kan."

[444] Biggest Sedition Trial of War Is Expected to Result from U.S. Indictments of 33. 1943, Jan 5. Santa Cruz Sentinel.

[445] Sedition Trial of 1944. Accessed 2022, Dec 28 from https://digital-library.csun.edu/in-our-own-backyard/sedition-trial-of-1944.

[446] Winrod Flees State. 1942, Jul 26. San Francisco Examiner. "FBI agents today extended their search to Wichita, Kas., after Gerald B. Winrod, sought on a federal indictment on charges of conspiring to undermine morale in the Navy and Army, slipped out of California."

[447] Murder Quiz in Captain's Death. 1944, Apr 3. Santa Maria Daily Times. "Mrs. Alice Schmidt, who reported her husband's death to police, said she fears he had been poisoned, but Dr. Stanley McCool, who had been treating Schmidt for pernicious anemia, said he believed the death was natural though he refused to sign the death certificate when Mrs. Schmidt expressed her fears that her husband had been poisoned."

Later, in November of 1944, Chief Justice Edward C. Eicher — the presiding judge in the case — died of a heart attack, and a mistrial was declared. Time magazine characterized the trial as *"biggest and noisiest sedition trial in United States history"* and reported that *"no one in Washington doubted that a ludicrously undignified trial had hastened the death of a scrupulously dignified judge."*[448]

The dismissal of charges against the white supremacists empowered Winrod and his associates even further. Their strategy of using religion to propagate their political agenda through the nation had been highly effective, and because of the United States legal system's separation of church and state for the purpose of religious freedom, many found sanctuary in what would soon become a new breed of "Christianity". With sermons, books, pamphlets, radio broadcasts, and other religious communications as a vehicle to distribute political agendas, fundamentalist Christianity quickly transitioned to "Political Christianity", the early stages of the "Christian Right".

In 1960, Winrod's son Gordon was named national chaplain of the racist and antisemitic National States Rights Party (NSRP), which was originally headquartered in William Branham's hometown of Jeffersonville, Indiana.[449] Under the auspices of the NSRP, Winrod toured the United States from coast to coast spreading the fear of "Jewish communism".[450] The NSRP at that time was operating out of Georgia, but still received official mail

---

[448] "Trial's End", 1944, Dec 11. Time.

[449] 90th Congress, 2nd Session, 1968. Present Day Ku Klux Klan Movement. "Originally headquartered in Jeffersonville, Ind., the organization moved its national office to Birmingham, Ala., in 1960."

[450] The Winrod Legacy of Hate. Anti-Defamation League. Accessed 2022, Dec 26 from https://www.adl.org/sites/default/files/documents/assets/pdf/combating-hate/The-Winrod-Legacy-of-Hate.pdf. "in the summer of 1960. Winrod was then ousted from his Arkansas position and suspended from ministerial functions by the Missouri Synod of the Lutheran Church. Subsequently, Winrod was named National Chaplain of the racist and antisemitic National States Rights Party (NSRP), led by J. B. Stoner. Although in this position only for six months, Winrod preached his anti-Jewish gospel coast-to-coast during an extensive speaking tour made under the auspices of the Georgia-based NSRP."

from a Jeffersonville post office box.[451]   There was another key figure, also inspired by Winrod, who was a leader in the NSRP. It was from this student of Winrod's work that William Branham learned the Christian Identity Doctrine, better known to his cult of personality as "The Serpent's Seed". That man was Rev. Wesley A. Swift.

[451] National States Rights Party. Accessed 2020, Oct 28 from http://jfk.hood.edu/Collection/Weisberg%20Subject%20Index%20Files/N%20Disk/Natio nal%20States%20Rights%20Party/Item%20069.pdf "Issue #19, dated June 1960, of "The Thunderbolt" announced the address of the headquarters of the NSRP had been changed from Jeffersonville, Indiana, to Post Office Box 783, Birmingham, AL."

CHAPTER 11

CHRISTIAN IDENTITY

❖

"The Federal FBI came by to see where I got the secrets. They thought that we had tapped the Pentagon and were giving away U.S. secrets. But, my friends, when it comes out in the U.S. News and World Report, it is no longer secret. If the FBI wants to do something good, they better keep their eyes on the enemy and let the Patriots alone." - *Rev. Wesley A. Swift*

One of the most significant figures in American history that was influenced by Gerald Burton Winrod was Angelus Temple student Wesley A. Swift.[452] Swift was one of the original leaders of the racist and antisemitic Christian Identity doctrine. Swift was trained in the doctrine while learning as a student in Rev. Philip Monson's Kingdom Bible School during the 1930s. Monson taught British Israelism as well as many of the racial teachings that Swift used as a basis for his Christian Identity theology.[453] Swift was first

---

[452] Barkun, Michael. 1997. Religion and the Racist Right: The Origins of the Christian Identity Movement. p. 68.
[453] Barkun, Michael. 1997. Religion and the Racist Right: The Origins of the Christian Identity Movement. p. 68.

introduced to the theology, however, from Winrod,[454] and used the Scofield Reference Bible.[455]

Swift influenced, was influenced by, and worked directly with a number of men and women associated with William Branham's ministry, both wielding influence over them, and being influenced by them. Some of these individuals were directly connected to William Branham, such as Rev. LeRoy Kopp. During the height of the Post WWII Healing revivals, Kopp would become an icon in William Branham's "Message" sect for his interview with Branham in the video "Twentieth Century Prophet"[456] Smith was a member of the Anglo-Saxon World federation at the same time that Branham's future campaign manager, Gordon Lindsay, was organizing and holding events[457] with Klan promoter Clem Davies.[458] Swift was also deeply connected to the cloak-and-dagger activities that went on behind the scenes during the revivals. For example, Swift was one of the white supremacist leaders present at the Little Rock Nine event in Civil Rights history,[459] an event that was heavily influenced by Roy E. Davis's

---

[454] Barkun, Michael. 1997. Religion and the Racist Right: The Origins of the Christian Identity Movement. p. 68.

[455] Swift, Wesley. 1965, Dec 3. The Times, the Measures, and the Climax of This Age. "If you have a Scofield Bible, that has a disciples, (Pedic) concordance, you note on page 57 of that concordance"

[456] Foursquare Church. 1954, Apr 17. Fresno Bee. "William Branham: 'The Story of a 20th Century Prophet: A Sound Film in Color".

[457] Annual Conference of Anglo-Saxon Christian World Movement. 1940, Aug 17. The Vancouver. "The convention will open with the British Israel church service in the auditorium on Sunday at 11 a.m. Rev. Gordon Lindsay of Portland, Ore., will deliver the address."

[458] Davies, Clem. The Racial Streams of Mankind. Accessed 2022, Apr 5 from http://www.colchestercollection.com/titles/R/racial-streams-of-mankind.html. This book presents a Christian Identity/Anglo-Israel perspective of the three streams of mankind flowing from Shem, Ham, and Japheth, the sons of Noah, and with the Bible prophecies which relate those racial streams to the nations of today. We must know the racial backgrounds of nations if we hope to understand the characteristics which they exhibit today.

[459] Cope, Graeme (2017). "The Master Conspirator' and His Henchmen: The KKK and the Labor Day Bombings of 1959". The Arkansas Historical Quarterly. The Arkansas Historical Quarterly. 76 (1): vol 76, no. 1, 2017, 49-67. JSTOR 26281884. Retrieved June 8, 2022.

Original Knights of the Ku Klux Klan.[460] Over time, Swift became an *"authority on the subject of race,"*[461] and his national lectures and radio broadcasts quickly spread Christian Identity theology.

Swift was a student at the Angelus Temple Bible School[462] during the time LeRoy Kopp was working with the Angelus Temple as a leader in the Foursquare Church sect led by Aimee Semple McPherson.[463] Kopp would later become the leader of the Angelus Temple Evangelists,[464] and finally, the head pastor of the Calvary Temple[465] which would frequently host William Branham's revivals.[466] While studying in the church, Swift's wife was nearly kidnapped by men who claimed Swift was a member of a wealthy family from Chicago.[467] Swift began shooting at the kidnappers,

---

[460] Office Memorandum 5900017. 1958, Oct 2. "The Original Knights of the Ku Klux Klan {...} On 9/15/58 LR [redacted] made available personal records of Imperial Grand Dragon Roy E. Davis of captioned organization {...} All of the individuals listed at Little Rock are known to be members of the captioned organization at Little Rock with the exception of J. R. English on Page 3"

[461] Rev. W. A. Swift to Conduct Services. 1944, Sep 23. San Francisco Examiner. "The Rev. Wesley A. Swift, southern California pastor, comes to the Kingdom Gospel Chapels of Oakland and San Francisco for a two weeks' campaign, beginning tomorrow and closing October 8. Mr. Swift is a nationally known lecturer and radio speaker, whose research in ethnology, archaeology and anthropology have established him as an authority on the subject of race."

[462] Husband Routs Kidnaping Band. 1932, Dec 14. Los Angeles Times. "Wesley A. Swift, 19, a student at the Angelus Temple Bible School"

[463] 4-Square Pastor Tells of Kidnaping. 1931, May 4. Wichita Beacon. "Rev. LeRoy M. Kopp, pastor of the Foursquare church, spoke on the alleged unfair treatment which Aimee McPherson, founder of the Foursquare gospel, had received at the hands of officials at the time of her alleged kidnaping last year over Station KFH late Sunday afternoon. Mr. Kopp pointed out the religious work, which was being continued at Angelus Temple, which Mrs. McPherson founded, in spite of all misrepresentations. Mr. Kopp was one of the Foursquare pastors who was in the Temple when Mrs. McPherson explained the various misrepresentations and declares she is worthy of a full vindication.

[464] Misc. News. 1936, Oct 22. Fairview Enterprise. "Rev. LeRoy Kopp, formerly of Fairview is now vice chairman of the Angelus Temple Evangelists

[465] Calvary Temple Anniversary Date. 1949, Feb 26. Los Angeles Times.

[466] ex: Evangelist Plans Return for New Revival Meetings. 1951, Apr 28. Los Angeles Times. "Evangelist William Branham will return to Los Angeles on May 1 to conduct another series of revival meetings at Calvary Temple, 123 N. Lake St."

[467] Husband Routs Kidnaping Band. 1932, Dec 14. Los Angeles Times. "Swift told officers he is of the opinion the kidnapers have been attracted to him in the belief he is a member of the wealthy meatpacking family of Chicago".

sparking an investigation by the Los Angeles police.[468] This was but one of many acts of violence in Swift's history and legacy. Swift retaliated doctrinally.

Swift *"pioneered a particularly insidious form"* of racism, which became *"the most distinctive element of Christian Identity theology:* that non-whites and Jews are the "biological offspring" of Satan.[469] Swift traced the lineage of non-whites through the biblical son of Noah, Ham, all the way back to Cain who, according to the doctrine, was the result of a sexual union between Eve and the serpent. Ham, according to many Bible scholars of the era, was the father of the races of people with black skin. Swift's specific version of the doctrine became popularized when Branham re-branded it as his "Serpent's Seed Doctrine" and spread the doctrine throughout the world in his revivals.[470] Like Swift, Branham traced the lineage of the "seed of the serpent" through Ham to Cain. Though Branham covertly removed the words "black" and "Jew" when he introduced the doctrine, many people in his audience would have been aware of the lineage and understood that he was referring to non-whites. In private, however, Branham trained leaders in his sect with the racially-charged version. According to Raymond Jackson, leader of a "sister church" in Branham's cult of personality, people with black skin were designed to be a *"laboring type of people"* because of the curse of Ham — exactly as was taught by Wesley Swift.

> *It was the descendants of Ham who first began to go out and really it is the descendants of Ham that began to want to*

---

[468] Husband Routs Kidnaping Band. 1932, Dec 14. Los Angeles Times. "Wesley A. Swift, 19, a student at the Angelus Temple Bible School, took a pot shot at a prowler and routed him from the Swift home, 1012 Mohawk Street."

[469] Schambers, Jon F. 2000. Mystical Anti-Semitism and the Christian Identity Movement. Accessed 2022, Dec 26 from https://files.eric.ed.gov/fulltext/ED447517.pdf.

[470] Branham, William. 1958, September 28. The Serpent's Seed (58-0928E). "The seed of the serpent comes along, and what does it produce? Now let's take the first few years. Now watch what takes place there. We'll read it right down, 'cause I've just checked it up. The seed of the serpent produced Cain. Cain went to the land of Nod, produced giants, and then they come to the land of Noah."

build an empire for themselves. This was mainly characterized through Nimrod, Noah's grandson. Yet it's through Ham's lineage. Now. Nimrod, he began to be a mighty one in the Earth. He was a mighty hunter. Before the Lord, wherefore it is said, even as Nimrod the mighty hunter before the Lord and the beginning of his Kingdom. It... he's the first one, after the flood, that even began to try to establish a man-made kingdom, a dominion. And what little secular histories declare about him, he was a vicious, cruel, evil character. And what little history can and is able to compile about Nimrod, he is the first one to build a city after the flood. He is the first one that began to introduce idolatry after the flood. He is the one that introduces the very beginning of Baal worship. And this Baal worship and idolatry spirit becomes characterized throughout practically all of Ham's descendants in the various areas and territories where they go.

This lets me know, brothers and sisters somewhere... It's why we're seeing a great breaking of the colored people today. From the old spiritual spirit back 100 years ago that they used to have and now brothers and sisters, they're taking on this modernistic spirit. 'Cause I can see rising in the colored people today, that same spirit of Nimrod. Not too long ago, a certain magazine published and showed pictures of different antiques and things that belong to the colored kingdom of ancient times, and that had to be Nimrod Tower. It lets me know as the anti-Christ spirit moves in to try to unify everybody into one great brotherhood. You can't, brothers and sisters, put all races in the same bed. God didn't put all races in the same bed when Jesus Christ came. But I'll tell you one thing, the love of God in your heart can respect each race in his proper respective calling. The sad part of it is we have too many races today trying to outlive beyond what really their race is to be in the great universal earthly sphere of God's plan for the earth. {...} And he said, cursed be Canaan, a servant of servants, shall he be unto his brethren? Many *people wonder even today or how come is it that the colored race has more or less always been a sort of a a laboring type people? It's because right there it is. It's right there, it's just as plain as the nose on your face and the modern world today is failing to recognize.*[471]

Swift's usage of the "Two-Seed Doctrine" was a significant threat to the political and religious landscape of the 1950s and 1960s, especially with the help of Branham laying the framework to unsuspecting listeners. Combined with the fears of nuclear war, communism, and other concerns of the era; the Christian Identity doctrine became a primary platform upon which white supremacists and antisemitic groups could base their mixtures of religious and political ideologies. Swift made huge strides towards embedding the doctrine in mainstream Christianity, and with the help of Branham and the Latter Rain Revivals, Christian Identity quickly became a "cult for the racist right".[472] Swift is charged with "baptizing Nazism" — blending it so deeply with Christianity that it is difficult to unravel — and ultimately producing Neo-Nazism in the United States.[473]

---

[471] Jackson, Raymond. 1975, Mar 20. The Sin of Ham.

[472] Justification by Race: Wesley Swift's White Supremacy and Anti-Semitic Theological Views in His Christian Identity Sermons. Accessed 2022, May 5 from https://jhs.press.gonzaga.edu/articles/10.33972/jhs.183/. "This article explores the discourses of Minister Wesley Albert Swift (1913-1970), one of the original and leading proponents of Christian Identity, a racial theology movement which emerged in the United States after World War II. It is not the aim of this study to analyze the discourse of Christian Identity as an isolated element, but to understand its interrelation with the political-religious culture of the country during the 1950s and 1960s. Christian Identity rhetoric may be understood based on its socio-historical context. During the formulative years of Christian Identity, nuclear anxieties, along with the fear of Communist infiltration, were deeply present within the white supremacist and their anti-Semitic views. At the same time, the civil rights movement of African Americans stimulated violent white supremacy politics and rhetoric by the extreme right. Combining the white hegemonic fear of minority advances in American society, Christian Identity was created as a cult for the racist right."

[473] Milwicki, Alon. 2019. Baptizing Nazism: An Analysis of the Religious Roots of American Neo-Nazism. Accessed 2022, Dec 31 from https://jhs.press.gonzaga.edu/articles/10.33972/jhs.183/. Thus, it is necessary to understand the movement and the man who is arguably most directly responsible for

During the 1940s, Swift began working with Detroit pastor Gerald L. K. Smith to revive the Ku Klux Klan in California.[474] Swift was Smith's private chauffeur and bodyguard.[475] Interestingly, both Roy E. Davis and William D. Upshaw were in San Bernardino at the same time,[476] building what would later become the third wave of the Ku Klux Klan. It is not clear whether Davis and Upshaw were assisting Gerald Smith, but in either case, the rebuilding of the California Klan was successful. The California Klan went public in April of 1946, and Swift took the lead during a cross-burning rally held in the Big Bear Valley. He said, "*The Klan is here in Big Bear Valley to stay. We intend to form restrictive covenants here and elsewhere in order to hold the line of pure Americanism*".[477]

It should, however, be noted that shortly prior to the California revival of the Klan, Upshaw held conventions on subjects such as "*Americanism that will save America*"[478] and Upshaw was the head of the "*department of Americanism*"[479] in the orphanage that he and Davis established as a front for the Klan. According to witnesses that testified against Upshaw and Davis, Upshaw helped Davis pose as a federal agent to create assumptions of federal

---

"Baptizing Nazism" and laying a foundation for Modern American Neo-Nazism to grow and thrive on the fringes of American society."

[474] Fiery Cross Burning Again: Ku Klux Klan out in open in California. 1946, Apr 6. Daily News. "Rev. Wesley Swift admits his membership in revived Klan: Posing before hunting trophy in Lancaster home, he names Gerald L. K. Smith as national leader."

[475] Pre-1956 News Note. 1954, Mar 2. Ventura County Star Free Press. Dr. Wesley Swift, described as 'an apostle of hate' in Los Angeles and a 'former bodyguard and chauffer' for Gerald L. K. Smith."

[476] Orphanage Benefactor Questioned, Pictured as 'Disillusioned'; Funds Raising Investigated. 1944, Feb 20. The San Bernardino County Sun. "She said she had met Davis through William D. Upshaw, evangelist and former congressman from Georgia, and had given or loaned Davis $8,600 of her life savings."

[477] Ku Klux Klan Activities at Big Bear Under Investigation. 1946, Apr 7. San Bernardino County Sun.

[478] Downtown Evangelistic. 1944, May 27. The San Bernardino County Sun. "Americanism that Will Save America', William D. Upshaw former Georgia Congressman."

[479] 1943, Aug 8. The San Bernardino County Sun. "Former Representative William D. Upshaw is taking an active part in the organization of the institution and is to be in charge of the department of Americanism."

authority.[480] Combined with the fact that Swift worked with Roy Davis's Original Knights of the Ku Klux Klan during the Little Rock Nine event in 1957, and Upshaw's work with Gerard Winrod, it is difficult to imagine a world where the men were not connected. At a minimum, they knew *of* each other and held similar religious and political views.

It should also be noted that Wesley Swift is linked to several extremist groups. His "Church of Jesus Christ Christian" was renamed by Richard Girnt Butler to "Church of Jesus Christ Christian - Aryan Nations", later shortened to "Aryan Nations" and bore the Third Reich symbolism.[481] Through Butler's influence, Swift's sect would devolve into hyper-militant terrorism.[482] Convicted bank robber Morris Gulett, also linked to Swift's sect; organized the "Skinheads", "Klan-connected 'Knights'", and outlaw-biker "SS-MC" splinter groups.[483] Swift's right-wing religious theology was, like all of those linking him directly or indirectly to William Branham, very militant. The religious leaders at the

[480] Pastor Denies Charge of Posing as F.B.I. Man. 1944, Apr 21. The Los Angeles Times. "Upshaw denied testimony of government Witnesses that he had told Upland residents Mr. Davis was an F.B.I. man.

[481] Wesley Swift and the Church of Jesus Christ - Christian. 2015, Jan 26. Accessed 2022, May 5 from http://califias.blogspot.com/2015/01/wesley-swift-and-church-of-jesus-christ.html?m=1. "In Idaho, Butler renamed Swift's organization the Church of Jesus Christ Christian – Aryan Nations, although it would become best known as simply "Aryan Nations." To befit the neo-Nazi implications of the name, Swift adopted a standard for the Church that combined the cross-and-sword and Rebel-flag motifs of the American Christian Far-Right, with the Wolfsangel – the "hook rune" associated with Third Reich symbolism."

[482] Wesley Swift and the Church of Jesus Christ - Christian. 2015, Jan 26. Accessed 2022, May 5 from http://califias.blogspot.com/2015/01/wesley-swift-and-church-of-jesus-christ.html?m=1. "Before his departure, however, Gale introduced Swift to a middle-aged, Los Angeles-based aerospace engineer who would later, help make the Church of Jesus Christ - Christian, under an appended name, synonymous with American White-racist crime and terrorism."

[483] Wesley Swift and the Church of Jesus Christ - Christian. 2015, Jan 26. Accessed 2022, May 5 from http://califias.blogspot.com/2015/01/wesley-swift-and-church-of-jesus-christ.html?m=1. "Louisianan Morris Gulett leads the most visible Aryan Nations rump group. A convicted bank robber, Gulett has organized his own faction with tripartite membership for "Skinheads," Klan-connected "Knights", and outlaw-biker "SS-MC" subgroups."

Sharon Orphanage formed "Joel's Army", a militant form of Christianity opposed to both government and Christian denominations,[484] and like both Swift and Gerald Winrod, Branham preached sermons exciting crowds about a "super race"[485] that would overthrow the United States Government. With the help of Branham, and heavily influenced by Gerald Burton Winrod, Swift's theology would explode into a movement called "Joel's Army" in the late 1940s and early 1950s.

Swift was the West Coast Representative of the National States' Rights Party[486] which was formed in Jeffersonville, Indiana[487] and which continued to receive mail to a Jeffersonville post office box. He was also a member of several white supremacy groups connected to Roy Davis such as the White Citizens Council. In fact, FBI Intelligence documents confirm that Swift was suspected to be a key figure in almost every white supremacy organization existing in America at that time.[488] Intelligence documents also confirm that Swift had mastered the weaponization of religion — he *used his church not only to proselytize but also to recruit and screen potential 'soldiers' for more*

---

[484] Sanchez, Casey. 2008. TODD BENTLEY'S MILITANT JOEL'S ARMY GAINS FOLLOWERS IN FLORIDA. Accessed 2023, Feb 24 from https://www.splcenter.org/fighting-hate/intelligence-report/2008/todd-bentley%E2%80%99s-militant-joel%E2%80%99s-army-gains-followers-florida.

[485] Branham, William. 1962, March 18. The Spoken Word Is the Original Seed These last days, true Church-Bride comes to the Headstone, will be the super Church, a super Race.

[486] Milwicki, Alon. 2019. Baptizing Nazism: An Analysis of the Religious Roots of American Neo-Nazism. Accessed 2022, Dec 31 from https://jhs.press.gonzaga.edu/articles/10.33972/jhs.183/. "Swift was also the West Coast Representative of the National States' Rights Party, which allowed him to exert nationwide influence."

[487] 90th Congress, 2nd Session, 1968. Present Day Ku Klux Klan Movement. "Originally headquartered in Jeffersonville, Ind., the organization moved its national office to Birmingham, Ala., in 1960."

[488] Milwicki, Alon. 2019. Baptizing Nazism: An Analysis of the Religious Roots of American Neo-Nazism. Accessed 2022, Dec 31 from https://jhs.press.gonzaga.edu/articles/10.33972/jhs.183/. "FBI intelligence documents have divulged that agents tracking Swift suspected his involvement in nearly every white supremacy organization in America at the time, including the White Citizens Council, American Nazi Party, and the John Birch society."

militant organizations, such as the Rangers, Minutemen, and National States' Rights Party."[489]

After President John F. Kennedy met with Dr. Martin Luther King in the Oval Office, Swift launched a massive rally of protests inciting anger against the President. Swift spread the word that the Judeo infiltration of the United States was confirmed, and that the role of the "Negro" as foot soldiers would soon be employed.[490] "Wanted for Treason" pamphlets with the face of Kennedy were printed and distributed among white supremacists. Roy E. Davis was the Grand Dragon of the Ku Klux Klan at the time,[491] and authorities traced the pamphlets to Bobby Joiner and the White Citizen Council. Roy Davis was a member of the Council, along with Joiner and Swift. Witnesses claimed that the purchaser of the printers Joiner and Davis used looked like Lee Harvey Oswald in a wig.[492]

As it relates to the Post WWII healing revival, however, Swift's later views on the impending race war is critical to understanding key elements within the Latter Rain theology. Swift was a major proponent for the coming race war, and his "Church of Jesus Christ Christian" transitioned from a vehicle using weaponized religion to indoctrinate followers into a full-fledged

---

[489] Milwicki, Alon. 2019. Baptizing Nazism: An Analysis of the Religious Roots of American Neo-Nazism. Accessed 2022, Dec 31 from https://jhs.press.gonzaga.edu/articles/10.33972/jhs.183/.

[490] Milwicki, Alon. 2019. Baptizing Nazism: An Analysis of the Religious Roots of American Neo-Nazism. Accessed 2022, Dec 31 from https://jhs.press.gonzaga.edu/articles/10.33972/jhs.183/. "The fact that both Presidents Kennedy and Johnson invited Dr. King into the Oval Office confirmed for him and his followers-- – including Stoner–of the Judeo infiltration of the United States as well as the role of the "Negro" as their foot soldiers."

[491] Assassination of President Kennedy. 00-2-34030. "On December 9, 1963, Inv. Brumley, Intelligence Unit, Dallas Police Department, discussed this case with the reporting agent, and he through that Earl Thornton, Klansman, and former associate of Rev. Roy Davis, might be suspect in this case. Thornton offered to allow Davis to use his printing equipment when Davis was in business as Grand Dragon of the Ku Klux Klan. Brumley, who knows Davis personally, doubted however that Davis printed these leaflets."

[492] Assassination of President Kennedy. 00-2-34030. "He still thought the purchaser looked more like Oswald's photo, except that he had dark curly hair."

paramilitary organization. FBI documents tracked Swift's purchases of large quantities of handguns, shotguns, and rifles, and Swift began preaching that *"every Christian should get a rifle, shotgun, ammunition, and some shells and lay them in, they're going to need it to protect themselves and their homes."*[493]

In the late 1940s, however, this doctrine was in its early stages, and Swift's religious theology was not the primary delivery method for the white supremacy agenda. Swift, at that time, was simply one cog in a much larger wheel. Another key figure was rising into prominence in the United States and Canada in the mid 1940s who would become the catalyst for one of the biggest opportunities to weaponize religion in American history. That figure was William Branham.

---

[493] Milwicki, Alon. 2019. Baptizing Nazism: An Analysis of the Religious Roots of American Neo-Nazism. Accessed 2022, Dec 31 from https://jhs.press.gonzaga.edu/articles/10.33972/jhs.183/. "Swift was a major proponent of the coming race war and spoke for the necessity for white men to arm themselves and prepare for this war. The FBI suspected that "the use of the church of Jesus Christ Christian" was "a front for paramilitary activities" for organizations connected to Swift and his Identity message.451 The California Attorney General observed that Swift had a "rifle range in his backyard," and as a zealot of Swift, it is plausible that Potito's rifle practices happened at Swift's residence. FBI documents also tracked Swift for his purchase of large quantities of handguns, shotguns, and rifles. In this regard, Swift stated that "the day has come when every Christian should get a rifle, shotgun, ammunition and some shells and lay them in, they're going to need it to protect themselves and their homes.

CHAPTER 12

THE SERPENT'S SEED

❖

"How many of you people has heard years ago down here when they was going to have me arrested down here for preaching on that 'mark of the beast'? When I said that Mussolini, when he first come in power twenty-some-odd years ago, I said, 'If Mussolini ever goes towards Ethiopia, mark this down, there will never be peace till Jesus Christ comes.' And I said, "There'll be three great isms, Communism, Fascism, and Nazism." And I said, 'They'll wind up in one ism, and that one ism will dominate the world and will burn the Vatican City.'"
- William Branham

The British Israel Doctrines of Gerald Burton Winrod and the Christian Identity Doctrines of Wesley A. Swift were widely popular among white supremacists and certain groups of fundamentalist Christians, but they were not so well received among members of mainstream Christianity. The notion that these isolated groups of extremists had esoteric knowledge about sex between Eve and the serpent was largely rejected by Christian scholars and historians, especially those familiar with Gnosticism and ancient heresies. As early as 180 A.D., Christian apologist and bishop Irenaeus of Smyrna labeled the doctrine as heretical in his book, *Against Heresies*.[494]   Leaders of white supremacy needed a way to limit the influence of church historians and convince the general public of their white supremacy views. Through the Post WWII healing revival, both British Israelism and Christian Identity were gradually, subtly, and covertly introduced into churches around the world. William Branham, leader of the revival, strategically re-branded them under different names and injected the doctrines into mainstream using the framework of a doctrine of his own creation: "The Manifested Sons of God."

When historians examine the biographies of William Branham, they often seem to communicate that he was the least likely to push a racist agenda forward. Historical accounts of Branham are typically based upon the descriptions that Branham himself presented to his audiences while promoting his stage persona in the revivals. These ideas are often conflicting and inaccurate.[495]   Branham is usually described as a Baptist minister, uneducated, who was raised in the hills of Kentucky. During the years leading up to the Great Sedition Trial of 1944, according to Branham, he had never heard of Pentecostalism.[496]   He admitted that he had heard of the Christian Identity doctrine from elders in his first church, but he claimed to have rejected it.[497]   Historians describing Branham usually fail to mention that Branham was mentored by Roy Davis, high-ranking Klansman, leader of multiple

---

[494] "ANF01. The Apostolic Fathers with Justin Martyr and Irenaeus - Christian Classics Ethereal Library". Ccel.org. 13 July 2005. Retrieved 15 July 2014.

[495] List of Issues with the Message. Accessed 2023, Feb 24 from https://en.believethesign.com/index.php/List_of_Issues_with_the_Message

[496] Branham, William. 1952, Jul 20. Life Story. "It was at a church house. And I stop and goes in. Come to find out, it was a convention where there was a group of the Pentecostal people, was holding a convention over there. And they had to hold it in the north, because of the race conditions they couldn't hold it, and it was a international convention. They was holding it in a big tabernacle at Mishawaka. 211 So I–I never seen the Pentecost before, so I thought, "Well, believe I'll go and see what it looks like."

[497] Branham, William. 1957, Oct 6. Questions and Answers on Hebrews #3. "The first time I ever met anyone in my life, after I had been converted…I was…met Brother George DeArk and them down there. And I was walked, and the Lord led me to a little place. And they was discussing where the colored man came from. And they were trying to say that the colored man…That Cain married an animal like an ape, and through there come forth the colored race. Now, that's wrong! Absolutely, that's wrong"

white supremacy groups, and future Imperial Wizard of the Original Knights of the Ku Klux Klan.[498] Nor do they mention that Branham was nearly arrested for holding speeches similar to Winrod's verbal attacks against Mussolini.[499]

William Branham played a part in Roy E. Davis's strategy of invading Indiana Pentecostalism. When Davis established his Pentecostal Baptist Church of God sect in Jeffersonville and appointed new apostles and evangelists in 1930, Branham had already been working with Davis for well over a year. Branham was with Davis as early as 1929, when the Pentecostal Baptist church was headquartered in Nashville, and possibly even earlier. Davis had worked with Evansville, Indiana native John Roach Straton[500] who mixed race and politics under the banner of "The Supreme Kingdom",[501] a white supremacy group started by short-

---

[498] Klan Opens Membership Drive in Northwest Louisiana. 1961, Feb 11. Arkansas Gazette. "R. E. Davis, self-styled national imperial wizard of the original Knights of the Ku Klux Klan"

[499] Branham, William. 1953, Mar 26. Israel and the Church #2. "People, we're living in the end time. How many of you people has heard years ago down here when they was going to have me arrested down here for preaching on that "mark of the beast"? When I said that Mussolini, when he first come in power twenty-some-odd years ago, I said, "If Mussolini ever goes towards Ethiopia, mark this down, there will never be peace till Jesus Christ comes." And I said, "There'll be three great isms, Communism, Fascism, and Nazism." And I said, "They'll wind up in one ism, and that one ism will dominate the world and will burn the Vatican City." You remember me saying that years and years and years ago. And just exactly that way!"

[500] Dr. Roy Davis Holds revival in Bossier. 1937, Apr 23. Shreveport Journal. "Dr. Roy E. Davis, formerly connected with the late Dr. John Roach Straton, New York city, but who, for the last ten years, has given himself over to evangelism in the homeland and on foreign soil, is now conducting a revival in the Assembly of God's church, 425 Traffic Street, Bossier City."

[501] Battle for the Soul of a City: John Roach Straton, Harry Emerson Fosdick, and the Fundamentalist-Modernist Controversy in New York, 1922-1935. 2021, Aug 31. Accessed 2022, Feb 8 from https://www.cambridge.org/core/journals/church-history/article/battle-for-the-soul-of-a-city-john-roach-straton-harry-emerson-fosdick-and-the-fundamentalistmodernist-controversy-in-new-york-19221935/A0FAD484D9BB3CC54770971F8812CE54. "Straton's association with the group called 'Supreme Kingdom' proved to be the most vexing. It was the brainchild of Edgar Young Clarke, a former Ku Klux Klan member who founded the group in Georgia in 1926. It appealed to Southern fundamentalist evangelicals who felt under siege after the Scopes trial, and Clarke wooed them by promising to "protest modernism and the theory of evolution."

term Imperial Wizard Edward Young Clarke.[502] Davis used this connection to his advantage, advertising Straton's name for his revivals.[503] Dr. Caleb A. Ridley, Imperial Supreme Religious Chaplain, or KLUDD of the Ku Klux Klan,[504] was part of the Supreme Kingdom movement.[505] In 1929, Davis,[506] Branham, and Ridley held revivals near the Nashville Parthenon.[507] When the

[502] LARKE, EX-KLAN CHIEF, IN ANTI-EVOLUTIOIN WAR; Forms "Supreme Kingdom," Which Orders Several Georgia Teachers to Resign. 1926, Feb 14. New York Times. "Edward Young Clarke, deposed by the Klan as Acting Imperial Wizard and forced out of the order, is now organizing a new society, known as the Supreme Kingdom. The purpose will be to drive out of the schools and colleges of the nation all proponents of evolution, atheism, or revolution."

[503] Dr. Roy Davis Holds revival in Bossier. 1937, Apr 23. Shreveport Journal. "Dr. Roy E. Davis, formerly connected with the late Dr. John Roach Straton, New York city, but who, for the last ten years, has given himself over to evangelism in the homeland and on foreign soil, is now conducting a revival in the Assembly of God's church, 425 Traffic Street, Bossier City."

[504] Dr. Caleb A. Ridley Resigns as Pastor. 1925, Jul 27. The Atlanta Constitution. "Dr. Caleb A. Ridley, former imperial kludd of the Ku Klux Klan, tendered his resignation as pastor of the Third Baptist Church."

[505] Yaarab Temple Protests Name of Secret Order. 1927, Aug 24. The Atlanta Constitution. "An injunction to prevent E. Y. Clarke, Dr. Caleb A. Ridley, and others from organizing the 'Supreme Kingdom Shrine,' a new secret order, on the ground that it is an infringement of the name of the Mystic Shrine of North America, is sought in a petition filed Tuesday in Fulton superior court by members of Yaarab Temple of the Mystic Shrine."

[506] Pentecostal Baptist Church Rally Planned. 1929, Jul 6. The Tennessean. "The Pentecostal Baptist Church, located at Spring and Meridian, will have a rally Sunday evening under the large open-air dome on the same corner as the church building, in the interest of the new church building they are planning."

[507] Branham, William. 1962, Sep 9. In His Presence. NOTE: Branham says, "Memphis", but describes the Nashville Parthenon - When a man comes in contact with God, he recognizes himself "no good." How can a man walk around and brag about how big he is and what all he's done, when he's nothing? He's nothing to begin with. One day down in Memphis, Tennessee, or one...I don't think it was in Memphis. It was one of the places there. I was with Brother Davis and was having a—a revival. It might have been Memphis. And we was, went to a coliseum, and they had in there, not a coliseum, it was kind of an art gallery, and they had the—the great statues that they had got from different parts of the earth, of different, Hercules and so forth, and great artists had painted. And then they had the analysis of a man that weighed a hundred and fifty pounds. You know what, how much he's worth? Eighty-four cents. That's all he is. Eighty-four cents is all—all the chemicals you can get out of him. He's just got enough whitewash to sprinkle a hen's nest, and he's got enough, just a little bit of calcium, little potash. It would all sell for eighty-four cents. But we just take care of that eighty-four cents and baby it around.

organization moved to Louisville and eventually to Jeffersonville, Indiana, the new headquarters was actually in Branham's hometown. Though Branham claimed to have been raised in Kentucky,[508] the Branham family migrated to Jeffersonville before his third birthday.[509]

William Branham was raised in Utica on the grounds of liquor kingpin and president of the R. H. Wathen distilleries, Otto H. Wathen.[510] Branham and his father produced liquor in a homemade whiskey still[511] as did a number of others in the Wathen Liquor ring during prohibition. When his father was arrested in 1924, Otto Wathen tried unsuccessfully to gain his release from incarceration.[512] William Branham, at an age qualified to be tried as an adult in the state of Indiana, changed his birth year from 1907[513] to 1909,[514] the birth year of a deceased sibling. Branham then fled to Arizona for a period of time,[515] later joined Davis, and began touring the Midwest holding revivals.

---

[508] Branham, William. 1960, January 9. Sirs, We Would See Jesus (60-0109). "How many of you Southerners know what a fly bush is? I used to have to fan the flies at the table when company would come, you know, before we had screen doors, way back in Kentucky where we had to live poor. Little old cabin up on the side of the hill, seventy-five cents a day hauling logs, it was rough. No clothes"

[509] United States Census. 1920.

[510] Branham, William. 1959, Apr 19. My Life Story. "Later we moved to Indiana and Father went to work for a man, Mr. Wathen, a rich man. He owns the Wathen Distilleries. And he owned a great share; he's a multimillionaire, and the Louisville Colonels, and—and baseball, and so forth. And then we lived near there. And Dad being a poor man, yet he could not do without his drinking, so he—he went to making whiskey in a—in a still."

[511] Branham, William. 1953, Nov 8. Life Story. "I was packing water one day. you've heard that part of the story. Sorry to say, packing it to a moonshine still for my daddy, two little half-a-gallon molasses buckets."

[512] Asks Aid for Family. 1924, Mar 14. Courier Journal. "In addition to the jail sentence Branham was fined $100 and costs, which was stayed by Otto H. Wathen, but the commitment for thirty days cannot be suspended."

[513] According to most historical accounts and records, 1907 appears to be William Branham's actual birth year. This is the year that his parents used for census reports and was the year that was given for news articles. ex: Fourteenth Census of the United States.

[514] Fifteenth Census of the United States.

[515] Branham, William. 1960, Feb 28. Conferences. "Remember, my first visit to Phoenix, I was just about, well, I was about sixteen, seventeen years old. It's been around thirty years ago. And up on Sixteenth and Henshaw was a desert. That's where I stayed, up, just right out on an old country road."

Based on later descriptions of those revivals by William Branham, they were Pentecostal revivals. From 1910 to 1920, the poison drinking, snake handling Pentecostals were somewhat widespread.[516] The snake-handling Pentecostal movement appears to have started with George Went Hensley, a rural preacher from Grasshopper Valley near Cleveland, Tennessee, and quickly became popular among the Church of God, Cleveland. From there, it spread throughout Pentecostalism, though many Pentecostals rejected the practice. To test their faith, those who adopted the practice believed the ending of the Gospel of Mark to be a literal instruction rather than a blessing. They carried out that instruction by either drinking poison or handling snakes in their services. In some of the revival meetings Roy E. Davis allegedly drank sulfuric acid to win converts, and William Branham claimed that he and Davis had obtained written statements confirming this test by a *"notary public"*.[517] Davis's time in Nashville was brief, however, just long enough to spread the group into Kentucky, and finally to Jeffersonville in 1930.[518]

By 1934, the Pentecostal Baptist Church of God sect had gained a strong foothold in Indiana, and Roy Davis began efforts to relocate, announcing plans to move his headquarters back to

---

[516] Kelle, Brad. New Georgia Encyclopedia. Accessed 2022, Dec 23 from https://www.georgiaencyclopedia.org/articles/arts-culture/snake-handlers/. "The history of snake-handling churches extends back to the early 1900s in East Tennessee. Tradition attributes the practice to George Went Hensley, a rural preacher working near Cleveland, Tennessee, around 1909. From about 1910 to 1920 snake handling was widespread in the Church of God based in Cleveland, but by the end of the 1920s the denomination had renounced the practice. From then on, it existed only in independent churches in Appalachia."

[517] Branham, William. 1953, September 7. Lord, Show Us the Father and It Sufficeth Us (53-0907A). "But Brother Davis walked up to the platform. We got a notary public's statement on this. He walked up there. He said, 'Christian people,' about two or three thousand setting there, he said, 'I'm twenty-five years old.' He said, 'I'm a minister of the Gospel,' and he said, 'I–I know that my God is able to deliver me from that,' but said, 'nevertheless, if He does or does not, I'll never let that infidel stand there with that in his hand and challenge God's Word.' He said, 'I'll meet you in glory.'"

[518] Old Church on Watt Street has a Vexed History. 1931, Aug 08. Jeffersonville Evening News P 1.

Tennessee.[519]   That initiative quickly accelerated after an angry mob in Jeffersonville rose in opposition to Davis over a family estate. One of his wealthy converts died, and Davis claimed to have been written into her last will and testament shortly prior to her demise. When the family of Miss Laura Eaken objected, Davis sued[520] several church members, other churches, and even the cemetery in Jeffersonville.[521]   Coincidentally, during the course of the legal proceedings, Davis's church and printing presses burned to the ground.[522]   Davis left town, and began seeking to find another location for the headquarters of his sect.[523]   After his leaving Jeffersonville, the Indiana church body remained a satellite church under his leadership and gathered in the local Masonic temple.[524] Leadership in the church transitioned to William

---

[519] May Move Church Seat. 1934, May 15. The Commercial Appeal. "National headquarters of the Pentecostal Baptist Church may be moved from Jeffersonville, Ind., to Memphis, the Rev. Roy E. Davis, overseer, said yesterday."

[520] Rev. Roy Davis Sues to Claim Eaken Estate. 1934, Mar 30. Jeffersonville Evening News.

[521] 1934, Apr 17. Roy E. Davis vs. Et.al. Clark County Courthouse.

[522] Misc. News. 1934, Apr 3. Jeffersonville Evening News. "the city referred to City Attorney Warder a request that city authorities refuse to issue a permit for rebuilding the First Pentecostal Baptist church on Watt Street near Maple Street. The church recently was burned down. Seventeen property owners of the vicinity of the church site, who signed the petition, aver that rebuilding the church as it was before would create a dangerous fire hazard by reason of the proximity of the frame structure to other buildings."

[523] May Move Church Seat. 1934, May 15. The Commercial Appeal. "National headquarters of the Pentecostal Baptist Church may be moved from Jeffersonville, Ind., to Memphis, the Rev. Roy E. Davis, overseer, said yesterday."

[524] Branham, William. 1961, Aug 6. The Seventieth Week of Daniel. [NOTE THAT BRANHAM'S TIMELINE IS INCORRECT]: "Now, in 1933, when we were worshipping over here in the Masonic temple, where the church of Christ stands today, on one April morning, before leaving home, I was dedicating my car (I got a '33 model car, and I was dedicating it to the Lord's service.), and in a vision, I saw the end time (Now notice how striking this is, back yonder when I was just a boy, and you can imagine what a 1933 model car looked like, now, what it looked like.), and I went over there to the Masonic temple, where, some of you old-timers in here remembers, it's wrote down on old paper at home, it's already in print and went out around the world, see, that was in 1933, and I predicted that there would be some great tragedy happen to this United States before, or, by the year of 1977."

Branham[525]. From that point, William Branham's advance in his circle of influence moved very quickly.

In 1934, from a tent erected on 8th and Pratt Street, Branham held revivals with Cincinnati Pentecostal leader Frank Curts.[526] Days later, Branham attended the 1934 General Assembly held September 17-23 at Pentecostal Bishop G. B. Rowe's church in Mishawaka, Indiana.[527] Branham announced himself as a "Baptist" in the meeting,[528] representing the Pentecostal Baptist Church of God sect. The assembly was discussing the unification of several Pentecostal groups,[529] with delegates from each Pentecostal sect representing their group for the merger. For Davis, placing Branham in the meeting would have been strategic, though for one reason or another Davis's Pentecostal sect never officially joined the United Pentecostal Church International.

By October of 1935, Branham had gained thirty converts and began preaching from a building Branham called his

---

[525] Branham, William. 1964, April 27. A Trial (64-0427). "then, about seventeen years after that, I was, had become a minister, a Baptist preacher, of the Missionary Baptist Church. Dr. Roy E. Davis ordained me as one of the local pastors, give me rights then, by the state, to marry, bury, baptize, so forth. And the Missionary Baptist Church burned down, which I was assistant pastor, at the time. And Mr. Davis come back to Texas, which he was of Davis mountains, and—and down near Van Horn, Texas. That's where they come from. And so, while he was gone, I started to take over the congregation. Got a tent, and I begin to preach in the city, and just a boy preacher."

[526] Misc. news. 1934, Aug 15. Jeffersonville Evening News. "The Rev. Curts of Cincinnati Ohio will preach Wednesday evening at 7:45 at Pranham (sig) Pentecostal Tabernacle, 8th and Pratt streets"

[527] Wade, Bernie H. 2021. The Apostolic Faith & Pentecostal Timetable of Key Events 1930-1040 Volume 4. Accessed 2021, Dec 3 from https://issuu.com/charismata/docs/apostolic_faith_and_pentecostal_tim_f1466ac0c35c7 7. "General Assembly held at Bishop G. B. Rowe's church. William Branham reportedly visited this meeting driving a panel truck with advertisements about his 'healing revivals'. Later Branham would claim this is where he first saw Pentecostalism."

[528] Branham, William. 1958, May. The Eagle Stirring Her Nest. "Why, I remember the first Pentecostal meeting I ever went into; it was at Mishawaka, Indiana. And they had about five hundred preachers on the platform. And they said, 'We want every man up here, just to stand up and say what church he belongs to, what his name is.' And I just stood up and said, 'Evangelist William Branham, Baptist,' set down."

[529] Branham, William. 1959, Apr 19. My Life Story. "Well, it come my time, I said, "William Branham, Baptist. Jeffersonville, Indiana." Walked by. 155 I'd hear all the rest of them call themselves, "Pentecostal, Pentecostal, Pentecostal, P.A. of W., P.A.J.C., P.A.W., P…"

"tabernacle", which was located at a local arbor[530] owned by Roy Davis's brother Dan[531] on Eighth and Graham streets.[532] In 1936, the group purchased the adjacent grounds on Eighth and Penn streets to form the "Billie Branham Pentecostal Tabernacle",[533] which would be the revival headquarters for several decades, and later would be renamed the Branham Tabernacle.[534] He had held some services at that location as early as August, 1935,[535] suggesting the congregation used two buildings while the Billie Branham Pentecostal Tabernacle was being completed. Audiences were entertained with an *"anthem by choir of 25 voices"*,[536] a stringed band,[537] an orchestra,[538] an award-winning band,[539] and *"plenty of fans"*.[540] Newspapers also advertised healing revivals at the Billie Branham Pentecostal Tabernacle in 1936,[541] which would become a theme for Branham's revival meetings and eventually for

---

[530] Baptized Church of God Pentecostal. 1933, Jul 8. Jeffersonville Evening News. "every night at 8th and Graham streets, plenty of safe parking anywhere on the lot, all services will be held at the arbor except Thursday morning which will meet at the hall."

[531] Baptized Church of God Pentecostal. 1933, Jun 24. Jeffersonville Evening News. "we have decided to postpone construction of our arbor at Eighth and Graham.

[532] Revival at Tabernacle. 1935, Oct 2. Jeffersonville Evening News. "The Rev. William "Billy" Branham Sunday began a Revival at his Eighth and Graham Street tabernacle which already has claimed thirty converts, according to the tabernacle workers."

[533] Warranty Deed. 1936, Nov 9. (Billie Branham Pentecostal Tabernacle Deed)

[534] 1945, Oct 13. Jeffersonville Evening News P 3. (First Mention of Branham Tabernacle). "Branham Tabernacle, the Rev. William Branham, pastor"

[535] Jeffersonville Evening News Aug 17, 1935. Pentecostal Tabernacle. 8th and Penn St. Rev. Wm. Branham, Pastor.

[536] 1936, Jun 13. Jeffersonville Evening News P 4.

[537] 1939, Jun 03. Jeffersonville Evening News P 3. "Evening worship and sermon in charge of pastor, assisted by choir and stringed band."

[538] 1937, Jun 05. Jeffersonville Evening News P 3. "The Henryville Orchestra will be feature of the Sunday Evening services of the Pentecostal Tabernacle, Eighth and Penn streets."

[539] 1936, Jul 10. Jeffersonville Evening News P 4. "Our choir will sing one of the songs they won the contest at Carwood Tuesday evening the 7th.

[540] 1936, Jul 10. Jeffersonville Evening News P 4. "We have plenty of fans, so come spend the evening with the Lord."

[541] 1936, Sep 19. Jeffersonville Evening News P 4. "Our revival is still going on. We have had 57 conversions this week. Tuesday night had 26 conversions and 18 people healed."

the Post WWII healing revival.[542] Branham's Pentecostal Tabernacle held almost constant revival meetings, both in the Eighth and Graham Tabernacle[543] and later the tabernacle on Eighth and Penn streets. By 1937, the Billie Branham Pentecostal Tabernacle was holding *"indefinite"* revival services every single night.[544]

In 1940, Branham began planting satellite churches[545] for the Pentecostal Baptist Church of God, one of which appears to have been a collaborative effort with E. Howard Cadle. When the pastor of the Milltown, Indiana Baptist church was involved in a gun battle and left the church vacant,[546] Branham and Cadle filled the void.[547] Branham held revivals throughout Indiana for the Pentecostal Baptist Church of God, quickly becoming Indiana's face for Davis's sect. As late as 1953, long after Branham's focus shifted

---

[542] The healing revival 1947-1958 - An Overview. Accessed 2022, May 27 from https://www.revival-library.org/revival_histories/neo_pentecostal/healing_revival/general_introduction.shtml . "William Branham is the person universally acknowledged as the revival's 'father.'"

[543] Revival At Tabernacle.
Jeffersonville Evening News Oct 2, 1935. "The Rev. William 'Billy' Branham Sunday began a revival at his Eighth and Graham Street tabernacle."

[544] Revival Services at Pentecostal.
1937, Oct 13. Jeffersonville Evening News P 1. "Revival services at the Pentecostal Tabernacle, 804 Penn Street, are being held each night, at 7 o'clock, by the Rev. William Branham, pastor of the church, it was announced. The meetings, which are open to the public, will be held for an indefinite period, it was stated."

[545] Rev. Branham to Leave for Summer. 1940, Apr 29. Jeffersonville Evening News. "The Rev. William Branham, pastor of Pentecostal Tabernacle, 8th and Penn Streets, has vacated his pulpit for the summer, to devote his time to a series of evangelistic engagements, it was announced. During his absence, the Rev. N. C. Guthrie, of Louisville, will officiate at the local church."

[546] Branham, William. 1950, August 16. Looking To the Unseen (50-0816). "He said, 'Well, something went wrong here years ago. A minister got in some trouble, and there was a big shooting scrape.' And said, 'The church went down, and the—the church people turned it over to the city. They just have funeral services." I went up towards the door. And as I went towards the door, it seemed better. I tried to open the door, and it wouldn't open. And I–I said, "You go ahead. I'll wait here at the steps till you come back.' When he went up on the hill, I knelt down. I said, 'Lord, if this is the place You want me, you want me to hold a meeting here, open this door for me. Open the door.'"

[547] Branham, William. 1953, December 13. What Think Ye of Christ? (53-1213M). "A bosom friend of mine down from Milltown, Indiana, where I pastored a little old Baptist church down there. I'd say, 'Brother Cadle, I want you this morning, in the face of the Philadelphian Church, tell me Who you think the Son of God is?"

to the Latter Rain Movement, Branham held revivals under the auspices of the Pentecostal Baptists.[548]   To the general public, however, Branham presented himself as a minister ordained in the Southern Baptist Convention.[549]

His criminal past and his Pentecostal ordination were not the only aspects of Branham's ministry that were strategically hidden from public view while gaining new converts. Having been trained in a church planted by the Klan's second highest ranking official,[550] Branham had also been trained in the religious propaganda to be spread using Pentecostalism as the vehicle. Branham quickly rose to become the most influential evangelist for the Klan's Christian Identity doctrine, which Branham covertly introduced without mentioning race, under the name "Serpent's Seed Doctrine". Similar to the official white supremacy doctrine, Branham trained his listeners to believe that the Original Sin in the Garden of Eden was a sexual union between Eve and the serpent and traced the resulting bloodline through Noah's son Ham, believed to be the origin of people with black skin by many fundamentalists.[551] This bloodline, according to Branham, could be traced all the way through time to Judas Iscariot.

> *Notice, now, the devil come down and got into the serpent. And he found Eve in the garden of Eden, naked, and he talked about the fruit in the midst. The midst means "middle," and so forth; you understand, in a mixed congregation. And he said, "Now, it's pleasant. It's good to the eyes." What did he*

---

[548] ex: 1953, June 11. Dearborn County Register. "quite a few from here attended the Pentecostal Baptist revival in Connersville last week. The minister was the Rev. William Branham."

[549] Branham, William. 1954, Dec 3. "I was converted and joined an–a Baptist church which I was licensed and ordained under the Missionary Baptist church, in a Southern Baptist convention."

[550] Knights Flaming Sword Asked to Lay Down Arms. 1925, Jan 19. Chattanooga Daily Times. "Believing I was entitled to the honor of the second degree I went to the colonel's home and while visiting with him was raised to the second degree and that day made his personal representative."

[551] Braude, Benjamin. 1997. The Sons of Noah and the Construction of Ethnic and Geographical Identities in the Medieval and Early Modern Periods

do? He begin making love to Eve, and he lived with her, as a husband. And she saw it was pleasant, so she went and told her husband, but she was already pregnant, by Satan. And she brought forth her first son, whose name was Cain, the son of Satan.[552]

Notice this now. And out of there, then, come Ham, Ham with his wife, and them. He had a curse put on him. From Ham come Nimrod, who built Babylon. Out of Babylon come the Catholic church, the beginning of it. Come on down through Ahab. Come on down from Ahab, into Judas Iscariot; wound it up, the antichrist.[553]

Though Branham admitted that he first learned the doctrine from elders in Roy E. Davis's church,[554] and frequently denied teaching the doctrine,[555] [556] Branham was instrumental in broadcasting the racist Christian Identity Doctrine to the masses. Privately, Branham taught the racist version to his elders, and they spread it through their own ministries. Branham's close associate and leader of the "sister church"[557] in Southern Indiana, Raymond Jackson, openly taught the Christian Identity doctrine.

---

[552] Branham, William. 1958, Sep 28. The Serpent's Seed.

[553] Branham, William. 1958, Sep 28. The Serpent's Seed.

[554] Branham, William. 1957, Oct 6. Questions and Answers #3. "Now, it's been said…And I hope that my colored friends that's in here will excuse this remark, because it's absolutely not right. The first time I ever met anyone in my life, after I had been converted…I was…met Brother George DeArk and them down there. And I was walked, and the Lord led me to a little place. And they was discussing where the colored man came from. And they were trying to say that the colored man…That Cain married an animal like an ape, and through there come forth the colored race. Now, that's wrong! Absolutely, that's wrong! And don't never stand for that."

[555] Branham, William. 1959, Jun 28. Questions and Answers. "Brother Branham: Would you please explain your theory that Eve conceived Cain of the devil? 172 I never said that; I said Eve conceived Cain of the serpent."

[556] Branham, William. 1957, Oct 6. Questions and Answers on Hebrews #3. "Adam and Eve was the father and mother, earthly, of every living creature of human beings that's ever been on the earth."

[557] Branham, William. 1959, Dec 16. What Is the Holy Ghost. "Brother Junie Jackson is pastor, and also out on the highway where Brother Ruddell is pastor), we and they're, sister churches of this tabernacle."

CHAPTER 13

JOEL'S ARMY

❖

"Joel's Army believers are hard-core Christian dominionists, meaning they believe that America, along with the rest of the world, should be governed by conservative Christians and a conservative Christian interpretation of biblical law. There is no room in their doctrine for democracy or pluralism." - Southern Poverty Law

In the months leading up to the Great Sedition Trial of 1944, the world watched as Gerald B. Winrod and twenty-nine others were exposed for antisemitism and opposition to the war with Germany and undermining the morale of the United States Armed Forces.[558] While all attention was on the thirty defendants, however, the movement shifted to covert religious operations. Gerald Winrod's Nazi version of the British Israel theology had a strong influence on Pentecostals and Fundamentalists nationwide, especially in Los Angeles. Los Angeles was the headquarters for the Western Gau, or western district, of the German American Bund.

The Bund was an attempt by Germans to "Nazify" German Americans and build support for the Third Reich, and in many

---

[558] Sedition Trial of 1944. Accessed 2022, Dec 28 from https://digital-library.csun.edu/in-our-own-backyard/sedition-trial-of-1944. On January 3, 1944, thirty opponents of American involvement in the war against Germany went to trial for charges of violating the Smit Act of 1940. The charges stemmed from their involvement in fascist movements and from cooperation with German forces. The defendants opposed war against Germany and espoused rabid anti-Semitism. A high percentage of the defendants came from California, including Noble, Jones, Schwinn and Diebel.

ways, it was aligned with Winrod's agenda. The group originated in Chicago in 1933 as "The Friends of New Germany" to support the National Socialist Party and Teutonia Society. In 1936, the group reorganized as the German American Bund and established three geographic districts, or "Gaus", one of which was in Los Angeles.[559]   Though the group had limited success, the Nazi influence upon British Israelism was profound. As the doctrine transitioned to Christian Identity, it became far more extreme.[560]

This was especially the case within Angelus Temple, where Wesley Swift began originating the Christian Identity Doctrine. Swift was trained in the Angelus Temple Bible School and became an Angelus Temple minister during the time that Angelus Temple openly supported the British Israel doctrine of Gerald Winrod. The doctrine was so prevalent that Aimee Semple McPherson appointed Winrod as her replacement when she became too ill to continue preaching.[561]   To say that Angelus Temple offered support to

---

[559]   German American Bund. Accessed 2023, Jan 16 from https://digital-library.csun.edu/in-our-own-backyard/german-american-bund. "The Bund began as the Friends of New Germany in Chicago in 1933. This group traced its roots to the Teutonia Society and National Socialist Party, both active in the United States during the 1920s. The success of the Third Reich fueled the organization's rapid growth. In 1936, the Friends regrouped as the German American Bund, an organization espousing to be "100% American." They professed to be for "constitution, flag and a white gentile ruled, truly free America." The Bund had two goals: to establish an effective power base by "Nazifying" the German American community and to sway American public opinion in favor of the New Germany. The Bund divided the country into three geographic districts, or "Gaus," with Los Angeles as the headquarters of the Western Gau."

[560] Berger, J. M. Extremist Construction
of Identity:
How Escalating Demands for
Legitimacy Shape and Define InGroup and Out-Group Dynamics. Accessed 2023, Jan 16 from https://icct.nl/app/uploads/2017/04/ICCT-Berger-Extremist-Construction-of-Identity-April-2017-2.pdf. "This Research Paper examines how the white supremacist movement Christian Identity emerged from a non-extremist forerunner known as
British Israelism. By examining ideological shifts over the course of nearly a century, the paper seeks to identify key pivot points in the movement's shift toward extremism and explain the process through which extremist ideologues construct and define in-group and out-group identities."

[561] Aimee Ignores Protests Filed: Self-Styled U. S. Fascist to Occupy Pulpit at Angelus Temple. 1938. Nov 13. El Paso Times. "Dr. Gerald B. Winrod, self-professed American Fascist, will occupy the pulpit at Aimee Semple McPherson's Angelus Temple despite

Winrod would be quite an understatement; Winrod's leadership of the Angelus Temple led to anti-Nazi protests and bomb threats.[562] When asked why the "Kansas Hitler/Jayhawk Nazi" was given temporary control of Angeles Temple, Foursquare leader Giles Knight said that *"Sister McPherson and I knew exactly what we were doing when we invited Dr. Winrod to occupy the pulpit of Angelus Temple"*[563]

Interestingly, it was shortly after Winrod's engagement that William Branham's campaign manager Gordon Lindsay was appointed to "field position work" for the Angelus Temple.[564] together with his wife Freda, who was a student in Angelus Temple with Wesley Swift,[565] Gordon and Freda worked as a husband-and-wife evangelistic team. They also co-pastored a Foursquare Church.[566] Lindsay toured Canada holding British Israel conferences, helping to spread Winrod's agenda in the years leading up to the healing revival. During the 1940 Anglo-Saxon Christian World Movement Convention in Vancouver, Lindsay was the keynote speaker.[567] Lindsay's district was adjacent to

---

protests of labor and anti-Nazi groups, Giles M. Knight, business manager of the Temple, said tonight. 'Sister McPherson and I knew exactly what we were doing when we invited Dr. Winrod to occupy the pulpit of Angelus Temple," Knight said".

[562] Kansas Pastor Preaches at Angelus Temple Despite Bomb Threats. 1938, Nov 14. Hollywood Citizen News.

[563] Aimee Ignores Protests Filed: Self-Styled U. S. Fascist to Occupy Pulpit at Angelus Temple. 1938. Nov 13. El Paso Times.

[564] Rev. Forsberg Arrives Here. 1939, February 9. The Tacoma Times. "Rev. Lindsay has been appointed to do field extension work for the Four-Square Organization in Montana under the supervision of Dr. Harold Jefferies of Portland, field supervisor of Four-Square Churches in the Northwest."

[565] Joy of Faith Marks Pentecostal School. 2006, May 1. Post Star. "The school's all-male board asked Lindsay's wife, Freda, to take over. She had been a partner in her husband's work, and as a young woman attended a school run by Aimee Semple McPherson, the famous female Pentecostal evangelist."

[566] Foursquare Church. 1938, August 28. The Tacoma News Tribune. "Rev. and Mrs. Gordon Lindsay, co-pastors"

[567] Anglo-Saxon Christian Movement Convention Opens -- United Church Council Meets Soon. 1940, August 17. The Province. " Rev. Gordon Lindsay of Portland, Oregon, will deliver the address. {...} Questions will be answered followed by discussion. Public meetings to be held Sunday, Monday, Tuesday and Thursday evenings. Mr. G. Fred Johnson, Rev. Gordon Lindsay"

Saskatchewan, where the Latter Rain Revival broke out in North Battleford at the Angelus Temple-funded Sharon Orphanage.

The Anglo-Saxon Christian World Movement, though likely not intended to be supportive of white supremacy from its inception, had attracted several white supremacy leaders by the time Lindsay was involved. One key figure of interest was Vancouver's Rev. Clem Davies. Davies was very public in his support of white supremacy, openly inviting British Israel representatives to speak at his Centennial Church. Davies widely advertised his sermons, many of which were fully aligned with Gerald Winrod's apocalyptic teaching of the coming race war.[568] Davies had been supportive of the Klan since the 1920s, weaponizing his sermons against non-white immigrants and threatening violence from the Klan.[569] He also had ties back to Los Angeles through Full Gospel Businessman's Fellowship International founder Demos Shakarian and the Kardashian family[570] — the same family that sponsored William Branham's early revivals.[571]

Leaders in the white supremacy movement were forced to go underground and organize under countless false fronts —

---

[568] "Milestones to Armageddon" - Lecture by Dr. Clem Davies. 1940, Nov 16. The Vancouver.

[569] Roy, Patricia. The Oriental Question: Consolidating a White Man's Province. "Late in 1924 Davies gave a sermon on 'British or Oriental Columbia — which?' Two thousand people, including many MLAs, attended while others heard him over the radio warn that the Ku Klux Klan was growing in the province and would "take the law into its own hands unless legislators realized the gravity of the economic and oriental problems."

[570] Oppenheimer, Jerry. 2017. The Kardashians. "Earlier, in the late forties, Robert and Tom's grandfather, Tatos Kardashian, then the family patriarch who dominated the Kardashian household, had helped sponsor and pledged to build a temple in Los Angeles for an Armenian faith healer and mystic, twenty-year-old robed and bearded Avak Hagopian. For a time, Kardashian had actually teamed up with another financial backer of the mystic, one Clem Davies, an avowed anti-Semite, whose books included such titles as The Racial Streams of Mankind, What Is Anglo-Israel? and Pre-Adamic Races. He was known as a member of the Christian Identity Movement, using strange interpretations of biblical scripture to "prove" white superiority and to demonize Jews."

[571] Branham, William. 1947, Nov 2. The Angel of God. "They flew a boy, who prays for the sick, by the name of Avak. They brought him from Cairo over to pray for a man by the name of Arakelian. The same time they sent for him, they sent up in Indiana and had me to come to a woman with cancer."

making the already secretive organizations even more clandestine.[572] One of the more interesting false fronts for white supremacy was the use of children's orphanages. There is some evidence that leaders in white supremacy were indoctrinating children with antisemitic, anti-Catholic, anti-black ideologies by hiding under the disguise of children's orphanages. It was very easy to do; the Klan had been establishing orphanages since the 1920s. The Klan Haven Orphanage in Little Rock, for example, was owned and operated by the *Women of the Ku Klux Klan*.[573] In the fall of 1925, another was organized in Little Rock, though it never fully opened its doors when the Klan began to implode.[574] Regardless, others were successful at both establishing the orphanage and raising large sums of money to fund Klan operations.[575]

---

[572] In the bombing's aftermath, don't abandon the Bill of Rights. 2005, Oct 3. Tampa Bay Times. "Too many Americans remain unaware of the Nazi-style white supremacy movement in our country. It has gone through many permutations in the past years, thus succeeding in masking its true face with innocuous-seeming false fronts. Through it all, its leaders continue to surface and to network, forming new groups and alliances as the old, discredited organizations are dismantled following criminal prosecutions and heavy money judgments in the civil courts."

[573] Klan Haven Orphanage. Accessed 2023, Jan 5 from https://encyclopediaofarkansas.net/entries/klan-haven-orphanage-17991/. "The Klan Haven (or Klanhaven) Orphanage in Little Rock (Pulaski County) was operated by the Women of the Ku Klux Klan in 1925 and 1926 to care for orphaned children of Klansmen and Klanswomen."

[574] Klan Haven Orphanage. Accessed 2023, Jan 5 from https://encyclopediaofarkansas.net/entries/klan-haven-orphanage-17991/. "In the fall of 1925, Klansmen and Klanswomen in Fort Smith (Sebastian County) had announced plans to build the Arkansas Protestant Orphanage in that city. A board of trustees was established, including men and women, and the board appointed as director the Reverend John Moore, a professional Klan lecturer and former pastor of First Baptist Church of Pine Bluff (Jefferson County). By the end of the year, however, plans for this orphanage were abandoned and contributions returned to donors."

[575] The Colorado Women of the Ku Klux Klan. 1921, Apr 14. Accessed 2023, Jan 5 from https://www.historycolorado.org/story/2021/04/14/colorado-women-ku-klux-klan. Records indicate that the club was able to amass $15,000 in Cotton Mills savings bonds designated to build a Protestant boarding school for orphans next to Cotton Mills Stadium.16 This orphanage was meant to keep orphan children out of Catholic-supported orphanages.17

While Lindsay, Davies, Winrod, and others worked the Anglo-Saxon conferences to "educate" Christians in the antisemitic British Israel doctrine, William Branham's mentor Roy E. Davis and his partner William D. Upshaw[576] began enacting plans to open a children's orphanage and school in Upland, California, just outside of Los Angeles.[577] Davis posed as an FBI agent, with former Congressman and Klansman William D. Upshaw confirming his claim.[578] Upshaw, an active part of the school, was indoctrinating children into "Americanism"[579] — the Klan's loaded language for white supremacy. Their orphanage scheme would ultimately fail when donors discovered two sets of accounting books and misuse of funds, but it was not the only orphanage of interest.

While Roy E. Davis and William D. Upshaw were setting up their base of operations in San Bernardino collecting money for the Ussher-Davis Children's orphanage that fronted their work towards sparking the Third Wave of the Ku Klux Klan, and while Swift was working with Detroit pastor and pro-Nazi, Gerald L. K. Smith, to revive the Ku Klux Klan in California,[580] and while William Branham was transitioning the Pentecostal Baptist Church of God sect from a Pentecostal group to operate under the disguise of a Baptist newly discovering Pentecostalism, Rev. Herrick Holt began his operation in Canada. Holt was a minister in Aimee Semple

---

[576] Orphanage Benefactor Questioned, Pictured as 'Disillusioned'; Funds Raising Investigated. 1944, Feb 20. The San Bernardino County Sun. "She said she had met Davis through William D. Upshaw, evangelist and former congressman from Georgia, and had given or loaned Davis $8,600 of her life savings."

[577] Orphanage, School at Upland Slated to Open Sept 15. 1943, Aug 8. The San Bernardino County Sun.

[578] Witnesses Say Davis Claimed to Be F.B.I. Man. 1944, Apr 22. The San Bernardino County.

[579] Orphanage, School at Upland Slated to Open Sept 15. 1943, Aug 8. The San Bernardino County Sun. "Former Representative William D. Upshaw is taking an active part in the organization of the institution and is to be in charge of the department of Americanism."

[580] Fiery Cross Burning Again: Ku Klux Klan out in open in California. 1946, Apr 6. Daily News. "Rev. Wesley Swift admits his membership in revived Klan: Posing before hunting trophy in Lancaster home, he names Gerald L. K. Smith as national leader."

McPherson's Foursquare Church sect,[581] and with a handful of other men, was raising funds to erect the orphanage in North Battleford, Saskatchewan.

The Sharon Orphanage was officially announced in October of 1943,[582] and the Davis/Upshaw orphanage in September of 1943.[583] Both orphanages were "faith funded", and both had plans to include a school that was isolated from the public-school system. By May of 1944, the Sharon Orphanage project had doubled in expense to a half million dollars.[584] In today's money, that is 8.6 million dollars.[585] In September of the same year, Herrick Holt announced his plans to purchase the Mounted Police barracks, along with 2,000 acres for the orphanage and connected facilities.[586] In just a few years, the Sharon Orphanage would become the epicenter of the birth of the Latter Rain movement.

Among the men who worked with Holt to establish the Sharon Orphanage was Rev. George R. Hawtin, frequent speaker at the Foursquare Elim Tabernacle[587] — a church that hosted Foursquare leader Aimee Semple McPherson and which strongly

[581] Foursquare Heads Named. 1943, Aug 18. The Province. "Aimee Semple McPherson and Giles N. Knight, both here from Los Angeles ... Other Canadian provincial superintendents appointed were Rev. Herrick Holt, North Battleford."

[582] Orphanage Scheme Under Way at North Battleford. 1943, Oct 30. Star Phoenix

[583] Old Upland Health Resort to Be Dedicated to Use as Orphanage. 1943, Sep 14. Pomona Progress Bulletin. "The former Mount Victor health resort property at the north end of Euclid Avenue will be dedicated Wednesday to operation as an orphanage by the Ussher-Davis Foundation, Inc., according to Roy E. Davis Sr., president and managing director of the new enterprise and pastor of the Upland Missionary Baptist church".

[584] North Battleford to Get Orphanage and School. 1944, May 13. Star Phoenix. "Proposals for an orphanage and trade school, that with affiliated farms and an irrigation project, will represent a $500,000 venture, were outlined to the city council Monday night by Rev. Eric Holt."

[585] $500,000 in 1943 is worth $8,604,364.16 today. Accessed 2022, Dec 27 from https://www.in2013dollars.com/us/inflation/1943?amount=500000.

[586] Prem. T. C. Douglas Inspects Northern Mental Hospital. 1944, Sep 5. Star Phoenix. And heard representations from Rev. H. Holt regarding the acquisition of the old Mounted Police barracks site to be used in conjunction with 2000 acres of irrigated land in the vicinity for the establishment of an orphanage and trade school."

[587] ex: Elim Tabernacle. 1944, Dec 2. Star Phoenix. "Speaker: Rev. George R. Hawtin".

supported her.[588] Hawtin was a strong supporter of Wesley Swift's Christian Identity doctrine, to the extent that he even published books on the subject. Hawtin's book, *The Living Creature: Origin of the Negro*, got him in quite a bit of trouble in later years when Hawtin was exposed as a racist. Hawtin helped establish the religious views of the orphanage and Bible school, producing students trained in the Christian Identity doctrine and End of Days theology.

> *George Hawtin of Battleford, Sask., issued a written apology for distributing the 40-page booklet after a complaint about it to the Saskatchewan Human Rights Commission. Entitled "The Living Creature: Origin of the Negro", the booklet says God created a superior race of whites who are meant to rule. Blacks were created "in God's wisdom" to serve whites, it says.[589]*

Building upon Winrod's propaganda of the communist threat to the religious and political systems of the United States, leaders of the Sharon Orphanage also began training students to believe and teach that Communism had infiltrated the Christian faith resulting in *"cold formal churches"* and had infiltrated the government systems. Students of the Sharon Orphanage believed that their "non-apostate" form of worship was soon to be under attack.[590] In many ways the group was recreating a Pentecostal version of the Hitler Youth. It was very clear that the Sharon orphanage was being used to indoctrinate children into Pentecostalism. Considering the fact that Former Congressman and

---

[588] Collapse of the Conspiracy: A Review of the case Against Mrs. McPherson. 1927, Apr 1. The Elim Evangel: Foursquare on the Word of God.

[589] A Lesson for Racist. 1989, May 11. The Province

[590] Branham, William. 1949, Dec 25. The Deity of Jesus Christ. Accessed 2020, Sept 8 from http://table.branham.org. "I'm looking forward for a great hour. I see it coming. I see there is no hopes nowhere else. I see the age a moving up. I see the great red lights, of communism, swaying around over the earth. I see the formal churches taking their standard against Your Church, trying to condemn them, saying, 'Divine healing is wrong. It's a bunch of fanaticism.' A bill in our own White House, to close It down. "

Klansman William D. Upshaw oversaw the "Americanism department" in the Los Angeles orphanage,[591] and that Hawtin was spreading the white supremacy doctrines in the Sharon Orphanage, it was clear that both facilities were programming youth for the white supremacy agenda.

As the doctrine continued to develop in the orphanage's Bible school, leaders of the group developed the notion that God would be restoring the biblical roles held by ancients, from apostles to prophets and teachers, with the same authority over the Church as described in the Bible. The result of this thread of doctrine was authoritative control — not only for the leaders of the orphanage, but for all who were connected to them. What came next was doctrinally catastrophic with regards to Christianity. Spearheaded by William Branham,[592] the group repurposed the second chapter of the Book of Joel for their agenda, claiming that they were, in fact, the army of locusts being described by ancient biblical prophecy. The group called themselves the New Order of the Latter Rain, otherwise known as "Joel's Army".

In the Book of Joel, the locust invasion is described as an omen that an Assyrian army to the north may attack Israel if it fails to repent as a nation. But nowhere is the invasion described as an army of God. According to an Assemblies of God position paper: "It is a complete misinterpretation of Scripture to find in Joel's army of locusts a militant, victorious force attacking society and a non-cooperating

---

[591] Orphanage, School at Upland Slated to Open Sept. 15. 1943, Aug 8. "Former Representative William D. Upshaw is taking an active part in the organization of the institution and is to be in charge of the department of Americanism."

[592] Sanchez, Casey. 2008. TODD BENTLEY'S MILITANT JOEL'S ARMY GAINS FOLLOWERS IN FLORIDA. Accessed 2022, Dec 27 from https://www.splcenter.org/fighting-hate/intelligence-report/2008/todd-bentley%E2%80%99s-militant-joel%E2%80%99s-army-gains-followers-florida. "The story of how an ancient insect invasion came to be a rallying flag for 21st-century dominionists begins just after World War II in Canada. Out of a small town in Saskatchewan, a Pentecostal preacher named William Branham spearheaded a 1948 revival in which he claimed that his followers lived in a new biblical time of 'Latter Rain.'"

*Church to prepare the earth for Christ's millennial reign."
The story of how an ancient insect invasion came to be a
rallying flag for 21st-century dominonists begins just after
World War II in Canada. Out of a small town in
Saskatchewan, a Pentecostal preacher named William
Branham spearheaded a 1948 revival in which he claimed
that his followers lived in a new biblical time of "Latter
Rain."[593] - Southern Poverty Law Center*

Further expanding the works of Winrod, Swift, and others,
William Branham introduced the notion that God would "Manifest
Himself" into specific individuals in the last days, empowering
members of Latter Rain who achieved "perfection" to become *"like
gods"*.[594] Branham's Manifested Sons of God doctrine enabled
authoritative control far beyond what Hawtin could have ever
dreamed; men in spiritual authority under the Latter Rain's
religious hierarchy were revered as deities to those under their
manipulation and control. The faculty and students of the Sharon
Orphanage became *"the principal vehicle"* for spreading key
elements of William Branham's message throughout the United
States and Canada.[595]

---

[593] Sanchez, Casey. 2008. TODD BENTLEY'S MILITANT JOEL'S ARMY GAINS FOLLOWERS IN FLORIDA. Accessed 2022, Dec 27 from https://www.splcenter.org/fighting-hate/intelligence-report/2008/todd-bentley%E2%80%99s-militant-joel%E2%80%99s-army-gains-followers-florida.
[594] Sanchez, Casey. 2008. TODD BENTLEY'S MILITANT JOEL'S ARMY GAINS FOLLOWERS IN FLORIDA. Accessed 2022, Dec 27 from https://www.splcenter.org/fighting-hate/intelligence-report/2008/todd-bentley%E2%80%99s-militant-joel%E2%80%99s-army-gains-followers-florida. "The most sinless and ardent of his flock would be called "Manifest Sons of God." By the next year, the movement was so strong – and seemed so subversive to some – that the Assemblies of God banned it as a heretic cult. But Branham remained a controversial figure with a loyal following; many of his followers believed him to be the end-times prophet Elijah."
[595] 3-The Sharon Orphanage Connection. Accessed 2022, Dec 26 from https://abc-history.blogspot.com/2008/02/before-i-was-born-my-father-ramon-haas.html. "The principal vehicle for carrying some of Branham's message forward was the Sharon Orphanage and Schools in North Battleford, Saskatchewan, Canada. One student at this school was a man named George Hawtin; a man my dad knew personally. I had an opportunity to speak to George Hawtin on the phone not long before he passed away.

Throughout the years, this doctrine proved to be very deadly in the hands of religious leaders such as Jim Jones of Peoples Temple. Jones, an Indiana Pentecostal minister, was a leader in William Branham's sect during his early years as a Latter Rain revivalist.[596] In November of 1978, Jones and over nine hundred members of his cult of personality committed mass suicide by drinking cyanide-laced Kool-Aid. This level of control — control powerful enough to cause his faithful to lay down their own lives — was achieved using the Manifested Sons of God doctrine.

> *I swear to you that, this is that which was spoken by the prophet Joel. This is that which was and is to come. (Voice strengthens and rises) This is your salvation. You are looking at the Temple of the Holy Ghost. You are looking at the body of Jesus Christ. (Cries) Some are in the room, are sick and asleep because they don't discern the body of Christ. They don't understand the Godship degree. Jesus said, we all are gods, and I had to come back to remind you what I told you 2000 years ago. I'm on the scene to tell you, ye are gods. And not take it away. Won't let you take it away. So don't be judges of the fact, that my people say I am God. Jesus said, ye are gods. Ye all are gods.[597] – Jim Jones*

He was not happy with the outcome of the teachings that emanated from the Sharon Orphanage.

[596] Handwritten Notes of Jim Jones. Accessed 2022, Jul 14. "God sent you to Peoples Temple and you must not release yourself. I know there are things about the Message that you may not see but it is God."

[597] Jones, James. Annotated Transcript Q353. Accessed 2020, May 28 from https://jonestown.sdsu.edu/?page_id=62922.

CHAPTER 14

FRARY VON BLOMBERG

❖

"The Next Day, Baron von Pohl took me to see Hitler, with whom I shook hands." – Baron William Frary von Blomberg

While the Sharon Orphanage operation was underway, William Branham was busy growing the Indiana Pentecostal sect and making critical partnerships for expanding into other states. Branham began shortening the name "Pentecostal Baptist Church of God" to "Baptist", though most of his peers at that time would have realized that he was a Pentecostal minister. Branham sometimes held revivals as "Pentecostal Baptist" revivals.[598] The Great Sedition Trial of 1944 now overturned; Branham started expanding his revival circuits as far as St. Louis.[599] By 1946, William Branham was a common name among Pentecostals in the Midwest. He joined Pentecostal Church Incorporated minister and promoter W. E. Kidson and became the Associate Editor of The Herald of Truth newsletter.[600] Kidson advertised Branham in a column entitled "The Voice of Healing", which would eventually

---

[598] 1953, June 11. Dearborn County Register. "Quite a few here attended the Pentecostal Baptist Revival in Connersville last week. The minister was the Rev. William Branham.

[599] Branham, William. 1945. I Was Not Disobedient to the Heavenly Vision. We arrived in St. Louis at 10:00 A.M. the next morning. We had prearranged to meet the Rev. Daugherty and he was waiting for us. We were then taken to his home where the little sick girl lay. Here I witnessed one of the most heart-breaking scenes."

[600] List of Editors. 1947, May. Herald of Truth. "William Branham ... Associate Editor"

transition into the name of Branham's own publication.[601] Kidson expanded Branham's revival circuit even further, touring with Branham all the way to the West Coast.[602]

Through those 1946 meetings, Branham connected with Demos Shakarian,[603] brother-in-law of Kardashian Family patriarch Tatos Kardashian. Kardashian was a strong supporter[604] of Canadian minister, Klan promoter, and antisemite Clem Davies who helped organized the Anglo-Saxon conventions with Gordon Lindsay. In June of 1947, Branham embarked on a series of revivals that W. E. Kidson had arranged starting in Jonesboro, Arkansas; moving to Vandalia, Illinois; Louisiana, Missouri; Winnipeg, Manitoba; and eventually landing in Saskatoon, Saskatchewan just southeast of the Sharon Orphanage.[605] The revival tour continued into Edmonton, Alberta, and finally landing in Vancouver, British Columbia. Several of the ministers and students from the Sharon Orphanage followed Branham all the way from Saskatchewan to British Columbia, and after returning to North Battleford, began making plans to recreate the Pentecostal excitement that took place at Azusa Street in 1907.[606]

---

[601] The Voice of Healing. 1948, April. Herald of Faith.

[602] The Apostolic Temple - Los Angeles. 1947, May. Herald of Truth. "Recently, while with Brother Branham on the Pacific Coast, I had the privilege of a good visit with Brother Edward F. Smith and his wife. Brother Smith is the pastor of the Apostolic Temple, located at 3715 Whittier Boulevard in Los Angeles,"

[603] Shakarian, Demos. 1963, January. FGBMI Convention.

[604] Oppenheimer, Jerry. The Kardashians. 2017. "Earlier, in the late forties, Robert and Tom's grandfather, Tatos Kardashian, then the family patriarch who dominated the Kardashian household, had helped sponsor and pledged to build a temple in Los Angeles for an Armenian faith healer and mystic, twenty-year-old robed and bearded Avak Hagopian. For a time, Kardashian had actually teamed up with another financial backer of the mystic, one Clem Davies, an avowed anti-Semite, whose books included such titles as The Racial Streams of Mankind, What Is Anglo-Israel? and Pre-Adamic Races. He was known as a member of the Christian Identity Movement, using strange interpretations of biblical scripture to "prove" white superiority and to demonize Jews."

[605] Branham Healing Campaigns. 1947, May. Herald of Truth.

[606] 3 - The Sharon Orphanage. Accessed 2023, Jan 25 from https://abc-history.blogspot.com/2008/02/before-i-was-born-my-father-ramon-haas.html. "In the fall of 1947, a group at the Sharon Orphanage and School; some of whom had personally been at Azusa Street; traveled to Vancouver BC to hear Branham speak. They returned to

In the summer of 1948, thousands of Pentecostals from the United States and Canada — from at least twenty different states — made their way to the Sharon Orphanage and School to participate in the revival.[607] The men began claiming that the revival was an outpouring of *"The Latter Rain"*, referencing the same "Joel's Army" passage from Joel 2 of the Old Testament. As had happened in Los Angeles during the Azusa Street Revival, the religious ecstasy continued for several weeks until it eventually spawned a new religious movement. When the thousands of converts returned home and began spreading the news, curious Pentecostals and revivalists wanting to join in the revival invited men in attendance to come speak in their churches. Branham, one of the main catalysts for the movement, became such a hot commodity that he quickly rose to become the leader of the Post WWII healing revival which was directly connected to the Latter Rain Revival.

At the same time, and largely due to the efforts of his campaign manager, Gordon Lindsay, Branham's Voice of Healing revivals became increasingly popular. As a result, it became very difficult to distinguish the two. Evangelists in the Branham campaigns joined Latter Rain to see what all the excitement was about, while ministers participating in the Latter Rain Revival joined Voice of Healing revivals to learn more about Branham's unusual doctrines. F. F. Bosworth, who had been a leader in John Alexander Dowie's Zion compound and later transitioned to Charles Fox Parham's Parhamite sect with Gordon Lindsay's parents, began touring with Branham and playing the trumpet.[608]

Saskatchewan excited by the new ideas they heard so developed a plan to rebuild the "Latter Rain Movement" that had started at Azusa Street. "

[607] 3 - The Sharon Orphanage. Accessed 2023, Jan 25 from https://abc-history.blogspot.com/2008/02/before-i-was-born-my-father-ramon-haas.html.   "A significant event in the history of Sharon Orphanage and School was its July 7-18, 1948, Camp Meeting, during which thousands of people from Canada and the United States flocked in hopes of receiving something special from God. Residents from at least twenty states attended, and the great Latter Rain Movement burst upon the world."

[608] Branham, William. 1947, November. Fellowship. "At this time, we're going to have a trumpet solo by my good friend, Brother F. F. Bosworth: Brother Bosworth."

Sharon Orphanage, the epicenter of the initial Latter Rain "outpouring", became the same sort of Mecca to the Pentecostal world as the community on Azusa Street in Los Angeles was previously to Pentecostals. Those who were at the initial "outpouring" became heroes of the faith. They were mentors to those who were not at the orphanage during the revival and were viewed as individual conduits to receive the new "blessing". This gave the leaders of Sharon Orphanage and their silent partners a clear advantage; they had trained a number of students at the orphanage and schools with the British Israel and Christian Identity theology. The group was uniquely positioned to control the doctrinal teaching that flowed through Latter Rain since "Joel's Army" made up a large majority of the "original blessing". That theology, heavily influenced by George Hawtin, was perfectly aligned with the leaders at Angelus Temple, Gerald Winrod, Roy Davis, and others. Hawtin and his converts all believed and taught key aspects of the race war theology. In just a few short months, churches all throughout the United States and Canada believed that Christian churches had been infiltrated by "the enemy", had become "cold and formal" like the Catholic Church, and an invasion by Rome and the "Antichrist" would soon bring the End of Days.

At the same time, key figures of the British Israelism and white supremacy ideologies claimed leading roles in the movement. Gordon Lindsay, who had been a leader of the Angelus Temple's Foursquare church during the time Wesley Swift and Gerald Winrod were involved, became Branham's campaign manager — though Branham concealed this fact by describing Lindsay as having been *"from the Assemblies of God"*.[609] Former Congressman and Klansman William D. Upshaw embedded himself in the movement in Los Angeles, and eventually became connected

---

[609] Branham, William. 1947, Dec 7. Experiences. "Brother Lindsay was the campaign manager of the campaign in the north from the Assemblies of God."

to William Branham's ministry through Roy E. Davis.[610] Davis, who was soon to become the Imperial Wizard of the Ku Klux Klan, started claiming to have been bestowed with the gift of divine healing and started preaching at Assembly of God churches in the South.[611] Paul Kopp and the other Angelus Temple evangelists began hosting the Latter Rain revivalists. The connection was so strong that the Angelus Temple was chosen to host Latter Rain leaders at the 50th anniversary of the Azusa Street Revival. Ten thousand were expected to attend — big names such as Oral Roberts, Tommy Hicks, Jack Coe, William Branham, David Nunn, A. C. Valez, Demos Shakarian, and others.[612]

Of the campaign managers involved with William Branham and the Latter Rain revivals, the most interesting by far was William T. Frary, otherwise known as the German Baron William Theobald Frary von Blomberg. Von Blomberg was responsible for organizing many of William Branham's revival meetings overseas — including those held in Germany with Colonia Dignidad leader Paul Schäfer and his close associate, Ewald Frank.

In 1933, Frary was legally adopted by German Baroness Adelhard von Bromberg of Weimar Germany.[613] Frary had been a public relations representative of the World Fellowship of Faiths

---

[610] Branham, William. 1959, Apr 9. Mary's Belief. "But when I walked to the platform, and it happened to be that he knew the old Baptist preacher that ordained me in the Baptist church, Doctor Roy E. Davis. Doctor Davis told him to come, see me when I come to the coast, to have me to pray for him. And he moved in and was setting in his wheelchair. All of a sudden, I saw an old hay frame and a little boy fall, hurt his back, begin to relate just what I was seeing. Someone said, "That's the old congressman setting there, William Upshaw."

[611] Old-Fashioned Revival; Where? In the Assembly of God Church, Granary, Texas. 1950, Mar 16. Hood County News Tablet. "Evangelist R. E. Davis, of Fort Worth {...} Brother Davis has the gift of faith in praying for the sick, and since the bestowal of this gift a little over a year ago."

[612] Top Evangelists to Mark 50th Pentecostal Year; Angelus Temple Services to Commemorate Founding of Azusa Street Mission in 1906.
1956, September 16. The Los Angeles Times.

[613] He's Adopted Baron. 1933, Sep 30. The Evening Independent. "William T. Frary, 26-year-old Boston publicity man, has been transformed into a baron and heir to vast German estates through his legal adoption by the Baroness Adelhard von Bromberg, inset, of Weimar, Germany, and Boston."

working with her. The Baroness, who wished for this work to continue after her death, adopted Frary to become the sole beneficiary of her massive wealth and extensive properties in Weimar.[614] Von Blomberg was the cousin of the Commander-in-chief of the German Army, Werner Von Blomberg, the *"right hand man of Chancellor Hitler"*.[615]

Frary's adoption into direct connections to the German military leadership of the Third Reich was not well received, though. While the young Baron was seen as a rags-to-riches story by those interested in a fairy tale, others viewed the situation with a much healthier level of criticism. A letter from the editor of an Akron newspaper summed it up well:

> *A letter from the Goodwill Industries of America, with offices in Boston, is addressed to me and signed by George L. Burley. It says that the Honorable William Phillips, Under Secretary of State, suggested the letter he sent to me, to ask if I would permit the new Baron Wm. T. Frary von Blomberg to say about 150 words on my broadcast. The Baron is described as the recently adopted son of the Baroness von Blomberg, who is the cousin of the Commander-in-chief of the German Army and "right hand man of Chancellor Hitler." The purpose of the request, one presumes, is to create good will. Among everybody but the oppressed? At any rate, no, no, no, no, no, no, no, no, no, and NO!*[616]

This did not stop Baron von Blomberg from openly declaring his intimate connections with the Third Reich. As the Secretary for the World Fellowship of Faiths and a new member of German nobility, Von Blomberg published a letter describing his

---

[614] Curious Condensations. 1933, Nov 8. The Honolulu Advertiser. "William T. Frary, 26, Boston University graduate and public relations representative of a Boston charitable organization, will become Baron William Frary-von Blomberg and is destined to inherit extensive properties at Weimar, Germany. Through his adoption by the Baroness Adelhard and Eva von Blomberg, of Boston and Germany.

[615] Misc. News. 1933, Dec 27. The Akron Beacon Journal.

[616] Misc. News. 1933, Dec 27. The Akron Beacon Journal.

kinship to Lieutenant General and Minister of Defense, Warner von Blomberg.

My first sight of Germany was at Aachen, where I arrived from Belgium, and I soon had a foretaste there of what the Blomberg name means in Germany.

When I presented my passport to the examining official, he saluted and passed me through without a moment's delay. This was not the case with my fellow travelers, who underwent the regulation grilling.

The whole atmosphere in which I moved was different from anything I ever had experienced before. At home, a citizen is a citizen, whatever his name may be, but in this older country birth and tradition still count for very much.

I reached Berlin just after President von Hindenburg's death, and the whole place seemed under a great pall. The entire country was in mourning. High officials of the state, generals, admirals, foreign ambassadors were preparing to leave for Neudeck to attend the president's funeral.

I went to the headquarters of the Reichswehr, where my adopted mother's cousin, General von Blomberg, is the supreme chief, and presented a letter of introduction from her. An aide took it. That aide gave me a notion of some of the conditions of my new life. Stiff as a ramrod, perfectly courteous, but absolutely official, he bowed from the waist and informed me the general was overwhelmed with work and was preparing to go to Neudeck. The aide seemed to hint I might not be able to see his excellency at all, and I left the building rather heavy in heart.

I returned to my hotel and shortly afterward, a great official car, bearing the arms of the ministry of war, drew up outside. An officer stepped out and invited me to go back. I was taken straight into General von Blomberg's room, where I met him for the first time.

Tall, slim, every inch a member of the aristocratic Prussian officer caste, he made a profound impression upon me. He stood up and looked at me through a monocle. Speaking English, he asked about my foster mother. The thing I liked most about him was that, with great courtesy and tact, he refrained from commenting upon the combination of circumstances which had brought me into his family. He was sizing me up, in fact, and on the whole, I believe, I didn't come out badly under his scrutiny.

I had feared that my liberal views as honorary secretary of the World Fellowship of Faiths might have set the general against me, particularly as the German secretary of our fellowship, a Jewess, had been barred from Germany. Nothing of the sort happened. The general, in fact, offered me the use of an official car in Berlin and told me just to call his office if I wanted anything done.

My first and most dreaded contact with my new family thus passed off happily. My social life in Berlin then began. I went to dinners and luncheons, most of them rather formal. These, too, gave me an insight into my new life. It seems that everyone in Germany spends his nights at the restaurants and beer gardens. It is nearly impossible to obtain a table. The attitude seems to be — spend tonight, for tomorrow — who knows? It is rather a sad gayety.

My next anxious experience was when I met Baron Gustav von Pohl, another new relative of mine, who represented a wing of the family which had strenuously opposed my entry into the clan. But when I met him, he proved to be, not only a courteous gentleman, but a cordial friend. He accepted me without comment.

When I ventured to tell him, I regretted that some of the family had taken an antagonistic attitude toward me, he said, "You must realize that we were somewhat surprised by the action of Tante Trienne (Baroness Blomberg), but a little fight makes for fun and good feeling. You must come and stay with me at Dauchau."

The next day, Baron von Pohl took me to see Hitler, with whom I shook hands. A day or two later, I went to Dauchau, where I spent several days sampling German country life. Such was my introduction to my new life. That I shall like it and adapt myself to it I am quite sure, but my American citizenship still holds good and every year I shall look forward to the months I shall spend in the United States.[617]

- Baron William Theobald Frary von Blomberg.

Von Blomberg was a leader in The International Christian Leadership founded by Abraham Vereide (otherwise known as "The Family"). "The Family" has been labeled as an evangelical Christian cult sponsoring "The National Prayer Breakfast" in Washington, D. C., believed by some to influence key figures in Washington.[618] While many devout Christian men and women attend the Prayer Breakfast with good intentions, critics of "The Family" argue that the event is also used for the purpose of pushing certain agendas to Senators and Congressmen outside of the normal political process.

In 1944, Abraham Vereide founded the International Christian Leadership in Washington, D. C. and served as the executive director until he died in 1965. Baron Frary von

---

[617] Yank Baron Finds Nazis Are Cordial. 1934, Aug 29. Hartford Daily Courant.

[618] Larson, Jonathan. 2021, Sept 3. Bias, theocracy and lies: Inside the secretive organization behind the National Prayer Breakfast. Accessed 2023, Jan 29 from https://www.salon.com/2021/09/03/bias-theocracy-and-lies-inside-the-secretive-organization-behind-the-national-prayer-breakfast_partner/. "More recently, the FBI caught Russian operatives using the breakfast to pursue back-channel connections with U.S. politicians. But despite its dealings with international powers, The Family still enjoys the invisibility to which it attributes its influence."

Blomberg, who sponsored William Branham's international tours overseas, worked with Vereide in the early days of the organization and served as an executive member. Von Blomberg worked as a director for the International Christian Leadership, holding conferences for the group in Finland, Sweden, Norway, Denmark, France, England, Scotland, Ireland, and Wales. Von Blomberg was instrumental in organizing The International Christian Leadership in many of those countries.[619] Interestingly, William Branham's Seattle meetings coincide with the group's work in Seattle before migrating to Washington.[620] Whether Branham was a member of the group since 1946 or not, he openly admitted that von Blomberg sponsored his tours through those countries in the 1950s.[621] After Baron von Blomberg established the offices, Branham began claiming that he had fifteen offices, mentioning specific locations such as Sweden, Finland, Germany, Africa, Norway, Belgium, France, and Canada.[622] The establishment of

---

[619] Christian Leadership Group Organized in Fight on Reds. 1950, May 31. Greenville News. "Baron von Blomberg has been a leader in the International Christian Leadership program for more than five years and recently returned from a speaking tour in Finland, Sweden, Norway, Denmark, France, England, Scotland, Ireland, and Wales. He has held audiences with Prime Minster Attlee of England, the Pope and kings and prime ministers of many countries and have been instrumental in organizing International Christian Leadership groups in the parliaments of many of these countries. the organization was founded 15 years ago by Abraham Vereide, Von Blomberg explained, and added that many United States congressmen and senators are members, including Representative Joseph R. Bryson of Greenville. The Washington group holds weekly breakfast meetings he said."

[620] Branham, William. 1961, April 25. The Godhead Explained (61-0425B). "And so then, finally, it come to a showdown. And that showdown was at Seattle, Washington, about 1946. And one morning I was brought to the hotel lobby, something like this, with a–a breakfast of some ministers. And I had to talk to two main men."

[621] Branham, William. 1954, October 3. The Word Became Flesh (India Trip Report) (54-1003M). "And I could...that met many of the great celebrity of the country on this time, because Baron von Blomberg was with us, he was the manager of the meeting, and well-known by all the monarchs, and potentates, and so forth, of the world. In Lisbon, why, we met the governor of the parliament, had dinner with them. And in Rome, all the dignitaries there."

[622] Branham, William. 1953, May 6. Jesus Christ The Same Yesterday. "Since then, now, we got around about fifteen of those offices across the world: Sweden, Finland, Germany, Africa, Norway, Belgium, France, two in Canada."

those offices coincide with the Latter Rain years of William Branham's ministry.

CHAPTER 15

RICHARD NIXON

❖

"I am sure that this group of people, meeting as you have here and then spreading your influence all over America, into the big cities and small towns do very much to create in the minds and hearts of young people of America, dedication to those great ideals." – Vice President Richard Nixon

On January 25, 1954, foreign ministers representing the United States, Soviet Union, France, and Great Britain met for the first time in five years to resolve their differences over the occupation of Germany and Austria. The United States and Great Britain moved that Germany be unrestricted with free elections, albeit supervised by the United Nations. The Soviets refused to agree, pressuring France, Great Britain, and the United States to invite Communist China to the discussion and restricting free elections.[623] The Berlin Conference ended in stalemate, and tensions between Russia and the United States increased dramatically after it was realized that the Soviets did not want to relinquish control of Eastern Germany. By May of 1954, tensions between the United States and Russia were so high that the Joint Chiefs of Staff Advanced Study Group recommended that the United States consider *"deliberately precipitating war with the Soviet*

---

[623] 1954 Berlin Conference. History Central. Accessed 2023, Jan 26 from https://www.historycentral.com/Europe/4PwrMeeting.html.

Union in the near future.[624] Prior to the Berlin Conference, President Eisenhower considered issuing an ultimatum to the Soviet Union: *"come to terms or risk global nuclear war.*"[625]

The threat was certainly under consideration by Russia. The United States had been investing many resources into improving the nuclear capabilities of the Cold-War era submarines. In July of 1953, the first cruise missile was launched from a submarine, the vessel having been modified to carry the missile with a nuclear warhead.[626] Just days before the Berlin conference, the first nuclear-powered submarine, the USS Nautilus, was launched in Groton, Connecticut.[627] President Eisenhower flexed the muscles of the United States military under Operation Castle when a series of nuclear tests conducted over Bikini Atoll resulted in a successful detonation of a dry fuel thermonuclear bomb. The images of the mushroom cloud created by the detonation instilled such fear of destruction that the images would be used for decades in newspapers, magazines, movies, marketing images, and more.

The problem for Eisenhower, however, had nothing to do with the military. Engaging the United States in war — war that would likely result in nuclear war — would be political suicide. A

---

[624] Field, Alexander. 2014. Schelling, von Neumann, and the Event that Didn't Occur. "In May 1954 the Joint Chiefs of Staff Advanced Study Group recommended that the U.S. consider "deliberately precipitating war with the Soviet Union in the near future". Eisenhower would not go along with that, either, and in the fall of 1954, approved an updated National Security Paper which stated (as had NSC-68) that "the United States and its allies must reject the concept of preventive war or acts intended to provoke war."

[625] Field, Alexander. 2014. Schelling, von Neumann, and the Event that Didn't Occur. "In the spring of 1953, Eisenhower considered but ultimately rejected the recommendation of a high-level study committee headed by retired Air Force General James Doolittle that the Soviet Union be given a two-year ultimatum: come to terms or risk global nuclear war."

[626] Regulus I RGM-6 SSM-N-8. Accessed 2023, Jan 26 from https://www.globalsecurity.org/wmd/systems/regulus1.htm.

[627] USS Nautilus—world's first nuclear submarine—is commissioned. Accessed 2023, Jan 26 from https://www.history.com/this-day-in-history/uss-nautilus-commissioned. "on January 21, 1954, first lady Mamie Eisenhower broke a bottle of champagne across its bow as it was launched into the Thames River at Groton, Connecticut. Commissioned on September 30, 1954, it first ran under nuclear power on the morning of January 17, 1955."

rising number of people in the United States were either strongly opposed to war abroad or sympathetic to the Soviets as it related to keeping guard rails around Germany. To avoid lynching by a political mob, American citizens must not only be convinced to view the Soviets as a threat, but they must also be convinced that if the threat were not erased, it would result in the destruction of their way of life. It was a battle that must be fought in the mind, domestically. Given the power of persuasion flowing through the healing revivals, this was a challenge that was easily met. If the masses could be persuaded to believe certain races and ethnic groups posed a risk to the American way of life as was the case with British Israelism and Christian Identity, then those same doctrines could be adjusted to include Communism — especially if the "prophets" in the movement started including Russia in their "divine revelations". The United States government decided to enlist "Joel's Army".

In May of 1950, Baron von Blomberg organized a meeting at Bob Jones University under the auspices of The International Council for Christian Leadership (The Family) to rally evangelicals against communism. Moreover, Von Blomberg urged students and faculty to spread word that *"All Christian leaders, regardless of their individual faiths, find an increasing need to fight the advance of communism"*.[628] Von Blomberg was on the Board of Trustees for Bob Jones,[629] and his rally would have been seen as more of a directive than a suggestion. Whether that rallying cry was overheard by leaders in Washington, D. C. or inspired by those same leaders, the directive became a central focus for elected officials at the National Prayer Breakfast. In 1954, Vice President Richard Nixon spoke at the Full Gospel Businessmen's Fellowship International meeting in Washington, D.C., instructing Pentecostals at the National Prayer Breakfast to persuade Americans against

---

[628] Christian Leadership Group Organized in Fight on Reds. 1960, May 31. Greenville News.

[629] Christian Leadership Group Organized in Fight on Reds. 1960, May 31. Greenville News. "Baron von Blomberg is a member of the Co-Operating Board of Trustees of Bob Jones University."

Communism as the "battle of the mind". William Branham attended the breakfast[630] which was organized by founder Demos Shakarian.

Vice President Nixon urged the leaders of the healing revivals to use their influence to persuade participants in the revivals that Communism was a rising force against Christianity itself. While Communist Russia certainly posed a threat to world peace, the word "Communism" was loaded language to many of Nixon's listeners. For leaders of the Latter Rain Movement in attendance, this theme was perfectly aligned with British Israelism; they had been claiming for years that the "fraudulent Jews" were infiltrating the nation through Communism. For those in attendance who disagreed with the British Israel theology, Nixon's speech would have been seen as an indication that they had been wrong in their stance against the theology. The United States Government *must know something they did not.*

Thank you very much, my friend, Demos Shakarian for this much too generous introduction, and for this fine group this morning, meeting here in Washington. I want you to know I regret I haven't the time to stay here and greet all of you personally and allow people I see with cameras to get your snapshots. In any event, when I learned that this group was meeting here in Washington, our good friend Mr. Shakarian last week invited me to come. I told him that my schedule had been filled up for about three weeks before that, but that some way I would try to come. He said, "We meet every morning for breakfast." I said, "I believe I have a Breakfast three mornings of that week, but on one of the mornings, I will try to get by," and this happens to be it, and I am here, and I am very happy that I was able to come.

---

[630] Photograph: William Branham at the Full Gospel Businessmen's Fellowship International Prayer Breakfast. 1954.

I might say that after this meeting I am going down to a meeting at the White House; it will be at 9:30 this morning. I will have to be there a little early for briefings that will occur before the meeting. I believe that will be as good a theme as any to set for the brief remarks that I will make to you this morning. The meeting which I am to attend is a meeting of an organization called The National Security Council. You never read what the National Security Council does because it is the top advisory group for the President to deal with international policy and to deal with military policy. Its meetings are always confidential, or top secret – either of the phrases that may appeal to you. Its meetings are one in which grave problems confronting American and the free nations are considered and in which the solutions to those problems are worked out if they can be.

I don't need to tell you today the problems that confront America, do confront the free peoples, are as great as we have ever had in our history. We look across the world to Indo-China. We look down at the situation in Guatemala. We see revolution in some areas, subversion in other areas, even in the United States as my good friend Clyde Doyle can tell you. He has rendered a fine service in many of our American activities of which he is a member. But in all these areas of the world you see the godless, totalitarian doctrine of the communists pushing ahead and attempting to make gains against the free nations, and eventually threatening our nation as well.

Now in the National Security Council we consider, of course, the military policy, the economical policy, the political policies that the United States can adopt to meet this threat. But all of us know that the great battle in which we are engaged today is one which is not only military, economic, and political in character, and it is that, but in the final analysis it is a battle for the minds, and the hearts, and the souls of men. And I will tell you why it is.

Let us consider for the moment the problem we have in Indo-China. We have there a revolution, so called. A revolution against the existing government. But what kind of a revolution is it? It is a revolution which is greatly controlled, dominated, and inspired, not by the individuals within the country, individuals who are attempting to change their form of government, but is dominated, inspired, and controlled by the Communist rulers in Peking and Moscow, who use this method of extending their conquest all over the world. Now, what do we do to meet such a revolution?

As I pointed out in my address at Whittier College, obviously, we attempt to develop united action among our friends, other free nations in that area to see that the aggression does not go any further than it has already gone. But that meets the problem, generally too late. The major problem that we have is to find out what causes the revolution and then to meet it there. In other words, why is it that people are appealed to by this doctrine and what appeal can we offer which will be as effective? What appeal can we offer which will win the people in this battle for their minds, and their hearts, and their souls to decide for the free nations rather than to decide for the slave nations?

We are attempting, of course, to meet that appeal, not only in Indo-China, but in every other area of the world. Unless we do meet it effectively, we will be confronted with more revolution, Communist-inspired and controlled and directed. And so may I suggest that in meeting that appeal that there are a number of considerations that we must have in mind. We must of course associate ourselves with the causes people believe in, in these countries, with their aspirations. They want independence, they want equality, they want economic progress, they want peace. All those things are important to them.

There is one thing that I would emphasize above all others and that is that economic progress is part of the problem, but not all of it and that for any one to suggest, for example, that in Asia all that you have to do is keep the people from going Communist is to give them another bowl of rice is wrong. Wrong, because it is an insult to a proud and sensitive people. Wrong, because it is a false and superficial appraisal of a very complex problem. Because in Asia, as in the United States, as in every other section of the world, men are interested in economic progress, they are interested in military security to protect them from enemies abroad, but they are also interested in other things.

Ideals, we call them I mention two — independence and equality, I would mention another which this organization symbolizes, and that is that it seems to me one of the greatest advantages we have over the appeal that the Communists are able to make not only here but abroad, is that this nation was founded in a belief in God. This nation has become a great nation because its great leaders have believed in God. And it seems to me that it is extremely encouraging to see all over America, what I think is sense and that is a rededication of people to those basic principles which made America great in the past: a belief in God, combined with patriotism, and a belief in America and in that connection may I just close with one note.

About the only time I get to read the newspapers is when I am riding from one place to another. I sit in the car and read the newspapers and find out what is going on. In this instance I read a very interesting story this morning which you may have picked up in which President Eisenhower came out against giving a pension to Alger Hiss, who is, you know, serving a term in the penitentiary at the present for committing perjury, lying when he said he had not been a member of the Communist Conspiracy and had not indulged in activities which were detrimental to the United States of America. I believe the President was right when he made this

180

statement, I think you will agree that is right.

I would like to point out to you, something that you may have not known about Alger Hiss and all the types of people that he is a symbol of. I have often been asked, as my friend Clyde Doyle has been asked, "What kind of people become Communist in the United States?" "What makes them become Communists?" So, I thought in my own mind, let me analyze the ones that I know. What kind of people are they? So, I went back. I remembered the histories, I remembered the other young men. They were young then, six years ago when I was participating in the investigation of that case. The other young men who came before the Committee on un-American activities. There was Alger Hiss, Lee Preston, Nathan Witt, Victor Pruell, Harry White. These men came before the Committee and proof was established either by their own testimony or by corroborating evidence that they had been members of the Communist Conspiracy.

I tried to analyze them all and said, "What was it in their make-up, that made them members of the Communist Conspiracy?" And this is what I thought. Every one of them had the best advantages that America could give them. They were graduates of our great colleges. They were not poor. They had the best Government jobs that they could have, running eight to ten thousand dollars a year. They were individuals who had the advantages of coming from good families in the United States of America. They did not do what they did for money. Not one of this group that I have mentioned received money for what he did.

Then why did he do it? He did it because, somehow, somewhere, something went wrong. he lost faith in America. he lost faith in God if he ever had it. And in losing that faith, he transferred his loyalty and his allegiance to the totalitarian doctrine of Communism, and when he did that, once he does, he was willing to do anything: engage in

181

espionage, do things which would bring discredit to himself and to the members of his family, do anything to further that cause, a cause which will destroy his country and overthrow his government.

Now that is dedication. And whatever we say about the Communists, we must realize that they have made an appeal which makes dedicated men out of them. But on the other side, we have dedicated men too. And we need more of them, men who are dedicated to America, and men who believe in the free principles of this nation, men who have faith in God.

I am sure that this group of people, meeting as you have here and then spreading your influence all over America, into the big cities and small towns do very much to create in the minds and hearts of young people of America, dedication to those great ideals. And for that reason, I particularly appreciate the opportunity to meet with you here this morning and to speak to you informally, as I have. I hope that the balance of your visit to Washington will be pleasant and that we will continue to provide for you this magnificent California weather.[631]

- Vice President Richard Nixon, Full Gospel Businessmen's Fellowship International Breakfast

---

[631] Vice-President Richard Nixon's Message to the Full Gospel Businessmen's Convention. 1954, Sept. Voice of Healing.

CHAPTER 16

THE COLONY

❖

"He constantly stated that we were the only authentic faithful and, furthermore, supported that woman were an inferior creature; he did not express it so publicly, but every time a young man disturbed a young lady, she was the one punished, because, according to Branham, women had received their beauty from the devil, to seduce men." - Gerd Seewald, Official Statement

Near the end of WWII, the United States and Great Britain cooperatively engaged in operations to acquire the advanced military, scientific, and technological advancements from Nazi Germany. As the Allied forces seized control of research facilities in Germany, an advanced team trailed behind the military to seize documents and research. One of their greatest finds happened to be recovered from a toilet in Bonn University: a catalogue of scientists and engineers that had been put to work for the Third Reich. This catalogue, otherwise known as the Osenberg List, identified the greatest scientific minds of Germany.[632] This find quickly spawned a secret government operation, dubbed "Operation Paperclip". From 1945 through 1959 under Operation Paperclip, 1,600 German scientists and engineers were extracted from Germany to the United States to assist with the design,

---

[632] Schumm, Laura. 2014, Jun 2. What Was Operation Paperclip? Accessed 2023, Jan 30 from https://www.history.com/news/what-was-operation-paperclip. "One enlightening discovery—recovered from a toilet at Bonn University—was the Osenberg List: a catalogue of scientists and engineers that had been put to work for the Third Reich."

development, and manufacturing of weapons — including chemical and biological weapons.[633] The operation, approved by President Truman, was designed to *"ensure such coveted information did not fall into the hands of the Soviet Union"*.[634]

From 1945 to 1952, the United States Air Force engaged in transferring the largest number of German scientists. Two hundred and sixty Germans were brought to the United States to assist in creating an arsenal of weapons against the Soviets.[635] The operation blew up into controversy when it was learned that many of these German scientists were connected to the Nazi party. It was especially controversial in 1951 when the Boston Globe linked Walter Screiber to human experiments at Ravensbrück.[636] Screiber was quickly transferred to Argentina with the help of the United States Military.

After 1959, several other Nazis escaped directly to Argentina via an unusual cult compound in a remote area in the Maule Region of central Chile. The colony, filled with Pentecostal converts, was named Sociedad Benefactora y Educacional Dignidad ("Charitable and Educational Society 'Dignity'"). So many Nazis escaped through the colony that the Nazis in Germany referred to the location as simply, "the colony": the landing place in South

---

[633] Schumm, Laura. 2014, Jun 2. What Was Operation Paperclip? Accessed 2023, Jan 30 from https://www.history.com/news/what-was-operation-paperclip. "In a covert affair originally dubbed Operation Overcast but later renamed Operation Paperclip, roughly 1,600 of these German scientists (along with their families) were brought to the United States to work on America's behalf during the Cold War. The program was run by the newly-formed Joint Intelligence Objectives Agency (JIOA), whose goal was to harness German intellectual resources to help develop America's arsenal of rockets and other biological and chemical weapons."

[634] Wynne, Kelly. 2020, Feb 21. What Was Operation Paperclip? Accessed 2023, Jan 30 from https://www.newsweek.com/amazon-hunters-true-story-nazis-america-operation-paperclip-1488294. "In an attempt to beat Russia, President Harry S. Truman approved the operation that would "ensure such coveted information did not fall into the hands of the Soviet Union," reported the History Channel. About 1,600 Nazi-linked scientists were believed to have actively worked in America during the Cold War."

[635] Project Paperclip: German Scientists and the Cold War, 1975, Clarence G. Lasby, et al. page 257

[636] Jacobsen, Annie (February 11, 2014). Operation Paperclip: The secret intelligence-program to bring Nazi scientists to America (First ed.). New York. ISBN 9780316239820.

America in which to hide from the authorities and gain safe passage into Argentina.[637]   Surprisingly, the colony was led by a German Latter Rain convert selected to be on William Branham's security detail when Baron von Blomberg organized Branham's tour through Germany. Even more surprisingly, Richard Nixon — who had provoked the Latter Rain leaders in the 50s — conducted military operations against the Chilean government through the colony in later years during his presidency.[638]

When the Latter Rain Movement spread from Canada into the United States and Mexico, and Pentecostal leaders began to participate in what they thought to be the final chapter of the Book of Life on earth, news of the "Latter Rain Message" began to spread globally. This was largely due to printed materials with global mailing lists, such as The Voice of Healing, the Herald of Faith, and the Herald of Truth. Some of the revivalists had international ministries which added fuel to this fire. Readers in other countries were excited to watch the movement spreading through the Americas, and eager to hear more from revivalists who participated in the "outpouring". One such minister and evangelist who claimed to be a participant in the early days of Latter Rain was "Message" cult leader Ewald Frank of Germany.[639]   According Frank, he was converted to the Latter Rain by Hall Hermon while Hermon was engaged in an operation by the United States military in

[637] Infield, Glenn B. 1981. Secrets of the SS. "an enclave known only as 'the Colony' to outsiders but officially named Colonia Dignidad (Noble Colony) by the Chilean government."

[638] Hornberger, Jacob G. 2016. Accessed 2023, Jan 30 from https://www.fff.org/2016/09/19/colonia-dignidad/. "the CIA, operating on orders of President Richard Nixon (of Watergate fame), secretly poured fuel on the fire by making things even worse than they already were. For example, the CIA secretly bribed national truckers to go on strike to prevent food from being delivered across the country to the Chilean people. The CIA's goal? To improve the chances that the Chilean people would welcome the U.S.-inspired coup when it finally came."

[639] Frank, Ewald. Sixty Years in the Service of the LORD. Accessed 2022, Apr 29 from https://www.freie-volksmission.de/?lang=2&site=news. "As you all know, I dedicated my life to the LORD back in 1949 at the Pentecostal Conference in Hamburg. At the same time, I came to know of Brother Branham's special ministry."

Germany.[640]   According to Branham, Dr. Adolf Guggenbuhl engaged the United States Army and allowed him to enter Germany.[641]

In all research about Colonia Dignidad, Ewald Frank is of key interest. On October 17, 2005, Frank was denied entry into Chile due to his deep connection to the colony. He was placed under interrogation at the international terminal of the Arturo Merino Benítez International Airport. In his defense, Frank argued that Colonia Dignidad was a *"Nazi dictatorship"* and that it was he *"who in their first visit brought them their human dignity, human rights and freedom of faith."*[642] Government officials were surely surprised when Frank engaged Sergio Rodriguez Oro, a well-known defender of former members of DINA in Chile.

Dirección de Inteligencia Nacional (DINA), was the secret police under the ruthless dictatorship of Augusto Pinochet. It was established in 1973 as a Chilean Army Intelligence unit, but later separated from the army to become an independent administrative unit in June 1974. During the Pinochet regime, Colonia Dignidad — the commune of William Branham's converts in Chile — became the central hub of intelligence for DINA.[643]   The interrogators blocking Frank's entry to Chile would have most certainly made the connection between Colonia Dignidad and Oro. Frank insisted that he had only entered Chile three times, which was not in agreement with Chile immigration records. Frank had gained entry at least

---

[640] Frank, Ewald. 1997. I am a witness. "There came a man from America by the name of Hall Herman who preached in Hamburg, Germany. He was a great man in Hollywood, but after the two bombings on Hiroshima and Nagasaki he was hired by the US government to film the outcome of the bombings over Japan."

[641] Branham, William. 1955, October 3. Faith In Action (55-1003). "Doctor Guggenbuhl, a very smart lawyer (That's one of our sponsors there.), he didn't take 'no' for an answer. He went right on down to the Major in the United States Army; he said, 'tell Brother Branham to come on. If the rest of them can come, he can too.' So, it give me a chance to come into Germany."

[642] Basso, Carlos. 2022. La Secta Perfecta.

[643] Basso, Carlos. 2022. La Secta Perfecta. ""In his 1977 statement on the Parral sect, he stated that it was 'the central receiver of all the information from the "external apparatus of DINA,' among other things because it had a radio antenna that allowed it to connect with any part of the world."

seven times, one of which was only shortly after Colonia Dignidad leader Paul Schäfer's escape from the colony.[644]

In 1955, the year after Nixon's involvement with "The Family", Baron von Blomberg organized a series of revival tours for William Branham. One of the stops on the tour was his adopted country of Germany. Whether at the instruction of Von Blomberg or by chance, Ewald Frank joined the revivals in Karlsruhe,[645] met William Branham, and became a key figure in Branham's cult of personality. Also, whether by prearrangement or by chance, it was at this same meeting that Paul Schäfer met William Branham personally.[646]

The manner in which Frank and Schäfer participated in Branham's revivals in Karlsruhe would suggest that their involvement was the result of Baron von Blomberg's work in Germany rather than a coincidence. Frank was assigned to be Branham's translator in Germany.[647] Schäfer, a former member of the Hitler Youth and ex-Luftwaffe officer in the Nazi military, was assigned to the Branham party as Branham's personal security detail.[648] According to German journalist Ulla Frohling, the work that Frank, Schäfer, and their Latter Rain converts did with Branham forged strong alliances between key lieutenants at

---

[644] Basso, Carlos. 2022. La Secta Perfecta. "According to the lawyer Rodriguez, before 2005 Frank had entered Chile three times, but that is not consistent with the records held by the authorities, since his immigration record indicates that before 2005, he was in the country seven times, the first of them on a trip of just two days, in August 1998, a few months after Schafer's escape from the colony."

[645] Frank, Ewald. Sixty Years in the Service of the LORD. Accessed 2022, Apr 29 from https://www.freie-volksmission.de/?lang=2&site=news. "In 1955 I had the privilege of participating in his meetings in Karlsruhe, Germany, and there got to know him personally during our first conversation."

[646] Basso, Carlos. 2022. La Secta Perfecta. "He met Branham in person in the same activity in which the American and Schäfer met."

[647] Basso, Carlos. 2022. La Secta Perfecta. "Frank, as Winfried Hempel points out, officiated as his official translator".

[648] Basso, Carlos. 2022. La Secta Perfecta. "Schafer knew very well who the Jeffersonville preacher was and was elated by the prospect of his visit. So much so that, after much insistence, he got himself and his followers accepted as part of Branham's security detail."

Colonia Dignidad.[649] They were but one of many such "outposts" that Branham set up around the globe.[650]

In 1958, after Roy E. Davis had established himself in Dallas as the Imperial Wizard of the Ku Klux Klan and outspoken leader of the anti-Civil Rights white supremacy movement, Frank travelled to Dallas to attend a conference organized by Gordon Lindsay.[651] It was after this meeting that Frank established The Free People's Mission in Krefeld.

Interestingly, this meeting was shortly after William Branham went public with his "Serpent's Seed" rebranding of Wesley Swift's Christian Identity Doctrine. This doctrine heavily influenced Frank's ministry. As Frank began establishing cult communities in other countries, the Christian Identity Doctrine was fundamental to the communes — even among people with black skin that the doctrine was originally discriminating against. One of Frank's converts, a Branham cult "apostle" in West Africa, was imprisoned and ordered not to preach for five years after Branham's "Serpent's Seed" and other doctrines were deemed to be "hate speech".[652]

---

[649] Basso, Carlos. 2022. La Secta Perfecta. "According to her, during those days in Germany, strong ties were forged between him, Branham, Schafer, and some of their lieutenants, including Alfred Matthusen, Walter Laube, and Gerhard Micke."

[650] Branham, William. 1962, Jun 1. Taking Sides with Jesus. "And a church of this Faith can be set there, which will be an outpost in India, outpost in Germany, outpost in Switzerland. Why, right now, we should have had them all around the nations where I been. And the Message then, from there, comes another, from another comes another."

[651] Frank, Ewald. 1997. I Am a Witness. "Now we are coming to the year 1958 when I attended the "Voice of Healing" convention arranged by Gordon Lindsay in Dallas, Texas, who wrote this book: "William Branham, a man sent from God". In the German language it was also published: "William Branham - ein Mann von Gott gesandt". There I attended the convention in 1958. I came to know about 200 of the American evangelists. In the evening services brother Branham was the main speaker. "

[652] Kacou Philippe case: The prophet sentenced to one year of imprisonment. Accessed 2021, Jun 17 from https://www.linfodrome.com/societe/27085-affaire-kacou-philippe-le-prophete-condamne-a-un-an-d-emprisonnement-ferme. "The prophet Kacou Philippe, prosecuted for acts of incitement to religious hatred and intolerance, was sentenced to one (1) year of imprisonment. In addition to the 12 months spent at the Abidjan Detention and Correction Center (Maca), the religious guide is prohibited from preaching the gospel for five (5) years throughout the national territory. It was taken aback that his many followers listened to the deliberations of the judge, in charge of the

It is unclear whether Colonia Dignidad was one of the "outposts" that Ewald Frank established at the instruction of William Branham. Other Latter Rain evangelists working closely with William Branham established similar colonies in key locations. Jim Jones, who worked closely with William Branham and Joseph Mattsson-Boze in the same years, migrated to South America for the first time in 1962[653] — very close to the time Paul Schäfer began moving converts into the colony. Jones would later migrate Peoples Temple to Jonestown, Guyana, where the group of over nine hundred converts would commit mass suicide. Newly declassified documents concerning Colonia Dignidad out of Chile suggest that Frank may have been involved from the beginning — long before Frank's visits to the colony in 2005. According to the testimony of Colonia Dignidad leader Gerd Seewald during criminal investigations in Chile, recordings of William Branham and Ewald Frank were the only religious sermons heard in Colonia Dignidad from its inception.[654]

Before working with Ewald Frank, Paul Schäfer had organized a group of religious converts to support Nazis in post-war Germany. The group was initially located in Holporf, Germany, and later migrated to a town near Bonn. Schäfer and his converts assisted the defeated Germans with both material and spiritual needs, as well as providing a sanctuary for Nazis requiring anonymity. Combined with Schäfer's former rank in the Nazi military, this support network attracted several Schutzstaffel, or SS military officers who were hiding from the foreign militia

---

trial. On Friday, June 3, 2016, the deputy prosecutor, Abel Yéo, had requested, at the end of the trial, 10 years in prison and a 500,000 FCFA fine against the defendant. Deliberated for Monday, June 6, the verdict was rendered against the servant of God. And this, to the chagrin of his flock."
[653] 100 Events in History of Peoples Temple. Accessed 2023, Jan 29 from https://jonestown.sdsu.edu/wp-content/uploads/2013/10/Timeline100.pdf.
[654] Causa Rol N°2198-1998, episodio Asociación Ilícita Ex Colonia Dignidad, Corte de Apelaciones de Santiago, Chile. "Fifty years prior, and soon the sermons of Branham and Frank were the only presented to the population of Villa Baviera."

occupying Germany.[655] Schäfer and his commune would have been very appealing when the group migrated to Chile; not only was he a familiar face among Nazis in hiding, but the colony was also a safe haven for former German military leaders.[656]

When Schäfer and his cloak-and-dagger Nazi regime of religious converts began working as William Branham's security detail in a meeting with Baron von Blomberg — adopted cousin of Hitler's minister of war — Schäfer's group of converts enlisted in the Latter Rain. Ewald Frank, who had been established as a high-ranking cult leader of Branham's sect in Germany, became both Schäfer's spiritual leader as well as a spiritual leader for the Nazis in hiding. With the help of Frank, Schäfer implemented many of Branham's doctrines and began claiming that his converts were the "only true believers" of Branham's full set of doctrinal teachings.[657]

In 1959, Schäfer established the Private Sociale Mission, a charitable organization established as a front for the Nazi operation. It operated under the disguise of a children's home and school, very similar to that of the Latter Rain's Sharon Orphanage. That same year, however, Schäfer was charged with sexually abusing two of the young boys. A warrant was issued for his arrest, and he fled with his converts (and Nazis). Through some unknown twist of fate (or through the work of Baron von Blomberg), Schäfer

---

[655] Infield, Glenn B. 1981. Secrets of the SS. "Shaeffer guaranteed the defeated German citizens both the spiritual and material needs they craved during these harsh postwar years. He also promised anonymity to those Germans who joined his group. This was a powerful lure for many of the SS men on the run from Allied investigators."

[656] Infield, Glenn B. 1981. Secrets of the SS. "This was a powerful lure for many of the SS men on the run from Allied investigators. They quickly joined Shaeffer and when he moved the entire organization from Germany to Chile in 1961, his SS membership was pleased since South America was known to be a safe haven for unreconstructed Nazis."

[657] Basso, Carlos. 2022. La Secta Perfecta. "Schäfer had into practice several of his doctrines. , 'If you are wondering what these were, Seewald himself points out some of them: ,' He constantly maintained that we were the only faithful ones and, furthermore, he maintained that the woman was a lesser creature. She did not express it so publicly, but whenever a young man disturbed a girl, she was punished because, according to Branham, women had received her beauty from the devil, to seduce men."

connected with the Chilean ambassador to Germany, and was invited to Chile for safe haven.[658]

Schäfer arrived at Sociedad Benefactora y Educacional Dignidad in 1961 and began what from the surface looked like an agricultural society — very similar to the early beginnings of Jonestown, Guyana. Over time, however, the colony was fortified with barbed wire fences, a watchtower, search lights and weapons for a military-style fortification. Inside the walls of the colony, the military fortress included an orphanage and school, hospital, two airstrips, restaurant, and power station. Shortly after, in 1962, Ewald Frank claimed to have received a vision by God instructing him to leave Krefeld and preach to other cities. In just a short time Frank became a frequent traveler to all parts of the world.[659] During the investigation of human rights violations years later, it became apparent that Colonia Dignidad — which had become a *"state within a state"* was one of the "cities" he frequented. Authorities began to make the deeper connection when it was learned that Ewald Frank had been the minister who baptized Schäfer's right-hand man, Dr. Hartmut Wilhelm Hopp.[660]

One year into the CIA's involvement with Colonia Dignidad through Operation Condor, Paul Schäfer sent Hartmut Hope to the United States to study medicine at the University of California, in Davis, California. This university branch was operated by other Germans employed by the United States military. Francis H.

---

[658] Falconer, Bruce (1 September 2008). "The Torture Colony". American Scholar. Retrieved 2 April 2020.

[659] Frank, Ewald. 1997. I Am a Witness. "I looked towards the window, and from up, from the right, came the tremendous voice of the Lord where every word was spoken with direct precision in the German language. The Lord said these words: "My servant, your time for this city will soon be over, I will send you to other cities to preach my Word."

[660] Basso, Carlos. 2022. La Secta Perfecta. "One of those baptized, according to the same investigation, was Hartmut Hopp. In fact, when Martin Mathussen, one of the current controllers of the colony, was asked about the relationship between them and Frank, he stated that ,'we have nothing to do with Ewald Frank as an organization. I am a Christian, believer, and I do not declare myself from any religious institution.' When questioned about whether he was baptized by the German, he dodged the answer, declaring that 'I believe that...religious rites are part of private life and should not be a subject for the press.'"

Clauser, for example, started with University of California in 1965, a few short years prior to Hopp's enrollment. Clauser served as the academic vice chancellor, vice chancellor for science and engineering, and professor of applied science.[661] When Germany fell, Clauser was inducted into the United States Military as an *"instant full colonel"* under Operation Paperclip.[662] It was during his enrollment, in 1969, that Hopp acquired a degree for Paul Schäfer as a "Doctor of Theology". According to Hopp, he purchased the diploma with Schäfer's name for the sum of fifty dollars.[663] Hopp returned to Colonia Dignidad to become the head of the colony's hospital. It was later learned that the hospital was used for human experiments and torture.[664]

[661] Francis Clauser Memorial. Caltech. Accessed 2023, Jan 31 from https://www.eas.caltech.edu/events/francis-clauser-memorial. "He was invited to the newly created University of California campus in Santa Cruz in 1965 to set up the engineering school, and he served variously as the academic vice chancellor, vice chancellor for science and engineering, and professor of applied science."

[662] Francis Clauser Memorial. Caltech. Accessed 2023, Jan 31 from https://www.eas.caltech.edu/events/francis-clauser-memorial. "When Germany fell to the Allies in 1945, Clauser "was temporarily inducted into the U.S. military as an instant full colonel" as part of Operation Paperclip, says his son, John Clauser."

[663] Basso, Carlos. 2022. La Secta Perfecta. "'In another court testimony, he was asked about a diploma, found in a search, in the name of Paul Schafer and issued in the United States, which gave him the degree of Doctor of Theology. To this, Hopp replied that "in 1969, in circumstances that I was in the United States, for the sum of fifty dollars, I acquired this diploma with the name of Paul Schafer, and I gave it to him when I arrived in Chile.'"

[664] Basso, Carlos. 2022. La Secta Perfecta. "In this regard, Hopp "confessed that the violent psychiatric treatments that were applied in the villa to the rebellious settlers, which implied strong medication, the application of electroshocks and constant beatings, were used "as a way of breaking the will of the people who they opposed him (Schäfer)."

CHAPTER 17

MR. KREFELD

❖

"We don't want a big story leaking out that we are trying to overthrow the Government. We want his judgment on the possibility of a run-off election." – President Richard Nixon

In a letter dated June 6, 1970, addressed to former Luftwaffe officer Herman Schmidt, one of Paul Schäfer's early converts at the "Private Social Mission" in Germany and later Schäfer's lieutenants in Colonia Dignidad, an unknown author sent a message in secret code to the colony. It was written by *"your people from Sieburg"*, which was the location of Schäfer's first headquarters before migrating to Chile. The letter described the purchase and trafficking of arms for the colony and was a response to a request for *"INFRA RED special request"*. The letter replied to an unknown request stating, *"I immediately contacted Mr. Krefeld. I will send you the answers you ask me for"* and that *"in Germany these things are subject to strict controls, because they are only intended for the military and the police"*. The sender had evidently acquired technology for weapons but stated that *"The Special Box"* was out of funds and that *"these things"* must be paid for immediately. The sender requested that funds be deposited in the account of the Private Social Mission at Deutsche Bank. Among the things being purchased were eight helmets with masks, four infrared light barriers, radio receivers, an infrared camera, a small format camera with a roll of photosensitive film, nine voice inverters for radiophone, decoders, an infrared aiming device, a land mine detector, an underwater mine detector, and a night vision telescope.[665]

The letter was discovered in 2005, the same year that Ewald Frank was denied entry into Chile in October as a result of police agencies discovering weapons caches in the colony. Three tons of weapons, explosives, ammunition, and chemical elements for weapons manufacturing were discovered, as well as thousands of documents including letters, folders of papers, bank documents, and forty-six thousand intelligence files. These files connected the Chilean government officials with this "Mr. Krefeld", a German operative connected to Colonia Dignidad. Though the identity of "Mr. Krefeld" remains classified, there are many clues among the information that has been declassified to determine the identity of this operative. "Mr. Krefeld" was a person in Germany familiar with Schäfer's mission in Germany, entrusted to handle the financial transactions for criminal international arms deals.

In his book, La Secta Perfecta, University of Concepción professor and journalist Carlos Basso makes the case that this "Mr. Krefeld" is in fact Ewald Frank. Ewald Frank's Free People's Mission in Krefeld, Germany, was then and is today deeply connected to the leaders of Colonia Dignidad. When the Chilean government began investigating the colony for international arms deals, human rights violations, and an array of other crimes, some of them fled Chile to seek refuge in Frank's church. Hartmut Hopp — Schäfer's right hand man, for example, made world news when he started attending Ewald Frank's church in Krefeld.[666] A diamond-shaped sticker was discovered in Frank's church in

---

[665] Basso, Carlos. 2022. La Secta Perfecta.
[666] Ellrodt, Oliver. 2012. Insight: German sect victims seek escape from Chilean nightmare past. "To their horror, Schaefer's right-hand man, Hartmut Hopp, a doctor who received a five-year jail term in Chile in 2011 for his role in the abuse, also turned up there last May. Hopp, 67, had skipped Chile before his final sentencing, and Chile wants him back. But the German constitution forbids the extradition of its own citizens. So Schmidtke and about 120 other Colonia Dignidad survivors, backed by a German rights group, are now plaintiffs in a German investigation into Hopp,"

Krefeld with the words, *"Casino Familia, Villa Baviera."*[667]   One of the weapons caches identified in Chile was at the home of the Casino family of Bulnes.[668] Basso admits that unless the information is fully declassified, *"We cannot say with complete certainty that the person referred to by the author of that text as Mr. Krefeld was necessarily Frank, but it is useful to note that there are no other known connections of the colony with that city, much less with someone who lived there and in turn had ties to the United States, as the German pastor did."*[669]

A second document was identified that contained additional requests from "Mr. Krefeld" in Germany. An expense request for one hundred and twenty-six thousand Deutsche marks. (About $250,000 in today's money).

Indeed, this second list included intercoms, radar alarms, vehicle alarms, two bulletproof vests, another helmet, stethoscopes, five telescopic sights, more infrared light barriers, another small camera, another mine detector, "smoke" units., thirteen CS and five CN (tear gas) units, among other things, as well as a huge amount of ammunition for different weapons. At the end of the list appeared a couple of rather cryptic words, indicating that "three potato sorters and 1,500 potatoes" had also been purchased. Later, Kurt Schellenkamp confessed the meaning of some of those words and others that they used in these communications. Today we know that "eggs" and "potatoes" referred to grenades, while "fodder" was ammunition for Schäfer's favorite Rheinmetall

---

[667] Basso, Carlos. 2022. La Secta Perfecta. "there was a diamond-shaped sticker that read "Casino Familiar, Villa Baviera."

[668] Basso, Carlos. 2022. La Secta Perfecta. "a large arsenal that, originally, was found at the head of the airstrip of the town, which had been unearthed. and transferred to two points, one within the same headquarters of the colony, in Parral, and another in the family Casino of Bulnes. Thanks to these data, the police agencies were able to find the arsenals of the colony."

[669] Basso, Carlos. 2022. La Secta Perfecta.

machine guns.[670]

The date of the letter is significant, as it relates to the United States involvement with Colonia Dignidad. It was sent just thirty-four days after Salvador Allende won the presidential election in 1970. According to the letters identified, weapons were going into the compound rapidly using the colony as a munition hub to overthrow the Chilean government. The CIA and DIA (U.S. Defense Intelligence Agency) coordinated with Paul Schäfer and the Chilean ultra-nationalists to stage a coup d'état, though the CIA would not admit this until the year 2000.[671] "Mr. Krefeld" was involved as a means to acquire military supplies in both the US and in Germany.[672] One of the letters mentioned *"a good device to disinfect"*, and that the *"device is only sold to the largest pesticide factory in the United States and officially only to the armed forces and the Police"*. "Mr. Krefeld had requested that they send him a sample device for demonstration and mentioned that it would be six weeks before it could be delivered. The "disinfectant device" referred to tear gas.[673]

Paul Schäfer responded to "Mr. Krefeld, and his letter was just as cryptic. He mentioned that the colony needed *"a lot of practical and intellectual work, especially regarding chemistry and 'mass manufacturing' since we don't have much experience in it."* Based upon what government officials found in Colonia Dignidad, this referred to the weapons manufacturing of all kinds, including grenades, submachine guns, machine guns, rifles, flamethrowers,

---

[670] Basso, Carlos. 2022. La Secta Perfecta.

[671] Briscoe, David. 2000. CIA Admits Involvement in Chile. ABC News. Accessed 2023, Jan 31 from https://abcnews.go.com/International/story?id=82588&page=1.

[672] Basso, Carlos. 2022. La Secta Perfecta. "'Mr. Krefeld' was an important part in the acquisition of defense supplies, both in Germany and in the United States."

[673] Basso, Carlos. 2022. La Secta Perfecta. "This device is only sold to the largest pesticide factory in the "United States and officially only to the armed forces and the police. Through these institutions, Mr. Krefeld requested that they send him a sample device for a demonstration, and they promised to send it, but unfortunately it will never be before six weeks, because they have to go through several instances first. Then he referred, again, to the "cleaning liquid", which, judging by the comment he made next, was tear gas".

and chemical weapons including sarin gas.[674] Schäfer asked for additional equipment to monitor the radio devices of the Allende military. Schäfer mentioned the military coup before it was staged, which is significant in understanding the cult compound's relationship to the United States intelligence operations. Interestingly, his response letter stated that *"'Eduard' is participating and a large mass of civilians, and that Kennedy and the brother next door have made available the necessary utensils, the best fodder, is very comforting."* He also mentioned that *"a lot of red blood will surely be lost"* as he described the rifle-propelled grenades that had just arrived.[675]

As it turns out "Eduard" was likely a misspelling of "Edwards." In September 1970, Donald Kendall, CEO of Pepsi Cola, arranged for Chilean journalist Augustine Edwards to meet with the director of the CIA and the United States Attorney General to petition for U.S. involvement in Chile. Secretary of State Henry Kissinger discussed the situation with President Richard Nixon on September 12:

> *Kissinger: I had a call last night from McCane and Kendall this morning. McCane thinks it would be a catastrophe if we let it go. Latin American Bureau at State is against doing anything. Sorry has stopped all appointments unless they come to him.*

[674] Basso, Carlos. 2022. La Secta Perfecta. "In the same way, he said that they would need a lot of practical and intellectual work, especially regarding chemistry and "mass manufacturing", since "we don't have much experience in it", thus referring to the manufacture of weapons of all kinds: grenades, submachine guns, machine guns, rifles, flamethrowers and toxic gases, including sarin."

[675] Basso, Carlos. 2022. La Secta Perfecta. "Schafer indicated that a "coup" would take place and explained "that "Eduard" is participating and a large mass of civilians, and that Kennedy and the brother next door have made available the necessary utensils, the best fodder, is very comforting. Then there is a mention of what they say on the radio about "Washington and Chile", although it is not clear what it refers to. Later, he commented that ,'a lot of red blood will surely be lost,' before going into technical details about two types of fodder that had just arrived. Thanks to these details, everything indicates that it refers to rifle-propelled grenades."

Nixon: Did I see those instructions? I want to see them.

Kissinger: They came over here and one of my staff members agreed to it.

Nixon: I am following it and I want a personal note to State that I want to see all cables to Chile.

Kissinger: Maybe I should send a back channel to Kerry saying you are interested in keeping it open.

Nixon: By all means. I want an appraisal of what the options are. The options are having another run-off election.

Kissinger: [Redacted] sent someone down for a first-hand look to give their appraisal.

Nixon: Does State want to give them aid?

Kissinger: Let Allende come in and see what we can work out and work out opposition to him.

Nixon: Like against Castro? Like in Czech.? The same people said the same thing. Don't let them do that. Meyer knows better. Tell Kendall to call Meyer.

Kissinger. I did and he is beside himself. Augustine Edwards has escaped and is coming here Monday. I am going to meet with him on Monday for his feel of the situation.

Nixon: We don't want a big story leaking out that we are trying to overthrow the Government. We want his judgment on the possibility of a run-off election.

Kissinger: I will do that. That's essential.

Nixon: It's going to hell so fast. Their stock market is down 50%.

Kissinger: Sorry sent in a cable today that said while you meet in committees [unintelligible]

Nixon: Sorry may have wanted to put us on the spot. He is a Kennedy Democrat. Get a backchannel to him right away.[676]

Nixon was apparently convinced that the United States should intervene in Chile. In a recorded conversation between Henry Kissinger and former Secretary of State William Rogers, Kissinger relayed the President's directive that the Unites States should *"do the maximum possible to prevent an Allende takeover, but through Chilean sources and with a low posture."*[677] Nixon instructed Kissinger to *"do so discretely so that it doesn't backfire".*[678] U.S. involvement at that time was limited to election funding; money was funneled into the political campaigns of Salvador Allende's opponents. Impact to the campaign was limited, however, and Allende won by one percentage point.[679] The result was a runoff election in the Chilean Congress scheduled for October 24, 1970.

After the meeting in Washington between Augustine Edwards, Henry Kissinger, and Richard Nixon, the CIA (and DIA) were activated. Just two days before the runoff election, on October 22, 1970, a failed attempt at a military coup made matters much worse. The CIA "Task Force" worked with the Chilean

---

[676] TELCON President/Kissinger 12:32 p.m. 9/12/70. Accessed 2023, Jan 31 from https://nsarchive2.gwu.edu/NSAEBB/NSAEBB255/19700912-1200-Nixon2.pdf.

[677] TELECON Secretary Rogers 9/14/70 12:15 p.m. Accessed 2023, Jan 31 from https://nsarchive2.gwu.edu/NSAEBB/NSAEBB255/19700912-1215-Rogers3.pdf.

[678] TELECON Secretary Rogers 9/14/70 12:15 p.m. Accessed 2023, Jan 31 from https://nsarchive2.gwu.edu/NSAEBB/NSAEBB255/19700912-1215-Rogers3.pdf.

[679] The Allende Years and the Pinochet Coup, 1969-1973. Accessed 2023, Jan 31 from https://history.state.gov/milestones/1969-1976/allende. The U.S. Government used covert funds in Chile during this election period, not for any one candidate's use but to prevent Allende's election. U.S. support had some impact on the election, but Allende still received over one third of the popular vote. Alessandri also garnered over one third of the vote, trailing Allende by only one percentage point. A run-off election in the Chilean Congress was scheduled for October 24, 1970.

operatives and kidnapped the commander-in-chief of the Chilean army, René Schneider. Several extreme right-wing youths from some of the wealthiest families in Santiago joined with common criminals, and used the submachine guns, pistols, ammunition, and tear gas brought into Chile that had been delivered by DIA colonel Paul Wimert. The CIA considered Schneider *"a major stumbling block for military officers seeking to carry out a coup,"*[680] and by supplying the group with "sterile" weapons, the operation could easily be blamed upon Allende supporters.

According to Carlos Basso's observation, this tied Paul Schäfer and the Latter Rain compound at Colonia Dignidad directly to the early military coup attempts; not only were the weapons acquired by "Mr. Krefeld", "Eduard" is the spelling of the surname "Edward" in German.[681] And by understanding that the "comforting fodder" referred to weapons and ammunition, it was clear that Schäfer knew of the United States government sanctioned arms deal, and likely played a role in the delivery.[682] The question remains, however, what the letter meant by *"Kennedy and the brother next door"*. One can guess that Kennedy was being

---

[680] CIA Cable Transmissions on Coup Plotting, October 18, 1970, taken from Chile and the United States: Declassified Documents Relating to the Military Coup. Accessed 2023, Feb 1 from https://nsarchive2.gwu.edu/NSAEBB/NSAEBB8/nsaebb8.htm.

[681] Basso, Carlos. 2022. La Secta Perfecta. "Edwards traveled to Washington DC and, through the owner of Pepsi Cola, Donald Kendall, managed to meet with the director of the Central Intelligence Agency (CIA) and the United States Attorney General, who took Edwards' petition to Richard Nixon. Nixon agreed, remembering his old friendship with Kendall, and as a consequence the CIA put together a "Task Force", which finally designed an absurd coup plan, which would start with the kidnapping of the commander-in-chief of the Army, René Schneider. The kidnapping, which finally took place on October 22, culminated in a homicide. Its executioners were a group of extreme right-wing youths, belonging to the wealthiest families in Santiago, and some common criminals. In the operation, they used submachine guns, pistols, ammunition and tear gas grenades that were brought into Chile through the United States diplomatic bag and delivered by the head of the Defense Intelligence Agency (DIA) in Santiago, Colonel Paul Wimert, although the sending entity was the Central Intelligence Agency, the CIA. In other words, Schafer was aware of two key elements."

[682] Basso, Carlos. 2022. La Secta Perfecta. "fodder, which, he said, was a very "comforting" thing. In other words, she knew that there were weapons and ammunition available to the conspirators, provided by US intelligence, something that very few people in Chile knew about."

used as a code word for the United States, especially since Branham's Latter Rain doctrine from 1962 claimed that the election of Kennedy was the fulfillment of a prophecy that the Catholic Church would rule the United States.[683] Who was the "brother on the side"?

Regardless of the identity of codename "Mr. Krefeld", Ewald Frank continued to be a very active part of the colony and its escapees. Hartmutt Hopp was not the only executive leader of Colonia Dignidad that escaped into Germany. Albert Schreiber and Alfred Mathussen, for example, also fled into Germany and died there with impunity.[684] Schreiber, one of the most important fugitives of the colony, was identified in video footage from one of Ewald Frank's sermons at the missionary center in Krefeld. Both Schreiber and his wife were in the audience.[685]

---

[683] Branham, William. 1962, Oct 13. The Influence of Another. "No more than twenty years ago, right from this same building, it told of President Kennedy coming in. It told exactly what would take place, that the women and so forth would put this fellow in, and exactly what he would be. And we knowed it all along and told just exactly what would happen. And here it is today. And here is that conference coming up, the federation of church, and all coming together. Why, it ought to put us in action! That's right. Uh-huh. 166 Word by word, as He spoke, has been fulfilled right by us. It should put us in action."

[684] Colonia Dignidad leaders are sentenced. Accessed 2023, Feb 1 from https://www.dw.com/es/condenan-a-jerarcas-de-colonia-dignidad/a-16555676. "The lawyer Fernández criticized Germany's attitude towards the crimes that affected hundreds of its citizens, since Colonia Dignidad, which once had 400 inhabitants, was made up almost entirely of Germans who, after decades in Chile, did not even speak Spanish. Fernández recalled that two other leaders of the sect, Albert Schreiber and Alfred Mathussen, fled and died in Germany with impunity. The closure of this and other trials linked to the sect will also force the Chilean Justice to make public the 40,000 secret files that the judge in the case, Jorge Zepeda, found in the subways of the compound."

[685] Basso, Carlos. 2022. La Secta Perfecta. "a DVD that came from Germany came into the hands of the PDI. It was a record that contained one of Ewald Frank's sermons who, as in the case of Branham and Schafer, liked to be recorded. The official letter with which the Human Rights Brigade sent images to the judge specified that these images had been captured "in a missionary center in Krefeld, Germany, where the church, printing press and television studios of that ministry are located." The video was dated July 29 of that same year, 2005, and at the twenty-ninth minute it was possible to see Albert Schreiber and his wife in the audience."

CHAPTER 18

LITTLE NAZI GERMANY

❖

"I was released on the condition that I cooperate, they took me to Colonia Dignidad, a place about which he stated, 'there is a national intelligence training center run by Germans, that are nationalized Chileans'."

Of the events in Richard Nixon's presidency that would go from bad to worse, the installment of Chilean dictator Augusto Pinochet was one of the biggest failures of his administration. It was far worse than even his critics were aware when the Watergate Scandal was made public. While Salvador Allende was voted into office and began implementing sweeping socialist changes that impacted the economy, the CIA began working with Pinochet supporters to build political and military opposition within the country. Henry Kissinger, born *Heinz Alfred Kissinger* in Germany, worked with the CIA to assist the cultists, Germans, and Pinochet regime. The CIA worked to train and finance the terrorists,[686] and Colonia Dignidad quickly transitioned into a national intelligence

---

[686] Pinochet's Chile. Accessed 2023, Feb 1 from https://www.washingtonpost.com/wp-srv/inatl/longterm/pinochet/overview.htm. "The Chilean military, aided by training and financing from the U.S. Central Intelligence Agency, gained absolute control of the country in less than a week.

training center.[687] Along with the weapons cache, the colony soon had several aircraft, underground prisons, and torture and death chambers.[688] By 1977, it was *"the central receiver of all the information from the external apparatus of DINA"*,[689] the Dirección de Inteligencia Nacional. DINA was the central intelligence organization for Pinochet, but due to training by the Germans in Colonia Dignidad, it was referred to as "Pinochet's Gestapo".[690]

On September 11, 1973, the four branches of Chile's armed forces successfully overthrew the government of Allende. Allende was killed while defending presidential palace. In less than a week, the military established absolute control of the country, and silenced opposition through a series of raids, executions, "disappearances", arrests, torture, and murder of thousands of Chilean citizens.[691] According to Amnesty International and the U.N. Human Rights Commission, 250,000 people were detained for political reasons during this period. Looking at the expanding operation outside of Chile, it is estimated that at least 60,000 deaths resulted from Operation Condor.[692] The Archives of Terror

---

[687] Basso, Carlos. 2022. La Secta Perfecta. "I was released on the condition that I cooperate, they took me to Colonia Dignidad, a place about which he stated, 'there is a national intelligence training center run by Germans, that are nationalized Chileans'."

[688] Basso, Carlos. 2022. La Secta Perfecta. "they have a real regiment in Colonia Dignidad, where there is a hospital that has all the advances that any of the hospitals in Santiago would like, where there are ambulance planes, mail planes and underground prisons. There he trained me to interrogate people and to do counterintelligence tasks. {...} "'have engaged in tasks of hunting people, interrogating them, torturing, and killing."

[689] Basso, Carlos. 2022. La Secta Perfecta.

[690] Peterson, Brittany. 2011, Dec 1. Homage to a Criminal in Chile. Accessed 2023, Feb 1 from https://nacla.org/news/2011/12/1/homage-criminal-chile. "National Intelligence Directorate (DINA), Pinochet's Gestapo-like secret police"

[691] Pinochet's Chile. Accessed 2023, Feb 1 from https://www.washingtonpost.com/wp-srv/inatl/longterm/pinochet/overview.htm. "The Chilean military, aided by training and financing from the U.S. Central Intelligence Agency, gained absolute control of the country in less than a week. The new regime waged raids, executions, "disappearances" and the arrest and torture of thousands of Chilean citizens - establishing a climate of fear and intimidation that would remain for years to come."

[692] Bevins, Vincent 2020. The Jakarta Method: Washington's Anticommunist Crusade and the Mass Murder Program that Shaped Our World. "By the time Operation Condor ended in the early 1980s, as many as 60,000 people may have been killed."

list 50,000 killed, 30,000 disappeared and 400,000 imprisoned.[693] In Chile, where Colonia Dignidad was the central hub of intelligence operations for Augusto Pinochet, as many as 100,000 people were tortured.[694] Pinochet's military dictatorship quickly turned Chile into a country ruled by fear and eventually resulted in *"crimes of genocide and terrorism"*[695]

High-ranking Nazis began to enter Colonia Dignidad and help to establish facilities and technologies that were used during Hitler's reign in Germany. The CIA and Nazi-hunter Simon Wiesenthal claimed to have evidence that Hitler's "Angel of Death", Josef Mengele, spent time in Colonia Dignidad.[696] Mengele, whose infamous human experiments on torture, death, disease, and medicine on human victims made him the subject of several books and movies, was also known for visiting children's barracks to test various poisons on them. Infants were incinerated, the skulls of children were split with cleavers, and genitalia tortured under his command — very similar to what happened in Colonia Dignidad.[697]

---

[693] Chile. Accessed 2023, Jan 31 from https://cja.org/where-we-work/chile/. "Americans tortured and disappeared by the continent's combined security services. Based on this discovery, researchers have estimated Operation Condor's toll at 50,000 murdered, 30,000 disappeared (and presumed dead) and 400,000 incarcerated."

[694] Chile. Accessed 2023, Jan 31 from https://cja.org/where-we-work/chile/. "Under the 1973 to 1990 dictatorship of General Augusto Pinochet, the people of Chile were subjected to a systematic campaign of torture and state violence: an estimated 2,600 to 3,400 Chilean citizens were executed or "disappeared" while another estimated 30,000 to 100,000 were tortured."

[695] Nickelsberg, Robert. Augusto Pinochet. Accessed 2023, Feb 1 from https://www.history.com/topics/south-america/augusto-pinochet.

[696] Pisetta, Nicola. Colonia Dignidad: Pinochet's City-Lager in Chile. Accessed 2022, Jun 9 from https://www.vanillamagazine.it/colonia-dignidad-la-citta-lager-nel-cile-di-pinochet/. "Colonia Dignidad was therefore also one of the most ruthless places of detention for political prisoners in Chile: new bunkers, long underground tunnels and laboratories very similar to those of Auschwitz were born inside. According to the most recent documents, the well-known Nazi doctor Josef Mengele also found hospitality in the structure. Joseph Mengele Psychedelic drugs were tested on inmates and electroshock was common. In addition, the effect of sarin gas was also examined in the secret basement of the concentration camp. Those who died joined the long list of disappeared and ended up in mass graves."

[697] Basso, Carols. 2022. La Secta Perfecta. "They gave him green pills every day and also applied electroshocks to his genitals." https://itunes.apple.com/WebObjects/MZStore.woa/wa/viewBook?id=0

Helmuth Seelbach recounted having seen him several times injecting drugs into the penises of those who were detained in the "Neukra", where at one time they had many children and young people. Seelbach knew exactly what he was talking about, because for a long time he was part of the night guards. In this condition, he explained, one day Schafer gave him an electric baton with the purpose of applying it to the genitals of the boys[698]

Schäfer was in contact with pro-Nazi groups around the world, and large amounts of money were sent to Colonia Dignidad to fund military operations.[699] Some of those operations were on a global scale. Such was the case with Herbert Kappler, a former SS colonel serving a life sentence for the execution of 335 Italian citizens in German-occupied Rome in 1944. Former members of the SS helped him escape prison, and at least three of the ex-SS officers involved came from Colonia Dignidad.[700]

DINA helped to establish indoctrination courses in the colony, and many techniques of brainwashing and mind control were used on both converts and guests. According to testimony in court trials, Paul Schäfer and Gerhard Micke (Paul Schäfer's bodyguard) joined with the younger settlers for a course on explosives. Students were shown films, photos, and documents relating to WWII, including the destruction of tanks, bridges, and more.[701] The concept of "family" was completely dissolved.

---

[698] Basso, Carlos. 2022. La Secta Perfecta.

[699] Infield, Glenn B. 1981. Secrets of the SS. "There is also evidence that Shaeffer is in contact with pro-Nazi groups around the world and that large amounts of money are sent to Colonia Dignidad each year by such groups."

[700] Infield, Glenn B. 1981. Secrets of the SS. "The flight was planned and prepared by former members of the SS. One of them was an officer of the SS Security Service in Rome during the war. Three of the ex-SS officers involved in the escape came from Colonia Dignidad."

[701] Basso, Carlos. 2022. La Secta Perfecta. "Together with other younger settlers. They were shown films, photos, and documents related to the Second World War, where you could see the destruction of tanks, bridges, etc., in addition to the actions of the German intelligence services."

Children slept in the "kinderhauss" (Children's house) while the mothers lived in the basement. Words like "mother" or "father" were strictly forbidden. All adults were called "ankle" and "tante" (uncle and aunt). First names and nicknames were used instead of full names.[702] After marriage, couples were required to sleep in separate quarters. Those who procreated did so by secret encounters "in the corner of a shed or in a workshop ... so that no one sees them".[703]

Some of the new recruits in Colonia Dignidad were kidnapped. Dieter Scholz, for example, was stolen from his mother after he was born in the colony's hospital. Someone had told his mother, who lived in the Trabancura region, that the child was very sick and should remain in the colony. Weeks went by and the same answer was given. Weeks turned into months, and then years. Dieter was told that his mother had died during childbirth.[704] New "converts" were put to work in the colony after age ten. From that point, both day and night they worked on the machines with not even a few hours to play. They were told that "work is divine service".[705]

After dark the reign of terror continued. Men in the commune were required to sleep naked and watchmen stood guard to monitor sleep. If any children moved their eyelids, it was a sign that they were not sleeping properly, and they were beaten out of their bed. If their genitals moved, they were beaten with a cattle

---

[702] Basso, Carlos. 2022. La Secta Perfecta. ""in order to destroy the concept of family. They lived apart and the children were prevented from hearing words like "mama" or "dad". The "correct" thing within the sect was to call all adults "uncle" or "aunt" (onkel and tante, in German), even if it was the parents themselves, with whom there was no coexistence. The children and adolescents slept in the kinderhauss (children's house) and the women in the basement. The children did not know their last names."

[703] Basso, Carlos. 2022. La Secta Perfecta

[704] Basso, Carlos. 2022. La Secta Perfecta. "Dieter Scholz, a man in his fifties who was literally stolen from his mother shortly after he was born in the Colonia Dignidad hospital."

[705] Basso, Carlos. 2022. La Secta Perfecta. "the children of the colony were not entitled to even a few hours of play a day. The justification for these forced labors was of a religious nature, since the founders of the colony maintained that "work is divine service.""

whip on the testicles and put under a cold shower.[706]   Some children were trained to avoid sexual distraction in extremely painful ways.

> *There are testimonies of how Dr. Seewald gave young men injections into the testicles, which would swell and remain sore for weeks. Years later, Dr. Gisela Gruhlke, Gerd Seewald's wife, would end up confessing that she had instructions from Schafer to practice "treatments" on all young people who thought about sex and other distractions, consisting of medications and electroshock, as well as drugs, among which mentioned chlorpromazine, haloperidol, and diazepam. "Schäfer pointed out to me that these children had to be treated, because they did not pay attention, they were rebellious" and that the messianic leader "had the obsession that the children had demonic manifestations, which were healed with electroshocks that were applied to the forehead."[707]*

Schäfer's monitoring of the young males had a much more sinister purpose: they were his prey. According to Wolfgang Knesse, who escaped the colony after several failed attempts and brutal punishment, "If you don't know where Schäfer is, he must be with children, because he needs them like an animal needs meat."[708] Schäfer architected the structure of the broken family unit, religious doctrine, monitoring and more with the sole purpose of setting up a world where he could rape children with absolute impunity. He deceptively convinced many parents in Germany to send their children with him to Colonia Dignidad and performed illegal adoptions of several children from the local nearby areas.

---

[706] Basso, Carlos. 2022. La Secta Perfecta. "behind each bed or every two beds there was a watchman, among whom I was in the first period." If any of the children moved their eyelids, it was a sign that he was awake and therefore he was beaten out of bed. But "something moved in the genital area, then the child was taken out and beaten with the cattle whip, also on the testicles, and put under a cold shower."

[707] Basso, Carlos. 2022. La Secta Perfecta

[708] Basso, Carlos. 2022. La Secta Perfecta

Empowered by the Pinochet regime, Schäfer started a summer boarding school that allowed him to prey upon even more local children — at least until mothers started filing complaints.[709] Though Schäfer was involved with the mutilation, molestation, and rape of several young men in the colony, from a religious standpoint, he remained true to William Branham's Latter Rain theology — especially with regards to Branham's "Serpent's Seed" doctrine concerning Communism. As it related to the CIA operation in collaboration with Pinochet, the religious doctrine was both empowering and fulfilling to the religious converts. The sect was literally living out Branham's end-of-days scenario, and Branham's prediction of war against Communism was very real. Schäfer presented himself as an extension to Branham, a new religious leader appointed by God to carry on the work that did not end with Branham's death in 1965.

> *"I am here with the mission of the word of God, to preach the message, call everyone to repentance and conversion, and to move away from evil." "Put on your red glasses, those that the devil encourages." "If we agreed here and prayed now for communism to disappear completely from the earth, a new Antichrist would come."*[710]

The military components of Colonia Dignidad quickly increased after President Richard Nixon commissioned the CIA to work with the Branham cult compound under Operation Condor. While visitors to the surface of the compound watched Pentecostal holiness converts singing songs to Jesus and listening to recordings of William Branham and Ewald Frank, other converts worked to secretly establish fortification of the facilities to secure a joint

---

[709] Basso, Carlos. 2022. La Secta Perfecta. "Schafer deceived many parents in Germany to bring their children to Chile, as well as the illegal adoptions carried out in Catillo, Parral, San Carlos and other nearby areas, which were They started so that Schafer would have more children to abuse. When that strategy began to falter, at the end of the eighties, Schafer designed a new one: a summer boarding school that lasted for years."
[710] Basso, Carlos. 2022. La Secta Perfecta

military operation between rebel forces in Chile and the United States.

Visitors were surprised at the advanced technology inside Colonia Dignidad. Powerful communication equipment was installed, including intercoms in every room, cameras, and video equipment and more. Fully automated doors opened and closed as the cultists and military approached and entered.[711] What most visitors did not realize, however, was that this technology was used to secure a military operation the likes of which had not been seen since the Third Reich. One of the colonists named "Lindes", for example, was the former Nazi Gestapo officer Walter Rauff. Raugh was a DINA adviser and weapons specialist, as well as a teacher in karate mixed with judo for those assigned to Colonia Dignidad security. Rauff was the inventor of the famous "mobile gas chambers" and later head of the Gestapo in Northern Italy.

Evidence exists suggesting that Colonia Dignidad was producing sarin gas as early as the 1970s.[712] Sarin, a deadly nerve agent, was originally developed in Germany as a pesticide.[713] It is one of the most toxic and quickly fatal of all nerve agents. It was so deadly, in fact, that after the Nazis developed the chemical weapon, Hitler was afraid to use it.[714] By the end of WWII, Germany had produced over 12,000 tons of the gas, and high-ranking Nazis pressed Hitler to use it against military opponents. The gas would have contaminated the battlefield, however, crippling Germany's Blitzkrieg military strategy. On some

---

[711] Basso, Carlos. 2022. La Secta Perfecta. "They had technology that they didn't know about, powerful communication equipment, intercoms in every room, camera and video equipment, and fully automated doors that opened and closed on their own."

[712] Basso, Carlos. 2022. La Secta Perfecta. "sarin gas, which had been produced within the sect in the 1970s and perhaps even earlier."

[713] Facts about Sarin. CDC. Accessed 2023, Feb 1 from https://emergency.cdc.gov/agent/sarin/basics/facts.asp

[714] Pruitt, Sarah. 2019. The Nazis Developed Sarin Gas During WWII, But Hitler Was Afraid to Use It. Accessed 2023, Feb 1 from https://www.history.com/news/the-nazis-developed-sarin-gas-but-hitler-was-afraid-to-use-it

occasions, Schäfer himself sent assassins to use the deadly gas on his opponents.[715]

By the height of Augusto Pinochet's reign of terror in Chile, Colonia Dignidad had grown in military capacity far beyond that of simply an intelligence center and weapons depot. The cult compound began producing weapons of war, supplying them to Pinochet as well as other well-known international arms dealers. The property expanded to more than 16,000 hectares, and several weapons caches were discovered during the investigation of the colony after the fall of Pinochet. Among the weapons discovered were dozens of surface-to-air missiles, rocket launchers, machine guns, submachine guns, hand and cluster grenades, rifles, anti-personnel mines, automatic pistols and a large amount of ammunition.[716] Both chemical and biological weapons were being manufactured.[717] Evidence that the sarin gas was used in the basement of the concentration camp was found, as well as mass graves for those killed by members of Colonia Dignidad and DINA.[718]

---

[715] Basso, Carlos. 2022. La Secta Perfecta. "we started with a single mission: locate your car in Santiago and put sarin on the door or the steering wheel. But we searched all day and couldn't find it. When we got back, Schafer scolded us harshly. He told us that we were useless."

[716] The Investigation on the Mysterious German Enclave in Southern Chile. 2005. Clarin. Accessed 2022, Jun 9 from https://www.clarin.com/ediciones-anteriores/arma-mato-kennedy-oculta-chilena-colonia-dignidad_0_ByLg95_yRKe.html. "The arsenal includes dozens of surface-to-air missiles, rocket launchers, machine guns, submachine guns, hand and cluster grenades, rifles, anti-personnel mines, automatic pistols and a large amount of ammunition. The finding was the product of an inspection order of the property of more than 16,000 hectares of Judge Jorge Zepeda, who investigates human rights violations in the German enclave during the dictatorship."

[717] Wills, James. Dark secrets of Nazi paedo cult leader's commune where grisly torture methods were rife. Accessed 2022, Jun 9 from https://www.dailystar.co.uk/news/world-news/dark-secrets-nazi-paedo-cult-25089683. "It has also been claimed the site, which had its own armoury, was used as centre to create biological weapons."

[718] Pisetta, Nicola. Colonia Dignidad: Pinochet's City-Lager in Chile. Accessed 2022, Jun 9 from https://www.vanillamagazine.it/colonia-dignidad-la-citta-lager-nel-cile-di-pinochet/. "Colonia Dignidad was therefore also one of the most ruthless places of detention for political prisoners in Chile: new bunkers, long underground tunnels and laboratories very similar to those of Auschwitz were born inside. According to the most recent documents, the well-known Nazi doctor Josef Mengele also found hospitality in

Most of the cult members in Colonia Dignidad were aware of the military operation, though only certain members would have known the extent. It would have been difficult *not* to be aware; many new faces were entering the compound from Nazi elite to DINA and CIA agents and more. The three hundred and forty settlers of the colony supported and even defended the operation when confronted by investigators.[719] The politically and racially-charged doctrines of the Latter Rain empowered the leaders of Colonia Dignidad, especially when combined with the end-of-days prophecies on the recordings of William Branham taught by Paul Schäfer.

William Branham taught Latter Rain converts that Hitler's slaughter of Jews during the Holocaust was *"the tender hand of Jehovah."*[720] Branham claimed that he had seen a vision of how the world would end, and that one of the key milestones in that vision was the election of President John F. Kennedy.[721] According to Branham, Kennedy brought the end to democracy and entered the

---

the structure. Joseph Mengele Psychedelic drugs were tested on inmates and electroshock was common. In addition, the effect of sarin gas was also examined in the secret basement of the concentration camp. Those who died joined the long list of disappeared and ended up in mass graves."

[719] Was the weapon that killed Kennedy hidden in the Chilean Colonia Dignidad? 2005. Clarion. Accessed 2023, Feb 3 from https://www.clarin.com/ediciones-anteriores/arma-mato-kennedy-oculta-chilena-colonia-dignidad_0_ByLg95_yRKe.html. The secrets kept by the German enclave founded in 1960 by former Nazi corporal Schaefer, and which the 340 settlers zealously defended, are revealed little by little, with the help of the youngest settlers, who want to free themselves from Schaefer's sick tutelage."

[720] Branham, William. 1963, Jun 30. The Third Exodus. "Hitler and Stalin, Mussolini, who hated the Jew. They had to go back to their homeland. God, you got ways of doing things, that we don't understand. And You pressed them. No home in Germany; everything taken away from them. Also, in Italy, Russia, no place to go. And they were sent back to their homeland, just to fulfill the Word. 46 Oh, the loving hand of God! How, sometimes, it looks cruel, of the way that people suffer, but it, still, it's the tender hand of Jehovah, leading His little children. We thank You, Lord."

[721] Branham, William. 1964, April 3. Jehovah-Jireh #2. "He give seven things in 1933, would happen. And now every one of them has come to pass but two things, perfectly, just exactly. How that even President Kennedy would be taken in."

United States into a military dictatorship.[722] This, Branham claimed, would lead to a war between Communism and the Roman Catholic Church, and Communism would destroy Catholicism.[723] According to the timeline of Branham's doomsday prophecy, the world was in its final days. Branham predicted by *"Divine inspiration that 1977 ought to terminate the world systems and usher in the millennium."*[724] Operation Condor was officially declared in November of 1975, on Pinochet's 60th birthday.[725]

Depending upon which version of Branham's stage persona was being recorded, the outcome varied. When reading from a paper of the alleged prophecies that he claimed to have been written in 1933, Communism was the victor. When reading from a paper dated 1932, Communism was not the clear victor,[726] and Rome was to be the victor over Communism.[727] In either case, the end result was a war between *"both white and colored".*

> *Just—just like Hitler did, over in Germany, led them right into a death trap, them precious Germans. And they laid by the billions, or millions, piled up there on top one another. And that's exactly the same thing. And remember, I'm on tape. You'll see it, after, maybe after I'm gone. That's exactly what's going to happen. Them precious people will die down there, like flies. Starts a revolutionary, both white and colored will*

---

[722] Branham, William. 1963, Jun 30. The Third Exodus. "Said, "We'll not fight. No, sir." And said, "I hope the nation can find out that we're not living anymore under a democracy,"

[723] Branham, William. 1964, Apr 3. Jehovah-Jireh #2. "How that Hitler would rise up, and—and Fascism, and—and Nazism, and all to bind in communism, and communism would destroy Catholicism."

[724] Branham, William. An Exposition of The Seven Church Ages.

[725] Plummer, Robert. 2005, Jun 8. Condor legacy haunts South America". BBC. Accessed 2023, Feb 3 from http://news.bbc.co.uk/2/hi/americas/3720724.stm.

[726] Branham, William. 1960, Nov 13. Condemnation by Representation. "We will be in war with Germany. Watch Russia. Now, that, see, Communism, Nazism, and Fascism. Watch Russia, but that is not the main one to watch."

[727] Branham, William. 1962, Jun 24. Super Sign. "Show me one place where it said communism will rule the world. The Bible said Rome will rule the world, not communism."

fight again, and die like flies.[728]

The cultists in Colonia Dignidad would have seen the conflicting versions of prophecy as somewhat accurate as it related to their current set of events. In 1970, Chile was over ninety percent Catholic.[729] Allende's supporters were both Communist *and* Catholic. Almost all of them had dark skin and would have been viewed as the *"mongrel race"*. Combined with the fact that Nixon was sending militia to fight — Nixon who lost to President Kennedy in the 1960 election that Branham claimed to be fulfillment of prophecy — the Latter Rain converts in Colonia Dignidad would have believed they were fighting *Branham's war.* This is evident from the fact that nearly three hundred records in the intelligence files found in Colonia Dignidad were from *constant surveillance* of the nuns of the Little Sisters of Peace.[730]

Interestingly, in the middle of a massive hidden arsenal, investigators recovered two 7.62 caliber bullets, like the ones used in Lee Harvey Oswald's 7.62 caliber Mannlicher Carcano rifle. With the bullets was a piece of paper with a single word written: "Kennedy".[731]

---

[728] Branham, William. 1963, June 30. The Third Exodus (63-0630M).

[729] Religion and Churches. Accessed 2023, Feb 3 from https://countrystudies.us/chile/51.htm. "The 1970 census showed that about 90 percent of the population was nominally Roman Catholic, and a little over 6 percent was Protestant."

[730] Basso, Carlos. 2022. La Secta Perfecta. "Perhaps the most evident confirmation of this paranoia and the way in which it operated as an intelligence apparatus are the nearly three hundred records in which the constant surveillance of the nuns of the Little Sisters of Peace."

[731] The Investigation on the Mysterious German Enclave in Southern Chile. 2005. Clarin. Accessed 2022, Jun 9 from https://www.clarin.com/ediciones-anteriores/arma-mato-kennedy-oculta-chilena-colonia-dignidad_0_ByLg95_yRKe.html. "In the middle of a huge hidden arsenal, two bullets were found with a paper that had the name of the former president of the United States, assassinated in 1963, written on it. Now a possible connection between that assassination and the mysterious German enclave founded in Chile by the former Nazi Paul Schaefer."

CHAPTER 19

JONESTOWN

❖

"When I read about Jim Jones, I thought immediately of the Colonia Dignidad. We know there is strong indoctrination, but we don't know if there is total intimidation." – Charles Krause

On November 18, 1978, former Latter Rain minister Jim Jones and over nine hundred members of his Peoples Temple cult of personality committed mass suicide in Jonestown, Guyana. Jones, who had in the 1950s sponsored William Branham's healing revivals,[732] parted ways with Branham in 1957 after it was learned that Branham was teaching the Christian Identity doctrine. Several "Voice of Healing Evangelists" rose against Branham and issued an "Open Letter to William Branham" condemning him to death and destruction.[733] Jones joined the others, issuing his own prophecy against William Branham.[734] According to Jones, Branham

---

[732] Branham, William. 1956, Oct 2. Father, the Hour Has Come. "Happy to see, today, is our host pastor (Brother James Jones) from Indianapolis, back there."

[733] Christian FELLOWSHIP convention Replies to 'Open Letter' to William Branham. 1957, July. The Voice of Healing. "The fact that Evangelist William Branham was the main speaker at the Christian Fellowship convention in Indianapolis, Indiana, June 10-14, 1957, caused many brethren to be deeply concerned regarding the veracity of the statements in an open letter addressed to him and circulated widely. The convention decided upon an investigation of the matter in order to be able to give correct information to those who have been disturbed by this and other letters."

[734] Q612 Transcript. Accessed 2021, Jun 22 from https://jonestown.sdsu.edu/?page_id=27492. Some are listening. They won't tell you the

admitted to him that he didn't *"believe a thing in that Bible hardly. But he said, it's the way to make a living."* Jones continued his Latter Rain ministry, however, and by 1959 had changed his local "Peoples Temple Full Gospel" church to a "People's Temple International-Interdenominational Full Gospel Church".[735]

When news of the Jonestown Massacre spread into Chile, the Chileans were eerily reminded of the striking similarities between Jonestown and Colonia Dignidad.[736] Both communes initially started as "agricultural communities". Both were led by a narcissistic authoritarian figure. Both communes regulated (and deprived members of) sleep, sex, and more. Both resulted in horrific deaths of members. At the time, however, Chileans were largely unaware that the leaders of both communes were trained in the same extremist form of religion. Like Paul Schäfer, Jim Jones had integrated William Branham's Manifest Sons of God theology into his preaching, and used it as the foundation for authoritarian control.[737] Just as Branham used the phrase, "I am God's Voice to

---

truth, because the black book is the easiest gravy train that they've ever been on. Yet Allen [A.A. Allen, Pentecostal evangelist] came to me, Oral Roberts [Pentecostal evangelist] spoke this, Billy Graham came right to us - Ijames [Archie Ijames], Jack [Jack Arnold Beam], and me - in Claypool Hotel, said I don't believe a thing in that Bible hardly. But he said, it's the way to make a living. Billy Graham, who I prophesied his death, Billy Branham rather, said his head would be– I said he'd lose his head. His head was cut off in Texas. [Editorial note: The reference is to William Branham, an evangelical preacher and acquaintance of Jim Jones during the Temple's Indianapolis days. Branham died in an automobile accident on Christmas Eve 1965 in Texas but was not decapitated.] He said you can't preach the truth about that Bible, he said (tape cuts out about three seconds) preach reincarnation, you cannot preach the truth about the Bible, you will be in trouble. I said, I choose to treat th– preach the truth. He said, well, I'll be around, while you will be in trouble. Well, I'm still here, and his head is cut off from his body."

[735] Peoples Temple, 1959, Jul 11. Indianapolis Star. "Peoples Temple International-Interdenominational Full Gospel"

[736] Krause, Charles A. 1980, Feb 11. Nobody Comes, Nobody Goes Mystery Veils Colony in Chile

"When I read about Jim Jones, I thought immediately of the Colonia Dignidad," said a diplomat in Santiago, 200 miles to the north, whose embassy has had some contact with the colony over the years. "We know there is strong indoctrination, but we don't know if there is total intimidation."

[737] Colonia Dignidad and Jonestown. Accessed 2023, Feb 13 from https://jonestown.sdsu.edu/?page_id=67352.

You" or "The Spoken Word", Jones convinced his converts that he was also the "Spoken Word".[738] As it turns out, Jones was connected directly to William Branham during his years as a Latter Rain Minister.

In 1953, William Branham and Ern Baxter held a series of revivals In Connersville, Indiana at the Roberts Park Amphitheater. The ministers invited the public under the auspices of a "Plain Old-Fashioned Revival,"[739] but it was more than likely a means to spread British Israelism using the healing revivals as a vehicle. Branham and Baxter had recently held a similar series of revivals in New York, where Branham taught the Latter Rain message and British Israelism.[740] Not long after the Connersville revival, Jones changed the name of his Somerset Methodist Church to "Christian Assembly," and began advertising "Full Gospel Preaching" in the Sunday newspapers.[741] Within months, Jones became a familiar face in the local Indianapolis Pentecostal community, and was invited to preach for the first time at the Laurel Street Tabernacle, a Latter Rain church under the banner of the Assemblies of God.

Laurel Street Tabernacle's head pastor, Rev. Price, had announced that he would soon be retiring, and that Jones was a potential candidate to replace him.[742] Based simply upon the

---

[738] Q353 Transcript. Accessed 2023, Feb 13 from https://jonestown.sdsu.edu/?page_id=27429The Spoken Word is here. The Word is made flesh. We don't pray and beg anymore, we don't grovel around on our knees anymore, we can talk to God face-to-face, and we can hear God with our own ears, and with our own understanding.

[739] 1953, Mar 5. Plain Old-Fashioned Revival. Palladium-Item.

[740] Branham, William.1950, Apr 5. Expectation. "That's New York. See? 'Preach the Gospel to every creature. These signs shall follow them that believe.' He promised it. And then He promised the former rain and the latter rain. And we're living now, have been for years, under the latter rain. And just before God cut off relationship with the Jews, He put nine spiritual gifts into the Church. And just before the Gentile's age is over, He's restoring back in the Church those nine spiritual gifts, giving the Gentile church its last call before turning again to Israel."

[741] 1953, Nov 21. Christian Assembly. The Indianapolis News.

[742] Hall, John R. Gone from the Promised Land: Jonestown in American Cultural History. "In September 1954, Jones received an invitation to preach at the Tabernacle, the very time when the congregation's board was searching out a successor to the retiring minister, John Price."

number of times Jones shared the pulpit at the Laurel Street Tabernacle during his participation with Latter Rain, it is clear that Jones had become the *primary* candidate to replace Rev. Price. The church fully adopted Jones as an associate pastor and began advertising "Rev. James Jones" beside "Rev. J. L. Price" in their Sunday advertisements. It also changed the title to "New" Laurel Street Tabernacle and began advertising thousands of "miracles"[743] as was typical among ministers participating in the Latter Rain movement. They also introduced the slogan "Deliverance Center for All People." Price and Jones began holding "Miracle Services" advertising "1,000 Miracles in 2 Months," making waves throughout the Assemblies of God communities.

When the Assemblies of God became very rigid in their position against Latter Rain, however, sweeping changes came to the Laurel Street Tabernacle. It was announced that the Rev. W. L. Thornton would be replacing John L. Price as head pastor, and that he would be leading an "expansion and reorganization program." He had served for two years as the director of the youth organization of the main branch of the Assemblies of God after serving for three years as an evangelist in the Indiana area.[744] Thornton was strongly affiliated with the non-Latter Rain sect of the Assemblies of God, attending international conventions at the headquarters in Springfield, Missouri.[745]

As a result, on April 4, 1955, Jones had created his own business entity registered in the State of Indiana: Wings of Deliverance, Incorporated, and started his own church as the Laurel Street Tabernacle began to split. Several members sided with Jones,[746] and met briefly under the "Wings of Deliverance" name. Shortly after, they used the name "Peoples Temple Full

---

[743] 1955, Jan 1. New Laurel Street Tabernacle. The Indianapolis Star.

[744] 1955, Jan 1. New Laurel Street Tabernacle. The Indianapolis Star.

[745] 1952, Apr 4. Thornton Goes to Convention. Linton (Indiana) Daily Citizen.

[746] Hamlett, Ryan. 2014, Feb 25. The Devil in the Old Northside. Accessed May 27, 2019. "After leaving Somerset, Jones spent a short while as an associate minister at Laurel Street Tabernacle near Fountain Square, where he gathered the first few members of what would become the People's Temple."

Gospel," and eventually it transitioned to the shorter name of "Peoples Temple."

Jim Jones was also deeply impacted by William Branham's UFO and End of Days prophecy. In the 1950s, Jones frequently held revivals with Latter Rain evangelist Orval Lee Jaggers. Jaggers was an editor for Branham's Voice of Healing publication[747] and shared Branham's belief that UFOs were a *"revelation of God's power."*[748] The Voice of Healing publication thrilled its readers with doomsday countdowns,[749] clouds that allegedly looked like Jesus descending in an *"imminent"* return,[750] and *"spiritual"* explanations of the *"Mystery of the Flying Saucers."*[751] Leaders of the sect claimed that UFOs were *"celestial warnings of an impending Divine interruption of the course of world events"*[752] – or in simple terms, Armageddon.[753] These extraterrestrial *"wee men"* in *"flying saucers"* were not to be feared, but were sent to warn members of the sect that the End of Days was near. Those who did not heed their warning would be eternally doomed. Over time, the UFOs made their way into the sect's theology by interchanging the word *"sign"* in the Bible with *"flying saucer"*[754] when reading passages of

---

[747] 1951, Jan. Associate Editors. The Voice of Healing. (Listed as O. L. Jaggers).

[748] The Universal World Church (Hawaii Fellowship). Accessed 2019, May 27 from http://www.letusreason.org/Cults2.htm. His belief in astrology was confirmed through occult teachings which included that UFO's were a revelation of God's power.

[749] Ex: Lindsay, Gordon. November in Prophecy. 1948, Nov. The Voice of Healing. "The cold war is on now - the hour approaches for World War III to break in its fury."

[750] Ex: Signs in Earth, Air and Sky Foretell Imminent Return of Christ. 1951, Sept. The Voice of Healing (Front Cover).

[751] What Is the Mystery of the Flying Saucers? 1952, Oct. The Voice of Healing (Cover photo).

[752] Lindsay, Gordon. What Is the Mystery of the Flying Saucers? 1952, Oct. The Voice of Healing.

[753] Branham, William. 1953, Dec 1. God's Provided Way. "flying saucers through the air and everything else. Jesus said, "There'd be signs in the heaven above and in the earth below, pillars of fire and vapors of smoke; it shall come to pass before the great and terrible day of the Lord shall come."

[754] Branham, William. 1955, May 22. The Ark. "He is in the world today, showing signs and wonders {...} Signs! Signs of flying saucers through the air, where even the Pentagon and all don't know what to think of it, 'Signs in the heaven above. 'And on earth,' the healing of the sick, the raising of the dead, the opening of the blinded eyes, the casting out of evil spirits, the Gospel being preached, signs before His Coming! "Not willing that

apocalyptic prophecy.[755] Gordon Lindsay, Branham's campaign manager and publisher of The Voice of Healing, wrote several articles and books about UFOs to further promote the sect's doctrine of UFOs.[756] Branham began to claim that humans were made of *"cosmic light"* which would transition to another dimension,[757] and that dispensational *"ages"* were led by a prophet of *"light."*[758]

In 1956, when it was announced that Jim Jones would host the international convention of ministers at the Cadle Tabernacle in Indianapolis with William Branham as the headline act,[759] the Latter Rain sect began claiming that along with the UFO "signs" in the sky, God would soon be showing signs on the earth in the form of a tidal wave that would destroy Chicago.[760] According to William Branham, Chicago was the focal point of Nahum's prophecy[761] in

---

any should perish, but that all might humbly, sweetly bow to repentance.' But those who reject Christ, have to walk blind."

[755] Ex: Branham, William. 1955, May 22. The Junction of Time. "And it shall come to pass," saith God, "in the last days, I'll pour out My Spirit. Your sons and daughters shall prophesy," prophets promised. "Your young men shall see visions. And I'll show wonders in the heavens above," flying saucers and everything."

[756] Example Books: The Mystery of the Flying Saucers in the Light of the Bible, 1954. The Antichrists Have Come, 1958. The Signs of the Times in the Heavens, 1972. Example Voice of Healing articles: Signs in the Heavens, 1953. The Mystery of the Flying Saucers, 1954. Further Developments on the Flying Saucers, 1954. Men in the Flying Saucers Identified, 1954. Flying Saucers, Atomic Bombs and the Second Coming of Christ, 1955.

[757] Branham, William. 1955, Apr 3. Fellowship by Redemption. 55-0403. After you go out of this body, out of cosmic light and petroleums, and what you're made up of, and you go into the fourth dimension; out of that, into the fifth dimension, then the sixth dimension. Then, God is in the seventh. You're right under His altar."

[758] Branham, William. 1964, Mar 12. "Moses was the light of his age. Jeremiah was the light of his age. It was the God's light shining forth for the Word that was promised for that age. Every age has its promised Word. God sends His prophets and reveals that Word; vindicates His prophet, first, then reveals that Word and makes It live."

[759] Salvation-Healing Campaigns of the Voice of Healing Evangelists: William Branham. 1956, Jun. The Voice of Healing. "Host pastor: Rev. James Jones."

[760] Branham, William. 1956, Apr 4. The Infallibility of God's Spoken Word. A "flying saucers and everything, all kinds of mystic signs in the heavens above. Signs on the earth below, there'll be sea a roaring, tidal waves breaking along Chicago."

[761] Branham, William. 1957, Jul 14. As The Eagle Stirreth Up Her Nest. "That great eagle called Nahum, four thousand years ago, went up so high in the Spirit of God until he seen Outer Drive in Chicago, four thousand years later. Said, 'The chariots shall rage in

the Old Testament book of Nahum – instead of the city of Nineveh and the Assyrian Empire as described in the book itself.[762] Chicago had already seen a "freak wave" in 1954,[763] and because of its unexplained nature, the sect claimed that God himself was coming to destroy Chicago in the form of a much larger tidal wave.

In 1961, As Paul Schäfer began migrating to Colonia Dignidad from Germany, Jones began claiming to have seen a vision of Chicago and Indianapolis being destroyed by a nuclear holocaust.[764] By 1962, Jones had moved his family to Escola da Favela, Bello Horizonte, Brazil, and eventually to British Guiana[765] — years before the Peoples Temple migration to Jonestown, Guyana. At the time, both Paul Schäfer and Jim Jones were Latter Rain converts; it was not until 1964 that Jones would be ordained into the Disciples of Christ[766] in a somewhat failed attempt to distance himself from the Latter Rain sect. Jones continued teaching the Manifested Sons of God theology well into the 1970s.

> *I'm saying nothing more than what Jesus said. Jesus said, I am God. And they crucified him for it. They said, for that, we are going to crucify He said, why are you going to kill me? Because I'm teaching that ye all are gods. Because your ancient law says, it is written, ye all are gods and sons of the most high. So, we are sons of the most high, and that most high is a socialist non-violent revolution (John 10:34, "Jesus answered them, Is it not written in your law, I said, Ye are gods?" Psalms 82:6, "I have said, Ye are gods; and all of you*

---

the broad ways: they shall run like lightning, they shall seem like torches, they'll justle one against another.'"

[762] Nahum 1:1. "A prophecy concerning Nineveh."

[763] Briscoe, Tony. Lake Michigan's deadly 'freak wave' of 1954 is Chicago folklore. Turns out it was a meteotsunami. And they happen pretty often. 2019, Apr 25. Chicago Tribune.

[764] 100 Events in History of Peoples Temple. Accessed 2023, Feb 13 from https://jonestown.sdsu.edu/wp-content/uploads/2013/10/Timeline100.pdf.

[765] 100 Events in History of Peoples Temple.

[766] 100 Events in History of Peoples Temple.

are children of the most High."[767] *- Jim Jones, Summer of 1972.*

While leaders in Latter Rain worked with the Nixon and Ford administration to spread universal fear of Communism, Jones and Peoples Temple did not. In fact, Jones was supportive of Communism. In several speeches and sermons, Jones declared himself to be Marxist, and felt that Communism would help bring balance to the world. When Salvadore Allende became the first Marxist to be elected president in a liberal democracy in Latin America, Jones would have been supportive. At the time, however, it is unlikely that Jones knew that the CIA was working with the Latter Rain colony.

I'm a Marxist, whether the damn revolution wo— is won or lost. And I wonder sometimes whether Fidel [Castro] would've fought the fight if he thought he was gonna die. Would [Che] Guevara have fought the fight. Still, it don't make any difference whether they were pure communist or not. Uh, co— communism's got to win, and it's right if it didn't win, because two out of three babies going to bed hungry, it isn't right. And the only way you can stop two out of three babies going to bed hungry is to have pure communism. You got to share the wealth, or there's gonna be starvation, there's gonna be hunger, even— too much of it we see on the roads as we go back here. Poor children not in good— not in good shape, with their little pot bellies. (Pause) So communism's right. - Jim Jones, 1975

As news of the Chilean coup d'état began to leak to the United States media in 1973, and Jones became aware that there were hints of United States involvement in Chile, Jones decided to let People Temple share in the revolution. After the coup and

---

[767] ex: Jones, James. 2017, May 30. Annotated Transcript Q1057-5. Accessed 2017, May 30.

before Augusto Pinochet was officially declared the President of Chile, Peoples Temple leased the property in Jonestown and sent the first migrants to the new colony.[768]

In the summer of 1974, New York State professor Kyle Steenland published an article entitled "The Coup in Chile" in Latin American Perspectives. It came on the heels of the Associated Press articles describing U.S. involvement with Colonia Dignidad.[769] The journal article gave clear details as to what was going on in Chile, as well as the involvement by the United States. The article apparently made a significant impact on Jones; during a speech just weeks before the Jonestown Massacre, Jones mentioned both the article and the author.

> *There was a peasant revolt under [Salvador] Allende. The peasant question is central for revolutionary processes in most under-developed countries. In a recently-released book, Agrarian Reform under Allende – Dr. Allende was the socialist elected, non-violent leader of Chile – Kyle Steenland in his book gives a first hand look at the way– at the way in the mobilization of peasants, primarily Mapuche Indians – M-a-p-u-c-h-e – and land redistribution was handled, and handled properly, during the Chile's popular unity government under the socialist Dr. Allende from 1970–73 until the CIA, with our tax dollars that causes us considerable guilt, cruelly killed him with the seven million dollars that [Henry] Kissinger provided from our tax money. - Jim Jones, Aug 1978*

Steenland could not have predicted how much worse the situation in Chile would progress, nor how involved the United States was in the battle taking place in South America. He was, however, aware that something big was about to take place. The paragraph of "The Coup in Chile" referenced by Jones and written by Steenland mentioned the transfer of $400,000,000 by Henry

---

[768] 100 Events in History of Peoples Temple. Accessed 2023, Feb 13 from https://jonestown.sdsu.edu/wp-content/uploads/2013/10/Timeline100.pdf.
[769] GIs tied to torture of Chile inmates. 1976, Jun 2. Miami News.

Kissinger to the anti-Allende media campaign, as well as a silent influx of United States dollars into the country. Steenland noted that from 1973 to 1974, the black-market price of the dollar dropped significantly, which indicated a large inflow of dollars to the country.[770]

---

[770] Steenland, Kyle. 1974. The Coup in Chile. "It is likely that the CIA subsidized the owners' lockouts in both October 1972 and August 1973. At that time the black-market rate for the dollar dropped sharply, indicating a large inflow of dollars to the country".

CHAPTER 20

OPERATION CONDOR

❖

"That is right. And that is the way it is going to be played. But listen, as far as the people are concerned let me say they aren't going to buy this crap from the Liberals on this one. - President Nixon"

When Augusto Pinochet was installed as military dictator of the Government Junta of Chile, it was a silent victory for Nixon and the CIA. The covert intelligence operation had resulted in a "win" with regards to overturning a communist presidency, though it was not seen that way by the press. A government had just been *overthrown*, and critics of the situation saw the event for what it was: a hostile government takeover by a military dictator. Nixon was concerned that the plot would be exposed and instructed Kissinger to be sure *"our hand doesn't show on this one."* Both planned out *"the way it is going to be played"*: that the CIA only *"created the conditions as great as possible."* If confronted about the situation, no mention of the arms, vast intelligence network, and installation of Nazis at the primary training facility would be mentioned. Nor would any party involved mention the Latter Rain background of the leaders of that facility. The news media would have had a field day with the articles and photographs of then Vice President Nixon at the Full Gospel Businessman's Convention at the Prayer Breakfast.

Kissinger: Mr. President.

Nixon: Where are you. In New York?

Kissinger: No, I am in Washington. I am working. I may go to the football game this afternoon if I get through.

Nixon: Good. Good. Well, it is the opener. It is better than television. Nothing new of any importance or is there?

Kissinger: Nothing of very great consequence. The Chilean thing is getting consolidated and of course the newspapers and bleeding because a pro-Communist government has been overthrown.

Nixon: Isn't that something. Isn't that something.

Kissinger: I mean instead of celebrating — in the Eisenhower period we would be heroes.

Nixon: Well, we didn't — as you know — our hand doesn't show on this one though.

Kissinger: We didn't do it. I mean we helped them. [redacted] created the conditions as great as possible.

Nixon: That is right. And that is the way it is going to be played. But listen, as far as the people are concerned let me say they aren't going to buy this crap from the Liberals on this one.

Kissinger: Absolutely not.

Nixon: They know it is a pro-Communist government and that is the way it is.

Kissinger: Exactly. And pro-Castro.

Nixon: Well, the main thing was. Let's forget the pro-Communist. It was an anti-American government all the [obscenity] way.

Kissinger: Oh, wildly.

Nixon: And you're expropriating. I notice the memorandum you sent up of the confidential conversation [redacted] set up a policy for reimbursement on expropriations and cooperation with the United States for breaking relations with Castro. Well, what the hell that is a great treat if they think that. No, don't let the columns and the bleeding on that.

Kissinger: Oh, oh it doesn't bother me. I am just reporting it to you.

Nixon: Yes, you are reporting it because it is just typical of the crap we are up against.

Kissinger: and the unbelievable filthy hypocrisy.

Nixon: We know that.

Kissinger: Of these people. When it is South Africa, if we don't overthrow them, they are raising hell.[771]

Once Pinochet was installed, however, the size of the battlefield expanded to encompass a large part of South America. It was a battle that would continue long after President Richard Nixon resigned due to the Watergate Scandal and Vice President Spiro Agnew resigned after suspicion of criminal conspiracy, bribery, extortion, and tax fraud surfaced. When President Gerald Ford succeeded the presidency, he inherited Operation Condor. By that time, Operation Condor had turned into large scale war in South America.

In a monthly report in July of 1976, just months before the predicted 1977 Latter Rain doomsday, Operation Condor was rightfully named *"The Third World War and South America."* on

---

[771] TelCon: 9/16/73(Home)11:50. Mr. Kissinger/The President. Accessed 2023, Jan 31 from https://nsarchive2.gwu.edu/NSAEBB/NSAEBB255/19730916KP5.pdf.

classified documents[772] Chile, Argentina, Brazil, Bolivia, Paraguay, and Uruguay were all major battlefronts for Operation Condor. Representatives of West Germany, France, and Great Britain intelligence services visited the Condor organization secretariat in Buenos Aires in September of 1977 to discuss plans to replicate the operation in Europe.[773]

As the epicenter for the operation, Colonia Dignidad became of key interest and importance. Several different chemical products used to produce different gasses were purchased in Germany.[774] The chemical elements were sent to Chile in glass containers and metal cylinders through Lufthansa.[775] With the chemicals, workers in Colonia Dignidad modified forty to fifty flamethrowers for spraying napalm.[776] Some of the purchases included shrapnel and nitrin, a highly explosive powder for bombs.[777]

One of Paul Schäfer's close friends and former Nazi, Gerhard Mertins, was also involved with Colonia Dignidad. Until his death in 1993, Mertins was considered the biggest arms dealer

---

[772] Shlaudeman, Harry. 1976. 7616677

[773] Italian court jails 24 over South American Operation Condor. 2019, Jul 8. The Guardian. Accessed 2023, Feb 3 from https://www.theguardian.com/world/2019/jul/08/italian-court-jails-24-over-south-american-operation-condor.

[774] Basso, Carlos. 2022. La Secta Perfecta. "during the 1970s, different chemical products were purchased to produce gases of a different nature, in addition to fertilizers, as well as one (illegible) called "Pepper fox" (pepper injection), used to spray and disinfect."

[775] Basso, Carlos. 2022. La Secta Perfecta. "According to him, these elements were sent to Chile in glass containers and metal cylinders (oxygen tubes) through Lufthansa."

[776] Basso, Carlos. 2022. La Secta Perfecta. "According to his testimony, about ten were made and they emitted flames generated by a mixture of gasoline and detergents, propelled by compressed air. By the way, when he talks about a mixture of gasoline and detergents, what he is doing is lowering the profile of what they were really shooting through those devices: Napalm. As for other weapons, he noted that "I estimate that about forty to fifty were made.""

[777] Basso, Carlos. 2022. La Secta Perfecta. "cylinders of different diameters were bought, which corresponded to waste from grenades or ship ammunition, inside which they had thread; casings that were filled, among other components, with a powder called nitrin, which is highly explosive and could detonate without the need for an initiator or fuse."

in the world.[778] He was also Schäfer's primary international ally.[779] Interestingly, Mertins was also the contradiction to one of William Branham's Latter Rain predictions. Branham claimed to have prophesied that Benito Mussolini would face his final defeat after invading Ethiopia.[780] After invading Ethiopia in 1935, Mussolini forged an alliance with Nazi Germany. In 1940, Italy entered WWII on the German side and invaded British Somaliland.[781] Mussolini invaded several countries after Ethiopia, including Albania, France, Egypt, Greece, Yugoslavia, Tunisia, British Somaliland, Kenya, and Sudan. Mussolini was eventually captured, however, and imprisoned when the Allied forces invaded Italy. In 1943, Mertins participated in the Gran Sasso raid rescuing Benito Mussolini from prison in Italy.[782]

Mertins had been working with Iranian Secret Service SAVAK but earned his fame in the underworld for his sale of German F-86 Sabre jets to Pakistan. The jets were taken from German Air Force and shipped via Iran. Mertins had the support of the BND and other German authorities for the transaction.[783] When Mertins escaped several criminal investigations unscathed, he became involved in arms deals around the globe.

---

[778] Basso, Carlos. 2022. La Secta Perfecta. ""He was Paul Schafer's best friend. Former Nazi officer, he combined in his personality an extreme skill for business, unbeatable contacts in the world of intelligence and an astonishing lack of scruples. But not only that: until before his death in 1993, Gerhard Mertins was considered the biggest arms dealer in the world."

[779] Gonzalez, Monica. 2009. The day Manuel Contreras offered the Shah of Iran to kill "Carlos, the Jackal."

[780] Branham, William. 1960, Nov 13. Condemnation by Representation. "The President which now is, President Franklin D. Roosevelt," now remember, this is twenty-eight years ago, "will cause the whole world to go to war. And the new dictator of Italy, Mussolini, shall make his first invasion towards Ethiopia. And he will take Ethiopia, but that will be his last. He shall come to his end."

[781] Italy profile - Timeline. 2022, Dec 9. BBC. Accessed 2023, Feb 6 from https://www.bbc.com/news/world-europe-17435616.

[782] Romano Mussolini, My father, il Duce, Kales Press 2006, S.29: "For more than sixty years, my father's liberation from Gran Sasso was attributed solely to Skorzeny, even though Mors and Mertins played crucial roles."

[783] Mit Billetal und BND. In: Der Spiegel. 47/1974 vom 18. November 1974, S. 65.

In the 1970s, Mertins began selling arms produced by Colonia Dignidad, as well as supplying the colony with arms. According to the testimony of Erika Heiman, several tubes were sent from Germany filled with machine guns from Mertins. The colony referred to Mertins by code name "me", "Merich", or Meeretich".[784] Another testimony from Gerhard Micke confessed that Mertins had asked for 100,000 mortars.[785] To assist in the colony's funding for the manufacturing of arms, Mertins was the founder and president of "the Circle of Friends of Colonia Dignidad", a charitable organization founded in 1978 in Germany to help Schäfer's colony. Several right-wing Christian Social Union politicians participated including Franz Josef Strauss, the Minister-President of Bavaria.[786]

Mertins purchased a gold mine near Durango, Mexico, named Villa Parral. According to the testimony of Gerhard Mücke to the Chilean Justice System, a special antenna was installed in the mine that allowed Mertins to communicate directly with Schäfer from the mine. According to other testimonies, Mertins partnered with Schäfer in similar gold mines in the Nahuelbuta mountain range in Southern Chile.[787]

The expansion of Operation Condor beyond the Southern Cone of South America required an incredible amount of people, resources, and money. In 1976, Manuel Contreras, the former head

---

[784] Basso, Carlos. 2022. La Secta Perfecta. "the one he had in 1970 with Paul Schafer, according to the testimony of Erika Heimann, who pointed out, it will be remembered, that the famous tubes that were sent from Germany were "filled" with machine guns that were provided by Mertins, who in the colony was known as "Me", "Merich" or "Meeretich".

[785] Basso, Carlos. 2022. La Secta Perfecta. "Gerhard Micke confessed in 2005, when he said that "Mertins asked me on one occasion, as a result of my contacts with Famae, to ask if this company could send 100,000 mortars to Trak."

[786] Basso, Carlos. 2022. La Secta Perfecta. "Mertins was also the founder and president of del Círculo de Amigos de Colonia Dignidad, an aid organization for Schäfer created in 1978 in Germany, and in which several politicians linked to the right-wing SCU party, the Christian Social Union, participated, including Franz Josef Strauss."

[787] Basso, Carlos. 2022. La Secta Perfecta. "Mertins was not only interested in the mine he owned in Mexico, but also in the gold mines in the Nahuelbuta mountain range, where according to different testimonies he was a partner of Schafer."

of DINA, got involved with Gerhard Mertins and Paul Schäfer to help raise money. He traveled to Iran with Mertins, three Chilean officers, and one Brazilian general in hopes to convince Shah Reza Pahlevi to contribute in exchange for the killing of Venezuelan Ilich Ramírez, "Carlos, El Chacal" (The Jackal). "Carlos the Jackal" was an international terrorist and had angered Iran by kidnapping OPEC leaders.[788] On December 21, 1975, the world watched in horror as "The Jackal" and a handful of terrorists assaulted the headquarters of the Organization of Petroleum Exporting Countries (OPEC) in Vienna, taking sixty-three hostages. The operation was funded by Libyan leader Muammar Gaddafi.[789] It was later learned that the United States also supported the operation to assassinate "The Jackal", as well as two other well-known European leftists.[790] Ultimately, the mission did not succeed; Carlos was briefly

---

[788] Gonzalez, Monica. 2009, Aug 8. The day Manuel Contreras offered the Shah of Iran to kill "Carlos, the Jackal". "The expansion of Operation Condor beyond the borders of the Southern Cone required millionaire funds and the former head of DINA, Manuel Contreras, tried to obtain resources from powers interested in eliminating common enemies. For this he traveled to Iran in 1976, convinced that he would receive a large sum of money from Shah Reza Pahlevi if he offered to assassinate the Venezuelan Ilich Ramírez, "Carlos, El Chacal", the executor of the kidnapping of OPEC leaders. He was accompanied by former Nazi SS officer, arms dealer and Paul Schäfer ally Gerhard Mertins, three senior Chilean officers and a Brazilian general. They left photos and footprints at the Chilean embassy in Tehran that allow us to reconstruct a story that until now has remained unknown."

[789] Gonzalez, Monica. 2009, Aug 8. The day Manuel Contreras offered the Shah of Iran to kill "Carlos, the Jackal". "The horror that shook the world on December 21, 1975, was received by Manuel Contreras as a true gift for his plans to extend the borders of Operation Condor. Ilich "Carlos" Ramírez Sánchez, at the head of a commando of six people -militants of the Popular Front for the Liberation of Palestine (PFLP) and the Baader-Meinhof Group- assault the headquarters of the Organization of Petroleum Exporting Countries (OPEC) in Vienna, in a very daring and successful action, taking 63 hostages, including ministers and delegates from the countries gathered there, after shooting three security personnel to death. The operation, financed by Libyan leader Muammar Gaddafi."

[790] Gonzalez, Monica. 2009, Aug 8. The day Manuel Contreras offered the Shah of Iran to kill "Carlos, the Jackal". "In his investigation of Operation Condor, journalist John Dinges found a secret US Senate report ("Activities of certain foreign intelligence agencies in the United States") confirming the priority of that operation. After describing Phase Three of Operation Condor, the aforementioned report states: "Thereupon, the Condor planned an operation that had the objective of assassinating three well-known European leftists, one of whom was the famous terrorist 'Carlos'. "

detained and migrated to Yemen where he would start another terrorist organization in collaboration with Syrian, Lebanese and German rebels, as well as the Stasi, East Germany's secret police.[791]

Funding terrorists and ex-Nazis in Chile turned out to be problematic for the United States over time. The CIA was working with some very evil people in the Latter Rain commune, and many of them were also working directly with even worse people. The line between good and evil became even more blurred as the United States began using that evil to fight other evils in the world. Such was the case when the U.S. began supplying arms to Iran to fight Iraq and using the profit to fund the anti-communist guerrillas in Nicaragua "La Contra". When news broke that the Reagan administration was supplying arms to terrorists, the "Iran-Contra Affair" filled every newspaper, radio, and television broadcast, and became the subject matter for countless documentary series and television shows. Mertins helped facilitate the weapons deals between USMC Lt. Col. Oliver North and the Nicaraguan Contras.[792]

While it is difficult to ascertain *where* all the weapons were manufactured and shipped by to get into the hands of the Nicaraguans, there is evidence that Mertins was shipping weapons through Colonia Dignidad during this time. In 1987, Chilean customs discovered 1056 kilos of ammunition destined for Colonia Dignidad, shipped by Gerhard Mertins.[793] Interestingly, Colonia Dignidad's attorney Fernando Sanger admitted that Mertins was at

---

[791] "Rescued from the shredder, Carlos the Jackal's missing years" Archived 24 July 2017 at the Wayback Machine, The Independent, 30 October 2010. Retrieved 31 October 2010

[792] McFarren, Peter. Iglesias, Fadrique. 2013. The Devil's Agent: Life, Times and Crimes of Nazi Klaus Barbie.

[793] Basso, Carlos. 2022. La Secta Perfecta. ""In 1987 the Chilean customs detained the ship Nedlloyd Manila in Antofagasta, upon discovering that it was carrying one thousand fifty-six kilos of ammunition divided into eighty-two boxes, destined for Colonia Dignidad, which had been dispatched from Acapulco and Manzanillo, Mexico, bound for Valpara". Once again, the person behind the shipment was Mertins."

Colonia Dignidad in early 1987 as an *"industrial friend of people from Dignity"*.[794]

The number of weapons, chemical elements, ammunition, and equipment that was either produced by or shipped through Colonia Dignidad will never be known. Even that which remained after operations in the colony were halted is difficult to summarize; most of it was buried in very rugged terrain at depths of five or six meters. To date, investigators have uncovered forty-six thousand intelligence files, over forty-one thousand hand grenades, three hundred rifle grenades, five tear gas grenades, fifteen rockets, six rocket launchers, sixty-seven mortar bombs, thirty rifles, ninety-seven machine guns or submachine guns, forty-five pistols, four revolvers, five booby-trap devices, forty-four fuses, a camera hidden in a box, an ashtray with a hidden microphone, and eleven pistol pencils. Officials also uncovered 1,678 kg of pentolite, 9.7 of TNT, 900 g of Idemita and 250 of T4, as well as several chemicals used to make sarin gas. In addition to the technologically advanced facilities on the grounds at Colonia Dignidad, officials discovered a hidden bunker on the slopes of the Andes mountains that could only be reached by helicopter.

The operation was so advanced, with so many government and criminal organizations connected, that it seemed impossible that it could be stopped without invoking WWIII. Many governments around the world knew of the operation, some participating and some turning a blind eye. As information continued to leak to the press in other countries, however, and both citizens and politicians became informed of Operation Condor and its connection to Colonia Dignidad, motions to cease operations were slowly raised.

By 1980, very limited information about Colonia Dignidad began trickling through the news media in the United States. On February 24, 1980, the Washington Post broke the story of Latter Rain convert Erich Strohschein and his desperate attempts to reach

---

[794] Basso, Carlos. 2022. La Secta Perfecta.

his family in the colony.[795] In 1952, during the height of the Latter Rain Movement, Strohschein and his family migrated to Canada, and eventually to William Branham's home state of Indiana. His wife's sister, and brother-in-law, however, decided instead to migrate to Chile with Paul Schäfer.[796] In December 1979, Strohschein flew from Indiana to Santiago in search of their family, only to find what he described as *"nothing less than a concentration camp where simple people like the Schurgelis family are being held prisoner behind a barbed-wire curtain reinforced by fear, intimidation, and lies".*[797] Strohschein was initially turned away but was persistent. Eventually, his brother-in-law Walter was able to meet with him outside the perimeter. Strohschein was very surprised when Walter came to greet him wearing a heavy coat on what was an extremely hot midsummer day in Chile.[798] Instead of welcoming him, Walter instructed Strohschein to *"Go back to where you came from and make an appointment",* then returned to his job in the Colonia Dignidad quarry.

That same month, famous Nazi hunter Simon Wiesenthal informed news media that Josef Mengele, Hitler's "Angel of Death" had lived in the colony in 1979.[799] The FBI confirmed the claim. Hermann Schmidt, Colonia Dignidad's spokesperson, vehemently

---

[795] Krause, Charles A. 1980, Feb 24. Strange Encounter at a Chile 'Colony'. San Francisco Examiner. (Reprint from Washington Post)

[796] Krause, Charles A. 1980, Feb 24. Strange Encounter at a Chile 'Colony'. San Francisco Examiner. "Strohschein chose to emigrate with his family that year to Canada and later he moved to Warsaw, Ind. But his wife's sister, Matilde Schurgelis, and her husband, Walter, decided to join Schaeffer instead."

[797] Krause, Charles A. 1980, Feb 24. Strange Encounter at a Chile 'Colony'. San Francisco Examiner.

[798] Krause, Charles A. 1980, Feb 24. Strange Encounter at a Chile 'Colony'. San Francisco Examiner. "On December 18, Strohschein drove with a friend from Santiago to Colonia Dignidad and was told at the locked gates that his brother-in-law was then at work in a nearby stone quarry outside the barbed-wire colony perimeter. He went there, and finally, Walter Schurgelis appeared — dressed in a heavy coat on what was an extremely hot, midsummer day."

[799] Krause, Charles A. 1980, Feb 24. Strange Encounter at a Chile 'Colony'. San Francisco Examiner. "Last December, Nazi-hunter Simon Wiesenthal said that he had evidence that Josef Mengele, the Third Reich's infamous 'Angel of Death,' had lived in the colony for a time last year. The FBI had similar information.

denied that Mengele or *any other Nazi* had ever lived in the colony.[800] In the Washington Post article, the links to Pinochet and DINA were mentioned. Apparently, the West German branch of Amnesty International had publicly claimed that Colonia Dignidad had been used as an experimental torture center and prison camp by Chile's secret police.

---

[800] Krause, Charles A. 1980, Feb 24. Strange Encounter at a Chile 'Colony'. San Francisco Examiner. "A spokesman for the colony, Hermann Schmidt, vehemently denied, in a letter to El Mercurio, Chile's most important newspaper, that Mengele or any other Nazi had ever lived in the colony."

CHAPTER 21

INTERNATIONAL CRIMINALS

❖

"I don't know how many times my mother told me: "Take it with you to the grave." What she meant by that I have to tell you now. It seems that I cannot live with it no more and I am sure I couldn't die with it. I'm getting so nervous even thinking about it, simply cannot bare it any longer. - Sarah Branham"

In 1983, prominent Mexican journalist Manuel Buendía publicly exposed Gerhard Mertins and the arms deals. In his highly influential column, "Private Network" in the Excelsior newspaper, Buendía wrote that *"One of the main international arms traffickers, Nazi, ex-SS member, has established offices in Mexico."* Buendía informed his readers that Mertins was using his criminal network to "fight communism".[801] The column shocked readers as they suddenly learned that "many women, men, and children have died" because of Mertins, and that Mertins openly bragged about his having worked as a member of Hitler's elite.

---

[801] Basso, Carlos. 2022. La Secta Perfecta. "On January 3, 1983, the journalist Manuel Buendía, one of the most prominent political columnists in Mexico, exposed Mertins' actions in his country, through his influential column "Private Network", published in the Excelsior newspaper. With the suggestive title ," Sells Arms," Buendía wrote that ," one of the main international arms traffickers, "Nazi, ex-SS$ member," has established offices in Mexico. From here, according to his own words, he carries out operations in Central America to "fight communism." Sixty-three-year-old Gerhard Georg Mertins likes to recount his wartime exploits as a member of Hitler's select troops and now describes himself as a "logistics merchant." Many women, men and children have died."

That same year, Don Hancock, Chairman of the 3rd Annual Mayor's Prayer Breakfast in Portland Oregon, sent his official letter inviting President Ronald Reagan to the Full Gospel Businessmen's Fellowship International Prayer Breakfast in Washington, D. C. Hancock asked Reagan to schedule the "Day of Prayer Proclamation Ceremony" on either February 1st or 2nd to coincide with the National Religious Broadcasters Convention that was also being held in Washington.[802] At the time, Reagan could have never known that the dam holding the many government secrets in Chile was about to burst. Strohschein's heartbreaking account of visiting Colonia Dignidad had been almost fully contained.

In the spring of 1987, Dan Rather filled the airwaves with his coverage of the congressional hearings into the Iran Contra affair. It quickly turned into a media frenzy; the American citizens eager to learn why the United States had secretly been supporting terrorism to fund war on Communism in South America. CBS built a special glass booth on the top of one of the buildings in Washington that turned the capitol Dome into the perfect background for his reports.[803]

Whether due to the influence of the Full Gospel Businessmen or not, President Ronald Reagan had waged a very public political war against communism around the globe — especially in Central America. The Reagan administration supported a paramilitary group, the Contras, attempting to limit

---

[802] Hancock, Don G. 1983, Jan 14. Letter to White House, c/o Morton Blackwell, Special Assistant to the President".

[803] Iran-Contra Hearings. Accessed 2023, Feb 7 from https://danratherjournalist.org/anchorman/breaking-news/iran-contra-hearings. "The congressional hearings in the spring and summer of 1987 became a "mega-media event" on their own. As Karen Tumulty reported in the Los Angeles Times, CBS "had built a special glass booth atop a building near the capitol that will make the capitol Dome into a eye catching backdrop for Dan Rather as he anchors the opening of the hearings." Following the opening day, ABC, CBS, and NBC did short broadcasts when important witnesses appeared, such as Major General Richard Secord, or to summarize the main events of the day. Only CNN covered the hearings gavel to gavel. As Broadcasting pointed out, the broadcasting of the hearings by a multitude of networks such as PBS and C-SPAN illustrated the rapidly changing media landscape where satellite technology provided stations flexibility in such special event coverage."

the spread of Socialism in South America.[804] This, of course, was not received well by the American public having just learned that Iranian terrorists were being armed by the United States. The level of anger against the President intensified as news spread around the world.

At the same time, Augusto Pinochet's Presidency was in its final stages. In October of 1988, Pinochet was denied a second eight-year Presidency in Chile, essentially overthrowing his terroristic military dictatorship by the early stages of reimplementing a democratic process. All the secrets held by Pinochet were about to be aired to the Christian Democrat Patricio Aylwin's political party — and eventually to the public. That same year, Dr. Jürgen-Peter Graf, Germany's Generalbundesanwalt (Attorney General) began criminal proceedings against members of Colonia Dignidad.[805] The timing was far too coincidental; Germany was likely aware that the Pinochet regime would no longer be in power, and the door to investigate Chile's military operations could be opened through Colonia Dignidad.

It was also in 1989 that William Branham's daughter, Sarah Branham, publicly exposed the leaders of William Branham's cult of personality. In a letter addressed *"To the Bride of Christ – the followers of the message"*, Sarah exposed her brothers for what she claimed to be mishandling money that was *"indirectly"* connected to the death of William Branham.

> *I feel I should expose publicly several things that have happened all going back since the days when my father was killed. As you know my mother and I were the only survivors of it. Now she has passed away and I am the only living*

[804] Iran-Contra Hearings. Accessed 2023, Feb 7 from https://danratherjournalist.org/anchorman/breaking-news/iran-contra-hearings. "Reagan very publicly fought to eradicate communism around the globe, especially in Central America. In 1979, a revolution brought the Sandinistas, a socialist group, to power in Nicaragua. Fearing the spread of similar movements in the region, the Reagan administration decided to back a paramilitary group, the Contras."

[805] Note: In 1988, the German attorney general finally started proceedings against members of the colony.

witness of what happened in the car. I don't know how many times my mother told me: "Take it with you to the grave." What she meant by that I must tell you now. It seems that I cannot live with it no more and I am sure I couldn't die with it. I'm getting so nervous even thinking about it, simply cannot bare it any longer. In the way I look at it, it is indirectly connected with my father's accident.[806]

The most interesting part of her letter was a cryptic set of statements concerning Ewald Frank from Germany. Sarah mentioned the unusual amount of money flowing through the Branham Tabernacle, the head church of Branham's cult of personality, and its unusual handling. She claimed that Ewald Frank — the same German minister confirmed to have been visiting Colonia Dignidad — advised her not to go to the authorities concerning the finances.

Sarah then claimed that she had received divine inspiration to visit Frank in Germany and had *"confidential talks with him"*. At the end of the cryptic segment in the letter, Sarah mentioned that money from Frank was *"so generously given to the members of [her] family"*.

> *Up to this date the money given in the "Branham Tabernacle" in Jeffersonville goes in the church treasury. I was ready to take the whole matter to court, but Bro. Frank told me not to do it because it's against the Scripture (I Cor. 6).*

> *At this point I must mention that I had a very special experience in May 1989, when I was told to go and meet Brother Frank in Germany. Very clearly, and I say this before God Almighty, I saw a huge meeting where my father was preaching as usual. After the sermon a prayer line was called, and I was in that prayer line. When my turn came to be prayed for, I was told "Go and see Brother Frank." Of course,*

---

[806] Branham, Sarah. 1989, July. Take it With You (letter)

being taken by surprise, I asked spontaneously: "Brother Frank in Germany?" And the reply was quite commanding: "Yes, go and see Brother Frank in Germany."

At the beginning of June this year I spent a week at the Mission Center in Krefeld, West Germany. With my own eyes I saw how the stored-up food was made available in the different languages. Because I was told that I should go and see Brother Frank, I had confidential talks with him. As my husband and I could not go along with any of the strange doctrines we of course were pushed out from participating in the money that was so generously given to the members of the family as well as for Mission purposes.[807]

Sarah Branham's letter exposing the finances and links to the Mission Center in Krefeld came on the heels of a much broader examination of the finances among the Latter Rain leaders. A few months prior, Gerald Lee Walker, treasurer for the Full Gospel Businessmen's Fellowship, noticed huge discrepancies in the accounting. Walker initially accused Full Gospel Businessman's Fellowship founder Demos Shakarian of stealing almost $170,000 from the organization.[808] As his investigation into finances continued, an additional $267,000 was found to be missing.[809] Shakarian was placed on "administrative leave". Walker continued his investigation all the way into the Branham organization, and

---

[807] Branham, Sarah. 1989, July. Take it With You (letter)

[808] Scott, Christopher. Full Gospel's Head Accused of Illegality. 1988, Dec 31. Vero Beach Press Journal. "The ministry's internal audit committee, headed by retired Denver businessman Gerald Walker, ordered Mr. Shakarian in an Aug. 22 letter to reimburse $168,119 to the Full Gospel Fellowship. The money was used to pay Mr. Shakarian's legal, medical and insurance bills, Mr. Walker said in an interview."

[809] Worldwide Christian Body Divided Over Funds, Power. 1989, Jan 14. Los Angeles Times. "Last year, the board's audit committee notified the Internal Revenue Service that money spent for Shakarian from 1981 to 1987 was $276,000 higher than reported previously, said Gerald Walker, the fellowship treasurer and chairman of the audit committee. The total includes $168,119 in allegedly unauthorized insurance, legal and disability-related costs, and $107,916 in travel and entertainment expenses said to lack documentation."

noticed unusual transfers of property, civil and criminal lawsuits, and more.[810] Interestingly, all parties involved in Walker's investigation were untouchable. Both the leaders of the Branham organization and Shakarian retained their positions. Shakarian was fully reinstated. According to Walker, the reinstatement was a *"whitewashing of ... Demos without any documentation. He will have to answer to God and to the IRS, not necessarily in that order."*[811]

When Patricio Aylwin Azócar became the 30th President of Chile in 1990, his election marked the transition from dictatorship to democracy. One of Aylwin's primary initiatives was the National Commission for Truth and Reconciliation, a group of eight committee members working to produce what would become known as the Rettig report. The report had four objectives: 1) To create as complete a picture as possible of the most serious human rights violations. 2) To gather evidence to allow the creation of a list that identifies the victims' name, fate, and whereabouts. 3) To recommend reparations for the families of victims. 4) To recommend legal and administrative measures to prevent future violations.

The committee determined that there were two thousand one hundred fifteen victims of human rights violations and one hundred sixty-four victims of political violence between September 11, 1973, and the end of the Pinochet regime on March 11, 1990. Moreover, the commission found that most of the human rights violations were conducted in a sophisticated and systematic fashion, perpetrated by the National Intelligence Directorate (DINA).[812] The Rettig report was published February 1991, which spawned an even broader investigation into DINA and Colonia Dignidad.

---

[810] Walker, Gerald Lee. 1991. Intent to Sue William Branham Evangelistic Association, Voice of God Recordings, The Branham Tabernacle, The Tucson Tabernacle, Believers International, Roy E. Roberson, Paul Brewer, Angela Smith, Billy Paul Branham, Joseph Branham, Willard Collins, Pearry Green, George E. Smith, Fred Sothmann, Floyd Patterson, and Stephen Smith.
[811] Southern California File. 1989, Feb 4. Los Angeles Times.
[812] "Truth Commission: Chile 90". United States Institute of Peace.

Aylwin cut funding to Colonia Dignidad, revoking its nonprofit, charitable status, and began the process of auditing the business conducted by the colony.[813] The audit forced Paul Schäfer to privatize the business enterprises, moving large amounts of money through separate channels. This prompted a visit from German Chancellor Helmut Kohl, who urged the Chilean government to reopen the colony.[814] Using his political pull (and likely assistance from former DINA agents), Schäfer organized local protests against the closing of the hospital until the Chilean government was forced to reopen the colony.

The reopening of the colony, however, was a double-edged sword. To appear fully "transparent", Schäfer began allowing local children into the "Neukra" (short for "New Hospital" in German) — children he did *not* intend to steal from their parents while under the government's watchful eye. Some of the children from the parents of the colony were also singled out to be "patients" and were tortured. Werner Schmidtke, for example, was taken into the "Neukra", stripped naked and strapped onto a metal bed, blindfolded with wax plugs in his ears, and tortured with an electric prod. Children who were unable to remain silent during their "treatment" were dunked into tubs full of freezing water and further tortured with electric shock.[815]

Paul Schäfer became even more brazen, despite the situation that was quickly turning from controversy and speculation to a mob of angered Chilean citizens. He opened a new "Intensive Boarding School",[816] which invited local Chilean

---

[813] Falconer, Bruce. 2008, Sept 1. The Torture Colony" American Scholar.

[814] Colonia Dignidad. Aus dem Innern einer deutschen Sekte. Documentary by Annette Baumeister und Wilfried Huismann. Part 2: Aus der Finsternis ans Licht. ARD, 23 March 2020.

[815] Brown, Stephen. Ellrodt, Oliver. 2012. Insight: German sect victims seek escape from Chilean nightmare past. Accessed 2023, Feb 9 from https://www.reuters.com/article/us-germany-chile-sect-idUSBRE8480MN20120509.

[816] Falconer, Bruce. The Torture Colony. 2008, Sept 1. Accessed 2023, Feb 9 from https://theamericanscholar.org/the-torture-colony/. "He launched a new educational initiative called the "Intensive Boarding School," a kind of immersion program, in which

students to live, work, and study in Colonia Dignidad until they reached the age of 18. In the winter of 1996, however, a 12-year-old Cristobal Parada ended Schäfer's predatory ambitions with a single piece of paper. He slipped a secret note to his mother pleading, *"Take me out of here. He raped me."*[817]

Cristobal's mother managed to rescue him at considerable risk to Cristobal and herself. She drove him to a nearby medical clinic, where a physician verified that the boy had been raped. Cristobal's mother feared that the local police would be of no use, or, worse, that they would return her son to the Germans. She fled with Cristobal to the anonymity of the capital, where she sought out the chief of Chile's national detective force, a man named Luis Henriquez. As had happened in the past, Hartmut Hopp prescribed sedatives for the children, drugging them for Schäfer to rape them.

Fearing that the local police were compromised, Cristobal's mother fled to Santiago and sought Luis Henriquez, the chief of Chile's national detective force.[818] Henriquez opened an investigation into the compound, and before long, several other victims came forward. After twenty-six children reported that Schäfer had sexually abused them, a judge in Santiago issued a warrant for his arrest.[819] In 1996, Schäfer disappeared into the network of underground tunnels used by the Nazis to escape Germany and escaped criminal prosecution for raping the children.[820] Like so many of the Nazis that Schäfer had assisted in

---

select local Chilean students were invited to live, work, and study in the Colonia until they reached the age of 18. Local families proved eager to participate."

[817] Falconer, Bruce. The Torture Colony. 2008, Sept 1. Accessed 2023, Feb 9 from https://theamericanscholar.org/the-torture-colony/. "in the winter of 1996, a 12-year-old student named Cristobal Parada smuggled a secret note to his mother. He wrote, "Take me out of here. He raped me."

[818] Falconer, Bruce. The Torture Colony. 2008, Sept 1. Accessed 2023, Feb 9 from https://theamericanscholar.org/the-torture-colony/. "Cristobal's mother feared that the local police would be of no use, or, worse, that they would return her son to the Germans. She fled with Cristobal to the anonymity of the capital, where she sought out the chief of Chile's national detective force, a man named Luis Henriquez."

[819] Falconer, Bruce (1 September 2008). "The Torture Colony". American Scholar.

[820] Harding, Luke 2005, Mar 12. Fugitive Nazi cult leader arrested". The Guardian. London. Accessed 2023, Feb 7 from

the past, Schäfer disappeared into Argentina through the network of underground tunnels.

By 1997, Schäfer had made Chile's most wanted list.[821] Authorities declared Schäfer a fugitive, unaware that he had fled to Argentina. According to news media, Schäfer was hiding *"somewhere in the labyrinthine tunnels beneath this remote German-speaking village"*. He was charged with luring impoverished boys as young as eight years old to Colonia Dignidad and raping them.[822] The prosecution's case was also being made regarding the systematic sexual abuse, kidnapping, drugging, and torture of children for the past thirty-five years in the colony.

---

https://www.theguardian.com/world/2005/mar/12/warcrimes.chile. "Detectives in Argentina captured Paul Schäfer, an 84-year-old German, on Thursday on the outskirts of the capital, Buenos Aires. Schäfer has been wanted in Chile in connection with child abuse charges since 1996, when he disappeared. Last year a Chilean court convicted him in his absence of child abuse, together with 26 other cult members."

[821] Preacher accused of cult sex crimes. 1997, Jun 27. Gazette Sun. "But to the state police, Paul Shaffer is known simply as Chile's most wanted."

[822] Preacher accused of cult sex crimes. 1997, Jun 27. Gazette Sun. "Authorities allege that Shaefer lured a string of impoverished boys as young as 8 to his religious colony and raped them. Police are picking the latest accusations together with 35 years of testimony from former members of his religious sect who have recounted systematic sexual abuse, kidnapping, drugging, and torture of German and Chilean children inside this vast compound."

CHAPTER 22

ARMED AND READY

❖

"While Schäfer lived to serve only a fraction of his prison sentences, he will now face 'a divine justice' - Chilean President Sebastian Pinera"

On March 10, 2005, authorities arrested Paul Schäfer in Argentina. Schäfer had been living in a private, gated community in the Las Acacias neighborhood in Tortuguita, just north of Buenos Aires.[823] With him were three Chileans, two men and one woman, who were captured a few weeks later.[824] The Chilean government was in the early stages of discovering Colonia Dignidad's deeper involvement with the wars in South America, having at that time only recently discovered the arms cache inside the colony.[825] According to Deputy Interior Minister Jorge Correa, that arsenal was *"probably the largest ever found in private hands in*

---

[823] Ex-Nazi Schaefer Captured in Argentina. 2005, Apr 8. Latin America Data Base News & Education Services. Accessed 2023, Feb 18 from https://digitalrepository.unm.edu/cgi/viewcontent.cgi?article=14359. "Argentine police arrested Schaefer in a private, gated community in the Las Acacias neighborhood of the suburb of Tortuguita, north of Buenos Aires. "

[824] Ex-Nazi Schaefer Captured in Argentina. 2005, Apr 8. Latin America Data Base News & Education Services. Accessed 2023, Feb 18 from https://digitalrepository.unm.edu/cgi/viewcontent.cgi?article=14359. "Chile emitted an international arrest order for the two men and one woman, all Chileans, Argentine police arrested them in the outskirts of Buenos Aires on April 5."

[825] Second secret arsenal found near colony. 2005, Jun 24. Miami Herald. "Last month, police found another secret arsenal at the colony itself."

Chile." — It contained three containers with machine guns, automatic rifles, rocket launchers and large amounts of ammunitions.[826] After Schäfer's arrest, a second arms cache was found seventy-five miles south of Colonia Dignidad near a restaurant operated by the colony.[827]

The next month, Paul Schäfer, four former Chilean security agents and thirteen other members of Colonia Dignidad were indicted. Among the security agents indicated in connection to the colony were retired generals Manuel Contreras and Pedro Espinoza, the top commanders of DINA.[828] By the time of their indictment, Chilean officials were fully aware that the Latter Rain colony had been used as a torture and execution center for the Pinochet regime.[829] In May of 2006, Schäfer was sentenced to twenty years' prison time for the sexual abuse of twenty-five children in Colonia Dignidad.[830] He was also sentenced to pay $1.43 million to eleven of the children in civil suits.[831]

Schäfer's arrest brought an end to a very dark chapter of Chilean history and started a new chapter of transparency. In July

---

[826] Second secret arsenal found near colony. 2005, Jun 24. Miami Herald.

[827] Second secret arsenal found near colony. 2005, Jun 24. Miami Herald. "Police have found a second arms cache believed to belong to a secretive German colony in southern Chile, the Interior Ministry reported Saturday. No details were disclosed on the finding, but local radio stations said police found rocket launchers and grenades buried next to a restaurant operated by Colonia Dignidad – Dignity Colony – about 300 miles south of Santiago. Police were still working Saturday in the area, which is located 76 miles south of the sprawling farm occupied by the German colony."

[828] 18 from German colony indicted for abuses. 2006, Apr 11. Miami Herald. "Retired Chilean generals Manuel Contreras and Pedro Espinoza, the top commanders of Pinochet's feared security service known as DINA."

[829] Judge Seeks to Lift Pinochet's Immunity. 2005, Oct 8. Miami Herald. "Leaders of the German Colonia Dignidad – or Dignity Colony – have been accused of allowing its sprawling enclave 260 miles south of Santiago to be used by Pinochet's security services as an execution and torture center."

[830] Settlement leader convicted of abuse. 2006, May 25. Miami Herald. "The leader of a now-dismantled colony founded by German immigrants in southern Chile was convicted Wednesday of sexually abusing 25 children in the enclave and was sentenced to 20 years in jail."

[831] Settlement leader convicted of abuse. 2006, May 25. Miami Herald. "Gonzalez also sentenced Shaefer to pay $1.43 million to 11 of the children whose families filed a civil suit against the former leader of Colonia Dignidad."

2006, the Chilean government announced that at least twenty-two of the dissidents who disappeared under the dictatorship of Augusto Pinochet were executed in Colonia Dignidad, their bodies incinerated with chemicals.[832] In the years to come, Chilean citizens would come to know the true horror of what happened behind the gates of the colony that from the surface, appeared to be nothing more than a Pentecostal holiness community. On April 24, 2010, Paul Schäfer died in prison from heart failure. Under medical care in the Santiago de Chile's Ex-Penitentiary's Hospital, it was learned that Schäfer had been suffering from a cardiac illness for some time.[833]

At the time of Paul Schäfer's death, authorities were investigating human rights violations for the torture of political prisoners for the Pinochet regime.[834] Schäfer's second-in-command, Dr. Hartmutt Hopp, was placed under house arrest as officials prepared for trial.[835] Officials had not only tied Hopp to crimes for assisting Schäfer in the rape of several children, Hopp had been linked to a hundred prisoners of Colonia Dignidad that were tortured and murdered in the colony.[836] In 2011, Hopp boarded a

[832] Dissidents were killed at commune, paper says. 2006, July 24. Miami Herald. "At least 22 dissidents who disappeared under the dictatorship of Gen. Augusto Pinochet were killed at a secretive German commune and their bodies later burned with chemicals."

[833] Ex-Nazi Paul Schaefer dies at 88. 2010. France 24. Accessed 2023, Feb 20 from https://www.france24.com/en/20100424-ex-nazi-paul-schaefer-dies-88-chile-child-sex-abuse. Schaefer, 88, died just after 7:00 am (1100 GMT) amid worsening health due to heart disease, according to local media.

[834] Ex-Nazi Paul Schaefer dies at 88. 2010. France 24. "Schaefer was also charged with collaborating in human rights abuses during the regime of former Chilean dictator Augusto Pinochet's 1973-1990, including allowing Chilean military agents to use Colonia Dignidad to torture political prisoners who had disappeared."

[835] Reynoso-Pailey, Amanda. 2011, May 25. Colonia Dignidad Cult's Second-In-Command Flees Chile. Santiago Times. "Dr. Hartmutt Hopp, a top authority in the Colonia Dignidad cult of German immigrants, fled Chile on board a helicopter and is believed to be in Germany, according to investigative reporters at CIPER. Hopp was under house arrest in Chile while awaiting trial for human rights crimes committed during Chile's dictatorship (1973-1990)."

[836] Reynoso-Pailey, Amanda. 2011, May 25. Colonia Dignidad Cult's Second-In-Command Flees Chile. Santiago Times. "During the military dictatorship Schäfer, Hopp, and the colony's other exiles - many of whom were once members of the German Gestapo - aligned with Gen. Augusto Pinochet and the dictator's secret police, the DINA."

helicopter and fled Chile,[837] first landing in Paraguay, traveling to Argentina, and finally to Germany where he hid out for several months in Willich-Schiefbahn. In August of 2011, Hopp surfaced in Krefeld, home of Ewald Franks' Freie Volksmission Church.[838] [Interestingly, that same year, an unusual $100 million was donated to the Branham cult, and "The Jehovah Jireh Foundation" was created to move the money.[839]]

Hopp was not the only person from Colonia Dignidad to flee the colony to Krefeld. Colonists Albert Schreiber and others escaped Chile and found their way to Krefeld.[840] As Carlos Basso noted in La Secta Perfecta, Frank's mission church is over a hundred kilometers to the south of Schäfer's initial headquarters in Siegburg, suggesting that they were escaping to seek refuge in Frank's Latter Rain congregation. This was later confirmed when victims of Colonia Dignidad recognized the escapees of the colony

---

Around 100 prisoners were reportedly murdered within the colony compound. The Talca Court of Appeals also sentenced Hopp to five years in prison for being an accomplice to Schäfer's sexual abuses."

[837] Reynoso-Pailey, Amanda. 2011, May 25. Colonia Dignidad Cult's Second-In-Command Flees Chile. Santiago Times. "Dr. Hartmutt Hopp, a top authority in the Colonia Dignidad cult of German immigrants, fled Chile on board a helicopter and is believed to be in Germany, according to investigative reporters at CIPER. Hopp was under house arrest in Chile while awaiting trial for human rights crimes committed during Chile's dictatorship (1973-1990)."

[838] Long, Dietmar. 2011. After fleeing Chile: sect doctor Hartmut Hopp appeared in Germany. Accessed 2023, Feb 20 from https://latina-press.com/news/101659-nach-flucht-aus-chile-sektenarzt-hartmut-hopp-in-deutschland-aufgetaucht/. "The German doctor Dr. Hartmut Hopp wants to live on welfare in Krefeld in the future. This reports RP Online. Accordingly, Hopp has lived in Willich-Schiefbahn for the past few months and has already received state support there. The 66-year-old fled Chile in mid-May and claims to have fled to Germany via Paraguay and Argentina.

[839] Jehovah Jireh Foundation Form 990. 2012.

[840] Basso, Carlos. 2022. La Secta Perfecta. "In fact, the most famous fugitive from the colony, the doctor Hartmut Hopp, convicted in Chile for concealing sexual abuse against minors, did not settle in the German city of Krefeld by chance, but because Frank's church is there. It is also no coincidence that other important leaders of the colony who fled from Chilean justice, such as Albert Schreiber, have come to Krefeld, and that many others have done the same, despite the fact that Krefeld does not have many ties to Schafer's sect, whose initial headquarters was in the city of Siegburg, located one hundred kilometers to the south."

in Frank's church.[841] After news media in Germany made the connection, Frank filed legal action to halt reports of the Colonia Dignidad migrants attending his church. Chilean officials filed a request for extradition, but German officials refused to comply. Germany's foreign ministry declined to comment on the matter.[842]

In March of 2017, however, the German Bundestag officially acknowledged the German responsibility for the events that happened in Colonia Dignidad, and German parliament passed a resolution to investigate and publish information about the history of the colony.[843] In January of 2023, German and Chilean governments decided to turn Colonia Dignidad into a memorial site for murder, torture, and cult victims.[844] The full history, however, and the complete list of crimes committed by Paul Schäfer and leaders of the colony, may never be uncovered.

The full extent of crimes committed by extremist sects that branched from the Latter Rain movement may also never be known. Paul Schäfer was but one of thousands of Latter Rain evangelists, and Colonia Dignidad was but one of hundreds of

---

[841] Ellrodt. Oliver. Brown, Stephen. 2012, May 9. Insight: German sect victims seek escape from Chilean nightmare past. Accessed 2023, Feb 20 from https://www.reuters.com/article/us-germany-chile-sect/insight-german-sect-victims-seek-escape-from-chilean-nightmare-past-icUSBRE8480MN20120509. "About a dozen former sect members now attend an evangelical church in Krefeld run by Ewald Frank, who, like Schaefer before him, follows the teachings of Branham. Frank, who travels the world preaching, took legal action against local news outlets for reporting that his "Free Mission Krefeld" sheltered former sect leaders like Hopp. He said in a statement that his congregation shielded victims of the sect, not its leaders, and added in an email to Reuters: "For us, that unpleasant chapter for the time being is closed."

[842] Ellrodt. Oliver. Brown, Stephen. 2012, May 9. Insight: German sect victims seek escape from Chilean nightmare past. "Chile filed an extradition request for Hopp last August. The Chilean judge leading the investigations into Colonia Dignidad said he could not discuss the case. Germany's foreign ministry confirmed that Hopp could not be extradited but declined to comment further."

[843] Chase, Jefferson. 2018, Jun 18. Colonia Dignidad survivors demand German action. Accessed 2023, Feb 20 from https://www.dw.com/en/relatives-of-colonia-dignidad-victims-await-germanys-plan/a-44208686.

[844] Fischer, Michael. Farmbauer, Martina. 2023, Jan 30. Germany, Chile plan to turn Colonia Dignidad into a memorial. Accessed 2023, Feb 20 from https://starconnectmedia.com/germany-chile-plan-to-turn-colonia-dignidad-into-a-memorial/.

colonies and communes. Not all ware militant, obviously, but at the same time, not all were peaceful. Some, like Colonia Dignidad, were involved with government coups. William Branham "Message" cult leader Robert Gumbura of Zimbabwe, for example, worked with Albert Matapo to overthrow the Zimbabwe government in 2007[845] after having infiltrated the banking system.[846] Like Schäfer, Gumbura used his "Manifested Sons of God" authority to rape converts.[847] Gumbura did not learn this from Paul Schäfer; he was a convert of the "End Time Message" of William Branham, heavily influenced by Branham's "Serpent's Seed" (Christian Identity) doctrine.[848] In the Ivory Coast, "Message"

[845] 2015, Dec 4. Gumbura Plotted to Dethrone Govt: Witness. Accessed 2021, May 13 from https://www.herald.co.zw/gumbura-plotted-to-dethrone-govt-witness. "ailed Independent End Time Message leader Robert Martin Gumbura communicated with alleged coup plotter and former army captain Albert Matapo from prison cells planning on how "they" would dethrone the Government, the court heard yesterday. State witness, Claudius Mutizwa, a convict, told the court during cross examination by Gumbura's lawyer that the Church leader communicated with Matapo through one prison officer, Chinake's mobile phone. He said Matapo's role was to gather manpower and to get guns from Morris Depot's armoury adding that the rioting at Chikurubhi was not about food, but a political scheme. On Tuesday the same witness said Gumbura communicated with former Vice President Dr Joice Mujuru from prison cells through letters, strategizing on how they were going to form their political party."

[846] 2015, Jan 18. EXCLUSIVE: Gumbura Agents Infiltrate Stanbic Bank, Harare. Accessed 2021, May 13 from https://www.zimeye.net/2015/01/18/exclusive-gumbura-agents-invade-stanbic-bank-harare. "The Branhamites have infiltrated middle management and strategic junior positions to be fully made known in the part 2 of this investigation. All recruitment interviews are strategically attended by cult members, to ensure that cult members are taken in. This has led to the bank now being regarded as defacto controlled by the cult, leading to their boast at a cult meeting that the Church 'owns' the bank in Harare. Non-cult members are secretly viewed as 'of the devil' thus in subtle and obvious ways non cult members have their lives made miserable, knowing that when there is a conflict, cult members will be believed and sided with, and non-cult members corrected, even if wrong."

[847] 2015, Jan 24. Pastor Robert Gumbura who had unprotected sex with over 100 women bounces back. Accessed 2021, May 13 from https://web.archive.org/web/20171116050910/http://www.myzimbabwe.co.zw/news/24 03-pastor-robert-gumbura-who-had-unprotected-sex-with-over-100-women-bounces-back.html "Pastor Robert Gumbura who had 13 wives was slapped with a half a century jail term for having raped several women last year."

[848] 2015, Jan 24. Pastor Robert Gumbura who had unprotected sex with over 100 women bounces back. "The End Time Message dictates various disturbing beliefs which include claims that women are inferior to men all because "the first female, Eve, in the book of

leader Kacou Phillippe also manipulated and controlled victims[849] while also spreading Branham's "Serpent Seed" doctrine. Both Phillippe and Gumbura have black skin, making themselves both targets of Branham's white supremacy doctrine[850] and examples of the level of manipulation and undue influence in the sect. Phillipe was eventually arrested for hate speech and forbidden to preach in any part of Ivory Coast. Interestingly, Phillipe's sect was also influenced by Ewald Frank during the years that Frank left Germany.[851]

The criminal abuse and torture of cult victims in the Latter Rain communes were not only taking place outside of the United States. In the 1960s, as Schäfer was building out Colonia Dignidad,

---

Genesis, had intercourse with a live snake producing a half serpent, half human child, Esau". They also hold that their Church founder William Marrion Branham is the Last Prophet of the New Testament."

[849] 2021, Jun 16. Gumbura's Fifth Wife Deserts Over Abuse. Accessed 2021, Jun 17 from https://www.zimeye.net/2021/06/16/gumburas-fifth-wife-deserts-over-abuse/ "Polygamous End Time Message Church pastor's fifth wife is reported to have fled to a safe house over sexual and physical abuse in the hands of her husband. Innocent Gumbura, who is married to Sarah Wendy Romol has been described as hostile, over-controlling, excessively violent, verbally abusive, belittling and manipulative person in a probation officer's report to the magistrate court in a row over custody of four minor children which the former applied for."

[850] Ivory Coast: Philippe Kacou pardoned, continues to "insult" Alassane Ouattara. Accessed 2022, Mar 21 from https://www.koaci.com/article/2019/02/05/cote-divoire/politique/cote-divoire-philippe-kacou-gracie-continue-dinsulter-alassane-ouattara_127624.html. "The prophet Phillippe Kacou militates for a deterministic submission of the black man to the white man. Phillippe Kacou also reveals in his letter that it is up to the white men to validate the election of a president in Africa. "Any recalcitrant African leader who rebels against this must be transferred to the International Criminal Court," he said.

[851] KACOU 29: THE VOICES OF DISCREPANCY. Accessed 2023, Feb 20 from https://philippekacou.org/en/predications/predications-ecrites?NumPred=29. "Well. I was born on December 20, 1972, and at the same time, Ewald Frank, Alexis Barilier and Alex Baranowski were in Sikensi, in Ivory Coast; See circular letter of January 1973. And they all know that in that time, the angels had sung at Katadji, at the exact place where I was born. And far from exaggerating, the place where, they say, the singing of the angels was first located also includes our poor mud house. My parents who have no notion of the spiritual did not feel concerned by the Event. You see? The midnight Cry which is a celestial and world event deserves that. And it is in this small village that the evening Message was first mentioned in Ivory Coast. [Ed: the congregation says, "Amen!"]."

Branham's "scribes" (men who recorded Branham's sermons) were setting up their commune in Prescott, Arizona.[852] Gene Goad and Leo Mercer — familiar faces in the Latter Rain crowds — led what victims referred to as "the Park". Mercier employed various forms of punishment, from "shunning" members of the commune to physical and sexual abuse and torture.[853] Children were marched around the commune military-style and were physically beaten if caught talking during a march or not properly tying their shoes. Girls were punished by cutting their hair, which the cult believed to be an unforgivable "sin". Boys punished were forced to wear girls' clothing. Evidence collected by the police investigation confirmed that children were sexually abused.[854] As in the Colonia Dignidad compound, children were often stripped naked[855] and beaten or tortured.[856] Some families were forced to live separately, while others were forced to work as Mercer's personal servants.

Other Latter Rain communities, often in the same network, were found to be involved in criminal activities that could have

---

[852] Branham, William. 1964, May 31. The Oddball (64-0531). "Brother Leo, Brother Gene and pilgrims, I–I deem this one of the grand privileges that I've had, to come here to see for myself what you have here on these grounds. It's a...I have been blessed as I moved across the little creek there and see this court. And I...One time when Brother Leo was making tapes."

[853] Thibodeau, Deb Daulton. 2022. The serpent's Tail. "every morning before school a different Brother showed up to administer a beating, I never knew what was coming a belt, a switch once an electric cord that hurt worse than anything so far, I walked to school every day, striped throbbing pain neck to knees.

[854] People vs. Keith Thomas Loker. 2008, July 28. California Supreme Court. SCR-58212. "Leo Mercer, a self-proclaimed minister, ran the park. After Brother Branham's death in 1965, Mercer gradually became more authoritative, employing various forms of punishment. He would ostracize people from the community and separate families. Children were beaten for minor infractions like talking during a march or not tying their shoes. Mercer would punish girls by cutting their hair, and force boys to wear girls' clothing. There was also evidence that Mercer sexually abused children."

[855] Thibodeau, Deb Daulton. 2022. The serpent's Tail. "You will stay here tonight. In the morning you will be stripped naked, and you will march the roads until our Lord Jesus forgives you. Do not move. The Lord will show me if you do."

[856] Thibodeau, Deb Daulton. 2022. The serpent's Tail. "Ed, he took them to the creek, stripped them naked....and beat them, he shoved creek sand in their mouth and ears...up their nose, it's wrong and wicked what he done Ed.... he poked sand up in their rectum.... made them run home naked!"

financed global operations including those between Germany and Chile. On July 1, 2021, for example, Vinworth Dayal of William Branham's cult of personality was charged with laundering money for the sect.[857] In January of the prior year, government officials in Trinidad raided his Third Exodus Assembly church and the homes of family members to seize millions of dollars under the Proceeds of Crime act. Trinidad and Tobago was rated the highest country at risk for money laundering and terrorist financing in Latin America.[858] Almost thirty million dollars were seized during the raids.[859]

Over the years, most of the crimes have been forgotten, their critical information having been controlled and withheld from converts to the movement. The Latter Rain, as a movement or as a sect of Christianity, is almost non-existent today. As a framework for building new cult structures with similarly destructive and dangerous philosophies, however, it is very much alive. Events in Christian history, such as the dramatic climax of the Shepherding Movement, led by Latter Rain ministers and evangelists Don Basham, Bob Mumford, Derek Prince, Charles Simpson and Ern Baxter, for example, imploded after the authoritative nature of the

---

[857] Achong, Derek. 2021, Jul 1. $10 million bail as Pastor Dayal charged with money laundering. CNC3 News. Accessed 2021, Jul 2 from https://www.cnc3.co.tt/10-million-bail-as-pastor-dayal-charged-with-money-laundering/.

[858] Risk index score of money laundering and terrorist financing in Trinidad and Tobago from 2015 to 2019. Accessed 2021, May 30 from https://www.statista.com/statistics/876073/risk-index-money-laundering-terrorist-financing-trinidad-tobago/. "In 2019, Trinidad and Tobago was ranked as the country with the sixteenth highest risk of money laundering and terrorist financing in Latin America."

[859] Afield, Further. 2020, Jan 2. Trinidad: Pastor brings $28m in tithes to the bank. Accessed 2021, May 30 from https://antiguaobserver.com/trinidad-pastor-brings-28m-in-tithes-to-the-bank/. "According to the Trinidad Express, moments before the dawn of 2020, Financial Investigation Branch police went before a magistrate and secured a detention court order to impound $28,046,500 under the Proceeds of Crime Act. Sources said the money, which was brought to the Central Bank after 5 p.m. on Old Year's Day, was counted by police late into the night and was confirmed at $28,046,500 in old $100 paper bills. This is the most significant development so far in the currency changeover exercise."

movement was exposed.[860] Even after men and women working directly with key figures in the Latter Rain denounced the fruits of the movement, as Ern Baxter did who toured with Branham and denounced Branham's ministry in the 1970s,[861] splinter groups continue to emerge and become just as destructive. New branches from the same tree will continue to produce the same fruit.

The blend of religion and politics for the purpose of furthering agendas incompatible with core Christian values makes the "trunk of the tree" more difficult to identify. Each new branch that sprang from the movement claimed to have much different doctrinal positions than their predecessors — whether Word of Faith, the Prosperity Gospel, or the many other sects that ultimately emerged to form the New Apostolic Reformation. Many leaders in the new movements recognize elders of the past movements as "God's Generals" who had "gone astray" and claim theological differences as their distinguishing factors. At the same time many of the core political ideologies remain consistent.

The crimes against humanity that occurred behind the walls of Colonia Dignidad have ceased, and the many secrets once whispered in the shadows of the labyrinth of tunnels under the colony are now printed in journals and books for all to see. The questions raised by this knowledge, however, may never be answered. How much did Paul Schäfer's ties to Latter Rain

---

[860] Maynard. The Shepherding Movement. 2008, Feb 21. Accessed 2022, Sep 19 from http://subversiveinfluence.com/2008/02/the-shepherding-movement. "their prominence helped gain wide acceptance for their teaching, which included what was felt to be correctives to the charismatic movement at the time. Other charismatic leaders began submitting to the authority of the Ft. Lauderdale Five in what was known as 'covenant relationships.' A network of cell groups was formed, with members submitting to a shepherd who in turn was submitted to one of the five or a representative who was submitted to one of the five. At its height, it was estimated that some 100,000 people were involved in this network in the USA. In conjunction with this pyramidal authority structure, the movement taught that every believer needed to be under a 'spiritual covering' from a leader in authority over them."

[861] New Wine Magazine, "New Wine Interviews Ern Baxter", Christian Growth Ministries, Ft. Lauderdale, FL, pp. 4-7, 22-24. "I think there can be a lesson in this. Branham, as a miracle worker, had a real place. Branham as a teacher was outside of his calling. The fruits of his teaching ministry are not good."

contribute to the events that took place at Colonia Dignidad? Would the Nixon Administration have chosen the Latter Rain sect in Chile had they not been working with Latter Rain leaders at the National Prayer Breakfasts? Would the Germans have been as successful in escaping to South America without the Latter Rain connections back to Germany and the Latter Rain agricultural community? What role did Branham's campaign manager, German Baron von Blomberg, play in the initial colony settlement? What role did William Branham himself, or the other Latter Rain leaders, play in the colony?

It would be very easy to say that the religious extremism played no role in what happened in Chile. Like the CIA's denial of direct involvement, converts to Latter Rain and its various splinter groups could just as easily argue that Paul Schäfer's Nazi ties were to blame for Augusto Pinochet choosing Colonia Dignidad for the center of intelligence. If so, why did Schäfer continue preaching the doctrines of William Branham in the compound, and why did his cult faithful view Schäfer as a religious leader rather than a revolutionary? Did the Pinochet Regime further weaponize Schäfer's Latter Rain theology due to its control of followers' minds?

In terms of what happened in South America during the 1970s, Colonia Dignidad was but one sizable cog in a larger wheel. There were other military installations, and though others may not have had Latter Rain roots, similar trails to similar politically-charged movements or sects may later be identified in other areas. Paul Schäfer and Jim Jones were not the only religious figures who fled to South America.

In the end, only one thing is for certain. There was a long chain of events leading to Colonia Dignidad, and the links of that chain were constructed from weaponized religion. From the themes of white supremacy that emerged over time from the British Israel theology while weaponizing that theology for the Klan, to enhancing the theology in the 1960s to weaponize it against Communist Russia, to its deployment in the field as an actual weaponized military unit, if any single component had been missing, it is unlikely that Colonia Dignidad would have played such an important role in the darkest chapter of Chilean history. At a minimum, Paul Schäfer would not have had such mental control over his victims and upon the first sexual crime committed on South American soil, Schäfer would have been turned over to authorities by the German colonists.

The most unsettling question by far is when and how history will repeat itself. With a clear pattern emerging of other branches from the Latter Rain "tree", it is only a matter of time before another corrupt political administration takes notice of the power behind a weaponized army of militant converts and decides to use that "weapon". That weapon is mentally and often physically *armed and ready.*

ABOUT THE AUTHOR

John Collins is the author and webmaster of William Branham: Historical Research. He was born and raised in "The Message" cult following of William Branham, and is the grandson of Willard Collins, former pastor of William Branham's "Branham Tabernacle" in Jeffersonville, Indiana. From 1976 to 2012, John was unduly influenced to believe and practice many of the religious and cultural views expressed by William Branham and by men and women who were in Branham's inner circle.

After his escape in 2012, John began the process of deprogramming from the indoctrinated religious and world views Branham expressed on recorded sermons from 1947 to 1965. This process included re-evaluating every aspect of life, including personal experiences and beliefs that were core to his belief system, world view, and personality. In the early stages of this re-evaluation, John's worldview was centered around indoctrinated apocalyptic theology that resulted from William Branham's focus on doomsday through either doomsday predictions or alleged doomsday prophecies. As a result, early research focused upon differences between Branham's theological views and that of evangelical or fundamentalist Christianity with the intent to categorize Branham's doctrines into categories of Biblical, Extra-Biblical, and Anti-Biblical.

Once establishing the baseline for religious views, John began to research the historical life events of William Branham. Branham's "Life Story" was integrated into the religious views as core theology in "The Message", due to William Branham's usage of his accounts as the foundation for many doctrines expressed in his recorded sermons. While focused primarily upon William Branham, John found it necessary to also research the men associated with or influential to Branham, as well as notable events in the historical timeline of United States and World History. When this research was organized chronologically, John noticed patterns of data that appeared to suggest strategic usage of Pentecostal and fundamentalist extremism to advance the political views of men affiliated with or participating in the creation of William Branham's ministry. William Branham: Historical Research is an ongoing project to document and organize that research data for public usage.

John is the happily married father of three boys. He enjoys spending time with his family, playing his collection of stringed instruments, and visiting new places. His hobbies include music, art, video games, science fiction books or movies, or documentaries. When not writing, he relaxes by studying ancient world archaeology, geography, religion, and culture.

MORE BOOKS BY JOHN COLLINS

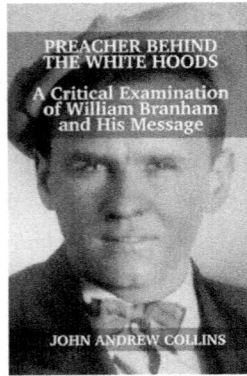

A shocking, pioneering eye-opener that blows the lid off the hagiographic "life-story" that has been blindly accepted by countless thousands of Branham followers through the decades. {...} Collins has left no stone unturned in his quest to uncover the truth in this meticulously researched study. It deserves to be widely read; apart from its historical value, it has much to say to the present-day church about the use of discernment.
- Tom Lennie. Prophecy Today (UK).

Collins has written an important and excellent book about Branham, entitled Preacher Behind the White Hoods: A Critical Examination of William Branham and His Message. Yes, "White Hoods" refers to the Ku Klux Klan (KKK). Collins also has a website devoted to informing people about The Message cult, as well as other destructive religious cults. His website serves as a place for ex-members to find information and support in their journey toward freedom of mind.
- Dr. Steven Hassan, Cult Expert

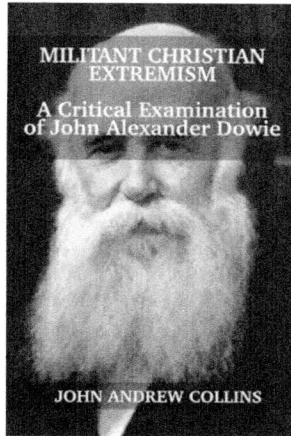

MILITANT CHRISTIAN EXTREMISM

A Critical Examination of John Alexander Dowie

JOHN ANDREW COLLINS

Thoroughly Documented Expose of an Early Charismatic Charlatan. I have spent the last 6 years studying Pentecostalism and started asking, who were the real pioneers of the modern-day signs and wonders movement. John Alexander Dowie truly is the grandfather of the American movement and sets the stage for every charlatan after. This book shows just how extreme, dishonest, and dangerous John Alexander Dowie was and why the movement following him continued to practice such manipulative tactics, such as Dowie's students John G Lake and Frank Sanford. Excellently written.
- Ralph E Brickley Jr

Outstanding research of a shadowy figure. I really love and appreciate this book! When I was involved in Pentecostal circles, for the most part they presented a sanitized version of Dowie's history. It seemed to me he was presented as a revered figure. Somebody to be emulated. As mentioned in the description of this book Dowie influenced directly or indirectly so many of the Pentecostal leaders and founders of the early 20th Century. (See the description for the names) And in turn I might add other luminaries who followed such as Hagin, Copeland, Price, and a slew of others. As well as so many televangelists of today.
- Steven Johnson

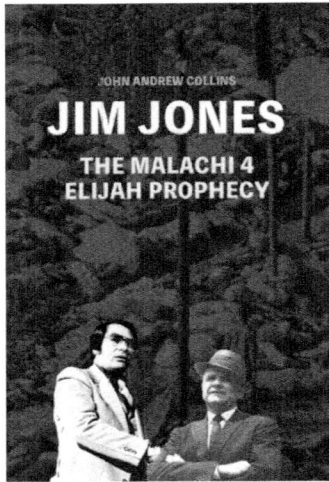

A Must Read for Charismatics. Very engaging from the very beginning! A must read if you are a Charismatic or Pentecostal. Really sheds light on why there is so much corruption and sin in the current Charismatic Movement, i.e., Todd Bentley, John Crowder, Jason Westerfield, Benny Hinn, David Tomberlain, etc. It's those who have and obey His commandments who will inherit the kingdom, not "miracle" workers who only say "Lord, Lord!"
- John Taylor

It was very insightful. Eye-opening to some of our American church Pentecostal history. I have bought multiple copies of this book. I think its content is so important. it warns us about the dangers of extra-biblical teaching and the following of personalities. In my opinion, it should be read by every Pentecostal- charismatic believer. We need to face the real history, of our movements, whether good or bad, I highly recommend this book! Couldn't put it down!
- Brian Pond

Printed in Dunstable, United Kingdom